Brenda DeVore Marshall

Brenda DeVore Marshall

CONTACT: HUMAN COMMUNICATION

and its history

Edited by RAYMOND WILLIAMS

CONTACT: HUMAN COMMUNICATION
and its history

Ferruccio Rossi-Landi
Massimo Pesaresi
Arthur D. Shulman
Robyn Penman
Donis A. Dondis
Jack Goody
Henri-Jean Martin
Ithiel de Sola Pool
Garth S. Jowett
Ederyn Williams

379 illustrations 57 in color   Thames and Hudson

Designed and produced by Thames and Hudson, London
Managing Editor: John Chesshyre
Design: Ruth Rosenberg
Picture Research: Georgina Bruckner
Diagrams and Maps: Peter Bridgewater
Translators: Brian McGuinness (Chapter 2), David Gerard (Chapter 6)

Grateful acknowledgment is due to the Editor and to individual
contributors for assistance in the selection and captioning of the
illustrations for the plate sections, which were otherwise the
publisher's exclusive responsibility.

Filmset in Great Britain by Keyspools Ltd, Golborne, Lancs
Color plates originated in Switzerland by Cliché Lux, Neuchâtel
Black and white origination by D S Colour International, London
Printed and bound in Portugal by Gris Impressores

First published in the USA in 1981 by
Thames and Hudson Inc., 500 Fifth
Avenue, New York, New York 10110

Library of Congress Catalog Card Number 81-50663

CONTENTS

I
INTRODUCTION
Raymond Williams

INTRODUCTION

For century after century, through all the many fluctuations of human fortune and endeavour, a distinguishing characteristic of man's existence has been his desire – and his ability – to communicate, to exchange meanings with his fellow men. Nearly two-and-a-half thousand years separate us from the civilization of Classical Greece, yet we can still find meaning in these lines:

> *Language, and thought like the wind*
> *And the feelings that make the town*
> *Man has taught himself, and shelter against the cold,*
> *Refuge from rain.*

These English words represent lines written by Sophocles in 442 BC as part of a choral song, now commonly known as the Hymn to Man. Their general meaning comes through to us clearly. Men have taught themselves language, thought, the sense of society and the means of material shelter, as the bases of human life. But then consider what has happened since Sophocles composed those words to be sung and danced by a chorus in his tragedy *Antigone*. We cannot be sure how he originally wrote them down, if indeed that is what he did; perhaps with a pen made from a shaped split reed, using ink made from lampblack, gum and water, on material made from the stem of the paper reed, *Cyperus papyrus*. But he was not writing the lines for what is now meant by publication. The verses would have been learned, by oral repetition, perhaps directly from their author, and he and the fifteen members of the chorus, divided into two groups of seven and a leader, would have been working out, in relation to the metre, the music and the dance movements which would accompany their singing.

We know that the lines became famous, by repeated public recitation and singing. Many years later, when there was a danger of the plays being forgotten or remembered only imperfectly, scholars and scribes, still reading aloud, made copies of seven of Sophocles' most famous plays; these seven are all we now have complete; more than a hundred others, which were not copied, are now lost and unknown. Yet the seven plays lasted, and can be read now in hundreds of editions. To bring them through to later times they have been translated and re-translated into all the major languages. What we now read as Sophocles has passed through this long and complex material and intellectual process.

We can reckon what we have lost, along the way. We can also know what we have gained: this remarkable communication between a great poet of the ancient world and modern readers speaking languages and living in conditions which, even in the great Hymn to Man, he could not have imagined.

This is just one striking example of the extraordinary story of human communication. There are also more immediate contemporary examples. We can press a switch on a machine in our homes and find ourselves watching a battle that was fought yesterday in Asia or a football match that is being played today in South America. On another machine we can, with a little preparation, talk directly to a friend half way round the world, and hear his replies. It is not so long since we called these possibilities the marvels of modern communication. But we have got used to them and, rather than talking about marvels, we are likely, often, to find ourselves complaining about the quality of reception, the standard of the camerawork, the badness of the connection. What was once extraordinary, and as such would have amazed, if they could now see it, the most farsighted of our ancestors, is now literally an everyday business, beyond which we are already looking to new possibilities and new machines.

It is undoubtedly the scale and rapidity of changes in methods of communication, above all in the 20th century, which have led to some new questions about human communication as such, and, as ways of trying to answer these questions, to new branches of scientific and humane inquiry. Most of us in the developed industrial societies have got used to the machines. Some of us take both them and their uses for granted. But many of us, at this point or that, see questions that have to be asked and, when we try to answer them, feel the need for more information and for ways of interpreting the information we already have. For example, it is obvious, when we think about it, that we are not seeing that battle in Asia by chance, or as a necessary consequence of some property of the machine. There are people, other than those directly concerned in the battle, at the far end and at the near end of what we are watching. It is, that is to say, no miracle. There is a specific advanced technology, which we can all in general principle come to understand. At the same time there are many people, at different stages of its operation, who are in specific social, economic and political relations to each other and to us. For we do not watch this battle like gods. A moment's attention will show us that we are not watching the battle from a neutral position above it, or from both sides, but typically from one side, where it was both possible to take film cameras and to link their film to the transmission system which ends in the machine in our house. If we had been, say, in a house in another country, pressing a switch on a very similar machine, we might well have seen quite different film, from the other side of the same battle, where other cameras, linked to a different transmission system, could be put in position. Thus what begins, apparently, as a technical marvel has to be seen, in the end, within whole social and political systems.

There are particular reasons why, in a battle, a neutral camera position would be very difficult to obtain: reasons of danger and of battlefield control. But look again at that very different event, the football match, being played as we watch it, on the other side of the world. Here the cameras can be neutrally positioned. We can watch the game with equal attention to each side. But then notice how often, behind the running players, we see not only the crowd – the immediate audience – but as it were accidentally placed the name of a chocolate, a beer, a washing machine. The camera positions are such that we can only watch the game if we see also, at some level of attention or attempted inattention, these

The novelty and marvel of modern communications: a group of Chinese watching television for the first time in 1949.

Modern communications taken for granted: a picture used to advertise a portable television set.

advertisement signs which have been placed, for a price, in exactly those positions. But this is only the most immediate problem. In what sense can we really say that we are watching the match as it is played? Are we seeing, as we might from a good position inside the stadium, the whole field and the patterns of play on it? Occasionally perhaps, but more often we are seeing, in varying degrees of close-up, selected local encounters, sometimes of several players, sometimes of just two, sometimes indeed of two or three disembodied legs or arms. What we actually see is being chosen, by cameramen or directors, of course with the intention that we should see what is most exciting. Yet, staring at their end-product, often putting aside our questions and other observations because are interested in the game, we can easily forget this, falling back on our assumption of the everyday miracle.

Yet we do not all forget it, all the time. It is from the questions that arise when we see and remember what is

actually happening that we have developed those new branches of scientific and humane inquiry that we can try to group as communications studies or the communications sciences. We shall see, as we look closer, that these branches of inquiry are often, in fact, very difficult to group, because in their developed forms they have such apparently different emphases and methods. Indeed, to come across any one of these branches in isolation is often to feel that we have strayed into another country, where we may know with luck what is being discussed but cannot really follow it, since the language is so often unfamiliar. It is especially ironic that this should be the case in studies of human communications. Yet there are discoverable reasons for it. The story is often told of an international conference of Latin scholars, at which it was innocently proposed that the language of the conference should be Latin, as the only language which all present could be expected to understand. The proposal failed, for an interesting reason. If all the conference papers had been in

Latin, they would indeed have been readily understood. But since Latin is not now a language spoken by an actual people, and is indeed a language that has to be learned from written texts, there is no agreed or authoritative way of speaking it, and the variations between speakers having different mother tongues could be enough to prevent them understanding each other when they spoke.

In the case of communications studies, the irony is as deep but the reasons are different. Instead of diverging from an ancient field, which was once held in common, the study of communications, in its modern forms, is a convergence, or attempted convergence, of people who were trained, initially, in very different fields: in history and philosophy, in literary and cultural studies, in sociology, technology and psychology. What all these people have in common, ultimately, is a field of interest. But it is not only inevitable, it is also in the end useful and necessary, that they should study this field in what are, at least initially, very different ways. For the problems, when closely examined, are neither simple nor special, and the necessary range of different kinds of knowledge and different kinds of analysis is beyond the scope of any single approach. Yet while we need these specialized approaches, we must obviously try, at times, to bring them together in the area of interest which they share with all those who, though they may not have studied communications, in any of its disciplines, have thought and are thinking about one of the central activities of the world.

The purpose of this book is to attempt and to illustrate this kind of comprehensive general approach. There is a diversity, from the beginning, in its selection of contributors, who not only come from six different countries but who now work, actively, in some seven different academic disciplines. It will be noticed that, as a result of this, several contributors have to try to define what communication is, within their own fields of reference. Thus in their particular contributions they write, understandably, from their own kinds of knowledge and perspective, but still the plan of the book is such that, within the necessary limits of a single volume, an attempt is made to look at the history and the processes of human communications as a whole subject. Thus in Chapters 2, 3 and 4 the three major processes of human communication – language, non-verbal communication and signs and symbols – are generally described and examined. Chapters 5, 6, 7 and 8 describe and examine the history and the social and cultural meanings of the major communications systems – writing, printing, extended sounds and extended images. Chapter 9 examines the relations between these systems and their technologies and the social institutions within and through which they are developed. The last chapter examines current and projected developments in communications technology, and their possible effects, taking the long story through to a coming generation, with quite new possibilities and problems.

The book as a whole is then at once analytic, historical and exploratory. It ranges in time from the beginnings of recorded human society to the end of the 20th century. This historical range is not its only emphasis, but it is worth saying, at the outset, why it has been so deliberately included. And to do this we must, paradoxically, begin by looking more closely at its latest phase.

Why communications matter
Access and action

As has already been said, it was the scale and rapidity of 20th-century changes in the means of communication which led to the intensive development of new kinds of communications studies. The effect of these changes can indeed hardly be overestimated. It is not only the provision of access, for hundreds of millions of us, to quite newly direct versions of thousands of distant events. That is the most commonly mentioned effect, often described as 'a window on the world'. But it is of course a very curious window. It is not the fixed view, from some place where we have chosen to stand. As was noted in the examples of the war and the football match, we are at once seeing and being shown. The window is not plain glass but a very complex process of technical and social production. And we must then make further distinctions. The war, we can presume, would have occurred whether or not there was television to report it. Our access to a version of what it is like can then range from simple spectacle – another thing to watch, without any real involvement – to concerned

Film editing: even when television seems to be merely reproducing 'reality', a window on the world, the window is not plain glass.

Television does not just happen to be looking in on this motor-race where the cars are moving advertising posters. (The picture shows a 60-in. projection television set.)

information, in which something of the reality of what is happening can be connected not only to our sense of the world beyond our everyday local experiences but also to our political perspectives and decisions. Access, that is to say, *as a viewer*, is already too simple a description. We can either rest content with this magic window or, at the other extreme, break the glass and get involved, because of what we have seen, in the actual events.

Events and pseudo-events

But this is only a variation in response to events that would, we suppose, have occurred in any case. The example of the football match is already to some extent different. In a majority of cases it would no doubt have been played, whether television was available or not. But an increasing number of sporting events – in golf and boxing most evidently – have from the beginning been arranged as subjects for television. Moreover this trend is increasing, with very

important effects on the organization and financing of most sports. The case is important in itself, but it is also an instance of those real processes which the description as 'access' – the 'window on the world' – obscures and is sometimes meant to obscure. A very high proportion of what is there to be seen was put there to be seen, and it is only when we consider communications as production, rather than reducing it to simple consumption, that we can at all understand its whole range.

In fact an emphasis on production is readily admitted, in certain specified areas. It is obvious that in the whole range of communications technologies – from publishing and the press through cinema to radio and television – most works are produced and, though then in highly variable ways, offered to others. A philosophical essay, a novel, a feature film, a radio play, a television variety show, are all in this sense manifestly produced. Moreover they are all forms governed by certain descriptions and conventions, which indicate, usually successfully, what kind of work is being offered. But there is then an initially simple contrast with another whole range of communications production, when what is being offered is not signalled as production at all, but as 'actuality'. Here the usual signals, of form and convention, which enable us to distinguish, on the whole successfully, between a novel and a biography, or a play and a recording of conversation, are not only not present; they are replaced by other signals, as most typically 'Here is the news', the explicit or implicit signal of newspapers and broadcast news bulletins.

It was the exceptional scale and intensity of this kind of communication that first attracted attention in the 20th century. Would not these new and powerful technologies offer opportunities for propaganda and brainwashing on a mass scale? Would they not slant and distort the news and monopolize opinion? These remain important questions. Nobody, looking at actual output, could simply dismiss them as hysterical. For we can see, if only in the contrast between different news and broadcasting services, a range of performance from some attempts at objectivity, especially in certain areas, to the most blatant distortion and propaganda. I say 'we can see', but in fact this contrast is only ever adequately available to people who have the means and take the trouble to compare different newspapers and different broadcasting services, especially – where the contrasts can jump at us – between different countries. Most of us, most of the time, have to make more internal comparisons, paying particular attention to reports of events of which we have some direct knowledge (the level of scepticism about these is significantly high) or to identifiable uses of words and images which carry or imply prejudice.

The window changes the world

But then the problem is deeper than this. It is not only a question of whether some independently occurring event is being reported with relative accuracy or with a decent range of opinions on its significance. It is also a question of the relations between such independently occurring events and specially arranged events. For it is not only in sport that events are arranged primarily so that they can be reported. In politics and in commerce such events are now regularly arranged. A camera does not happen to be present when a political leader happens to be taking what the French call a 'crowd bath' and what the British and Americans call a 'public walkabout' or 'meeting the people'. Elaborate schedules of time and logistics have in almost all cases made certain not only that the camera should be there but that the political leader and even, in some cases, the crowd should be there. What is then reported and shown may indeed be relatively accurate, and a claim to objectivity can be further staked if several alternative political leaders are shown in the same kind of crowd bath. Yet what is happening, beyond this, is a produced version of politics: that this, in at least one important way, is how leaders and people should relate, politically; indeed, structurally, and at a deeper level, that politics is wholly or primarily a matter of the relative generalized popularity of leaders or competing leaders. What is then happening, often without any local or immediate distortion, is the production of a version of politics, or of the electoral process, which in its repeated emphasis can override, or attempt to override, other versions: not just as a matter of opinion, but as a specific kind of produced event.

Medium as market

Similar processes of communicative production are now widely evident in commerce. A whole branch of cultural production has developed, within modern communications systems, with quite new quantitative and qualitative effects. Paid advertisements, or commercials, are now a significantly large element of most newspapers and most broadcasting services, to an extent where, in a majority of cases, the financial viability of the presumably primary service – the newspaper or general broadcasting – is directly determined by its performance in this area. Yet it is not only a matter of this now huge area of cultural production as commercial persuasion. In its most visible forms, specific signals – that this is a 'commercial'; that what is being said or shown has, if you take the trouble to think about it, been arranged, scripted, directed and paid for – are indeed present. Yet beyond this there is a range, as in politics, of apparently independent events, which are in fact also produced. The most widespread type is the sponsored event, in which something that might

have happened in any case is integrated with the naming of some basically irrelevant product, until the event and the product come to seem factually associated. Then there are other events which would never have happened unless they had been arranged to display or in association with the commercial product. One simple example is the increasing practice of 'product anniversaries' where what looks like news, that something or some name has been produced or marketed for some plausible number of years, over the available numerical range of ordinary social or personal celebration (the centenary, the jubilee, the twenty-first birthday), turns out, in most cases, to have been planned, paid for and in the fullest sense produced.

'Fact' and 'fiction'

These are major modern instances of a necessary concern with communications. But, profoundly important as they are, we should not make the mistake of limiting or reducing communications studies to matters of this kind. For the social processes involved, in these and in other less noticed cases, are on closer examination very complex. Thus we can become so used to descriptions of modern communications in terms of political or commercial propaganda or manipulation that we can fail to notice some equally widespread and perhaps equally significant cultural processes of an apparently different kind. The case of drama is an exceptionally strong example. For dramatic performance has been an important cultural practice, in many different kinds of society, for some twenty-five centuries, yet it is only comparatively recently that it has become an everyday event for what are in effect whole populations. In most earlier periods, drama was performed only on special occasions, such as festivals, and even when it became more regularly available, in city theatres and in touring companies, it reached only comparative minorities. Today, many old and new kinds of dramatic performances, not only in theatres but in cinemas, on the radio and on television, are produced in a truly astonishing number and frequency. On television alone many people in industrial societies can find themselves watching several hours of dramatic performance on most evenings. Indeed more time can be, and often is, spent in watching some kind of dramatic performance than in, say, eating.

Such a phenomenon can be interpreted, quite correctly, as an instance of an expanding culture. Similar kinds of expansion can be observed in other cultural activities such as reading and music. But is this the only relevant kind of interpretation? May there not be important questions, of a different kind, about the social and cultural significance of so large and regular an involvement, as spectators, in dramatic

A German cartoonist draws a satirical picture of total absorption in the products of television and radio broadcasting, Monday to Sunday, morning, noon and night.

performance and in other kinds of what we still, by habit, call 'fiction': fiction as distinct from 'fact'? Faced by a social fact of this magnitude, which does not fit in easily with our ordinary thinking about communications as news and opinions, we have to recognize the need for a kind of inquiry which does not simply begin from existing categories, but which is capable of examining the categories themselves.

The history of communications

One way of examining the categories, in practice, is to include, deliberately as I have said, the available historical range. The extraordinary developments of modern communications can so impress us that we isolate them, put them in a special field. And this is easily done if we adopt, uncritically, certain further current assumptions. Thus it is widely said that communications, in our time, are effectively 'mass communications', and that this is so because we live in a 'mass society'. But these definitions, which are discussed in more detail in Chapter 9, enclose our inquiry too much. Communication is thought of, within such definitions, in too functional and too secondary a way. The model of a small number of communicators using powerful technologies to address very large publics is obviously appropriate to many actual contemporary situations, especially in the cases of a heavily centralized press and of centralized broadcasting and cinema. But we may not be able to understand even this situation unless we have looked, very carefully, at the history of this kind of communication. The phenomenon of a minority addressing or controlling communication with a very large public can be quite quickly shown, when we have looked at the history, to be in no sense a singular 20th-century phenomenon. Or if we say that the singularity is a consequence of the 20th-century technologies, we have at once to notice that there are radical differences between, for example, the very large television audience – millions of people watching a single programme, but mainly in small unconnected groups in family homes; the very large cinema public – millions of people seeing a single film, but in audiences of varying sizes, in public places, on a string of occasions; and the very large actual crowds, at certain kinds of event, who are indeed (but only in this case) physically massed. In general, as we shall see from the history, the dispersed large public is much more typical of modern communications technologies than the large crowds and audiences – ('masses') – of many periods before these technologies were invented. Thus, instead of rushing into easy descriptions, before the full range of the evidence has been admitted, we find ourselves faced with the need to rethink our customary interpretations as well as to inform ourselves about what is, when looked at directly, the truly extraordinary history of human communications systems.

I asked the writers of the primarily historical chapters – Chapters 5 to 8 – to give a general account of the invention and development of the major communications systems, and at the same time to discuss their social and historical circumstances and consequences. Thus Professor Goody describes the development of systems of writing and, in addition to discussing the social and cultural situations in which the various developments occurred, considers the effects of an uneven literacy. Professor Martin takes up this story at the point of the invention of different kinds of printing, and follows the development through to the vastly expanded press and publishing of our own time. Professor Pool describes the development of the various systems which we can group as 'extended sound', in such different technologies, with different social origins and effects, as the telephone, radio and recorded sound. Dr Jowett describes the various systems which can be grouped as 'extended images', in different technologies but above all in the major systems of cinema and television. These chapters, taken together, introduce us to a new kind of communications history, deliberately large in scope and paying close attention, always, to the material history of the different means and systems of communications. This emphasis on the material history is again deliberate. For while it is possible to discuss communications – meanings and messages – at the level of simple *ideas*, it is impossible in the end to separate such discussion from that very important and indeed primary branch of social production which is the making of communications technologies and systems.

Communications in society

Thus it can be wrongly assumed that it is only with the coming of 20th-century technologies that communication has been at once systematized and mechanized. The real relations between techniques and systems, from the earliest experiments in writing and in other kinds of sign, through the application of printing to writing but also to other kinds of graphic reproduction, to the extension and combined extension of sounds and images in modern electronic systems, are at once more complex and more interesting. We do indeed, along the way, find major qualitative changes, crucial transformations in the nature of social communications. This is no simple history of continuity and expansion; within the systems and between the systems there are many kinds of unevenness, contradiction and mixtures of intended and unintended effect. But what most needs to be emphasized is that the communications systems have never been as it were an optional extra in social organization or in historical development. They take their place, as we read their real history, alongside other major forms of social organization and production, as they also take their place in the history of material invention and economic arrangement. It has been customary to think of communication as merely derived from other 'more practical' needs and arrangements. But while there are many such cases of applied communication, there are also, as we read the history, as many cases of the systems and the technologies becoming major elements in the nature and development of social orders as a whole. Some of the problems of the relations between communications systems and technologies and both their own institutions and other social institutions are discussed in my own Chapter 9, over the general field. Again, in Dr Ederyn Williams's account, in Chapter 10, of current and emerging communications technology, there is a deliberately close link between the material character of the new processes and the social and cultural questions — now not historical but in the broadest sense political, as decisions being taken and about to be taken — within which alone the significance of the new technologies can be assessed.

Messages, meanings, relationships

Thus from these connecting chapters of material and social history we can begin to assess, in some new ways, the past, present and future significance of human communications as one of our central and decisive activities. However, to grasp the fullest significance, we have to add to this historical account and analysis a different kind of discussion. I have said that communication is often understood as if it were only something that occurred *after* other more important events. Thus it is suggested that we build settlements, plant crops, fight wars, have thoughts, and after all this we tell each other about them. But in fact, when we look at any of these human actions, we can hardly fail to notice that communication, if in different ways, is from the beginning involved in them, and is indeed in many cases their necessary condition. We do not simply pass messages to each other after such events; we often precede and organize them by messages, of many kinds.

Yet the truth is more than this. Much of the activity of human communication is not limited to the passing of messages, in the simple sense in which that term is often understood. What we say and write and show to each other is in no way limited to the passing of certain definite quantities of information in its everyday sense. For before even the passing of information can happen, let alone the passing of

other material and other meanings, certain major processes must be available to us. Even the simplest communication depends on the existence or close possibility of significant relationships between those involved: sharing a language or certain gestures or some system of signs. Moreover these relationships are not merely available; in the course of communication they are themselves developed, and the means of communication with them. When this is realized we soon recognize that in all this vast complex of active communicating relationships we are doing more than speaking at or to each other; often, and indeed perhaps typically, we are speaking *with* each other, and the meanings that then emerge are often much more than some separable body of relayed information. Indeed, in the full sense, we cannot separate the relationships from this complex and active production and reproduction of meanings. In the same way, we cannot separate information — 'the facts' — or thought — 'our ideas' — from these basic processes through which we not only transmit or receive but necessarily compose what we have to say or to show.

Primary resources of communication

These basic processes are then of course necessarily complex. Since we are so deeply involved in them, it is easy to take them more or less for granted. But once we start thinking about the nature and processes of language, or of what we now call 'non-verbal' communication, or of the making of signs and symbols, we find that we are faced with some of the most difficult as well as the most central questions about ourselves. That is why, as a necessary preparation for any full reading of the historical development of communications systems, this book includes accounts of what can, at least in a preliminary way, be distinguished as the three basic communicative processes. Professor Rossi-Landi and Dr Pesaresi write of the social nature of language itself. Professor Shulman and Dr Penman describe the area which is now designated, in experimental psychology, as 'non-verbal communication'. Professor Dondis discusses signs and symbols.

Each of these kinds of communication is so important, and also at once so fascinating and so difficult, that it requires a chapter to itself. Yet something can also be said about the full range of such processes and about their interrelations. Thus we can see that, apparently from the beginning of human societies, men and women have drawn on two kinds of communicative resource. First, we have used and continue to use the resources of our own bodies. How much we do this, and at the same time the difficult problems of interpreting many such uses, can be seen in the account of 'non-verbal' communication in its now specialized scientific sense. Movements of our bodies and parts of our bodies can be related to both messages and meanings, and though some of these are simple, others are not. Then, second, we have used and continue to use non-human material objects and forces, which we adapt and shape for communicative purposes. This ranges from very simple uses – the mark on a tree, the significantly placed stone – through systems of an increasing complexity of shape, line and colour to the full complexity of systems we can differentiate and specialize as the visual arts and design. Between them these two kinds of resources – movements of our bodies and parts of our bodies; adaptations and shapings of non-human material objects – are composed into a vast and complex range of human communications.

Combination and elaboration of resources

Yet while we can distinguish these two kinds of resource, each of which can be used very significantly on its own, the full range, and then much of the history, of communications includes an interactive area between them. Thus the masked and painted dancer, or the robed figure carrying the significantly shaped and marked piece of wood or stone or metal, are basic examples of a powerfully combined use of human and non-human resources. But the interactions go much further. Language, initially, is a direct use and development of our own physical resources, in speech and song. But we have then not only combined these with other, non-verbal, bodily movements and gestures, and either or both with shaped and adapted non-human resources. In one major and transforming stage, we have developed variable graphic systems which can be seen, at least initially, as notations of other, more direct, kinds of use. Written language is still the major example. It can be seen as a way of recording and substituting for our directly physical speech. But we do not have to look far into the relations between spoken and written language to realize that while these direct relations are always important, the systems of notation become, in practice, more than that; become indeed, though always in variable degrees, means of composition, apparently in their own right. Writers, for example, have learned the intricate practical differences between writing for speech, or for being read aloud, and writing to be silently read. In this major area of communicative development, there are not only simple transfers, between one kind of system and another, but genuine and active transformations. Written language is not the only such case. The complex systems of notation of sound, as in musical notation, can be usefully compared and contrasted with written language; they

The combination of human and non-human resources of communication: a performance of the ancient Japanese Bugaku dance, with costume and mask.

The elaboration of resources: speech is transformed into writing as a Congolese schoolboy learns his lessons.

appear to remain more strictly notational. But the systems of notation of mathematical properties, for example, while retaining an important directly notational status, have long since passed the stage of simple transfer and include not only transformations but what appear to be new and irreplaceable means of direct intellectual composition.

Such interactions as these, in the combined use of human and non-human resources, are now central to human communicative activity. They raise, evidently, the most difficult questions: for example, about the relations between such material composition and the vital but extremely complex categories of 'thought' and 'experience', which can at one extreme be said to be merely 'expressed', as already formed wholes, by these means of composition, and at the other extreme be said to come into existence, or into substantial existence, only to the extent that they are articulated by systematic compositional means. These are, in varying forms, permanent philosophical questions, which underlie our thinking not only about communications but about many kinds of related human practices. We can find useful new evidence for thinking about them in the chapters on non-verbal communication and on signs and symbols, but especially in the chapter on language, on which, historically and understandably, much of this basic inquiry has been centred. These three chapters, taken together, help us to think through our most basic communicative processes, and, crucially, to think about their relations and interactions.

Magnification of resources

But the full extent of these relations and interactions goes beyond the development of representational and notational systems. Over a long period, the interaction between human and non-human resources had to do, primarily, with material *objects*: wood, stone, metal; materials for writing and painting. From each of these uses of objects elaborate communicative systems were developed. But already in some of these uses what was happening was more than adaptation or application: shaping a stick, carving a stone, selecting this or that object for this or that conventional significance. There was the development of tools and instruments for these simple uses, and then beyond that the development of means of transforming the objects, for new uses; by fire, as in the use of new metals; by chemical interaction, as in the later pigments and inks. From these productive developments we learned the possibilities – in communications as in other kinds of production – of the use of non-human forces as well as non-human objects. There have been many stages of this development, but the application of steam power to printing

and other graphic reproduction is one major example, with its extraordinary extension of range. The applications of electricity and magnetism have of course been even more extraordinary. For here there were not only more powerful ways of doing what had anyhow, by less developed means, already been done. In the extraordinary systems that were eventually developed from them, in the modern chemical, engineering and electronics industries, what seem not merely new devices but new forms of communication were developed. This history is traced in the relevant chapters, but especially in the chapters on extended sound, extended images and the new technology (Chapters 7, 8 and 10). It is, in itself, a fascinating history, and one too rarely told, in any systematic way. But then it is clear that the development of these new major systems – the adaptation of natural forces as well as of objects – requires the most careful reconsideration of our concepts as well as of our means of communication.

'Modern' communications, 'mass' communications?

The simplest response, as I argued above, was to separate off these new means and systems, as a modern area, and by calling them mechanical and electronic and then mass communications convert all previous history of communications to their implied opposites: human, natural and personal. But if there is one thing which the detailed histories show, it is that from the beginning the processes of communication have involved the use of both direct and indirect – human and non-human – physical resources. Similarly, the development of 'impersonal' communications – as distinct from the model of direct 'face-to-face' exchanges – is at least as early as the development of writing systems and indeed, in their graphic predecessors, much earlier. There is no future in attempting to reduce the many problems of modern communications to falsely absolute contrasts of that familiar kind. On the other hand, to fail to recognize changes of degree, in just this respect, would be to underestimate the problems quite hopelessly. This book, without attempting to impose any singularity or uniformity of view on its expert contributors, has been edited from the position that the full history of communications is indispensable to an understanding of either its contemporary or its recurrent problems, and that this history needs to be active: an account not only of what has been done but also of what is now being done and, in ways that we can hope to decide, is about to be done. That is why the historical chapters are there, and also why they are succeeded by an analysis of past, present and possible future relations between communications technologies and social institutions.

Communications and change

Meanwhile what can be said here, as a final introductory emphasis, has to do with the general significance of the book and with the relations between this kind of thinking and inquiry and our most general situation. I began by referring to some of the most obvious and most spectacular elements of modern communications systems, and went on to argue that we should look not only at this kind of spectacular consumption but at all communications as a form of social production. This general emphasis underlies the plan of the book, and is explicit, for example, in Rossi-Landi and Pesaresi's account of language. But it is more than a general emphasis. Communication, as we have seen and can confirm in all the detailed accounts, is involved from the beginning in the whole range of human practice. But this does not prevent us from saying – indeed it shows us a way of saying – that as an integral element of human practice it has, in itself and in its relations, a history. And there can be little doubt that the significance of this history has never, in all our long record, been more important.

For the processes of modern communications indicate, in many respects, a qualitatively new social situation. It is in practice impossible to separate them, in their present stages, from other ways of describing our qualitatively distinct contemporary situation. Thus it is impossible to separate the development, along particular lines and through particular institutions, of a potential and in some cases actual world communications system from the development of what, again along particular lines and through particular institutions, has to be seen as a relatively integrated world economy. Earlier and still continuing processes of the national organization of communications systems relate, in comparable ways, to the older and continuing processes of the formation of nation-states. Many current communications problems are indeed centred on the complex relations between these national formations and the powerful international market.

The important current controversy, for example, about the legal status of transmitting satellite stations, with its difficult questions about national and other forms of sovereignty in the air space above a territory and about national and other forms of reception and control of reception, is an exact case in point. It is a central issue in communications, and in the development of communications technology, but it is also a central issue in international politics, in its potential effects on the sources and controls of news and opinion, and in international economics, in its relations to the activities of para-national companies and the whole contested area of imports and exports, not only in ordinary goods and services but in cultural products, services and influences. Already, by developments in radio, we can, in all parts of the world, listen to political news and opinion from sources not only different from our ordinary political authorities but also, if we choose, disapproved of by them. The example reminds us that communications technology is used not only to bridge distances but consciously to implant alternative views in other societies and of course also to interfere with and jam alternative kinds of reception. Thus an issue in communications technology, about which we certainly need to inform ourselves, is at the same time a complex – and as we continue to consider it a very difficult – issue in international politics and economics, and indeed in some of our most basic thinking about political and economic questions and principles.

But then this issue turns up, also, in matters much nearer home. The origins and the control systems of the most public kinds of communications are major issues within our own most immediate societies. Indeed they cannot be reduced to issues between nations, though in some areas they are undeniably that, since it is a crucial question of any modern social order as to how the press or broadcasting or cinema or publishing are politically and economically organized and in that sense, directly or indirectly, controlled. These are questions with a long history of discussion, dispute and struggle. But increasing degrees of extension and magnification now make them especially urgent.

All these processes and changes have been occurring, moreover, in relation to other processes and changes which we are still struggling to understand. Two of these need special mention. First, there is now extraordinary mobility, of a physical kind. More people can and do move often and regularly beyond and outside their familiar communities. This actual movement relates in complicated ways to the means of cultural mobility in the developed communications systems, where forms of contact, but here mediated contact, with other peoples and cultures are now common. The effects of these different kinds of mobility, interacting as they do with still very powerful and relatively stable communications and other systems, in homes and families and workplaces and local communities and national educational systems, seem to require, for their understanding, quite new kinds of social thinking. The excited, merely rhetorical stress on mobility, which new systems of transport and communications can suggest, and in their own terms correctly suggest, cannot be allowed to run to the point where we underestimate, or simply fail to notice, these relatively stable persistences, with their undoubted capacity, as in all working communications systems, to reproduce, often very powerfully because apparently naturally, existing forms and relations. We need many kinds of evidence and inquiry to be able to understand these now exceptionally complicated relations between practical mobility and effective social and cultural reproduction, but clearly one essential area of any such inquiry is that of the communications processes through which so many of them are actually negotiated.

To this emphasis on the changing problems of mobility we can add an emphasis on the changing character of our labour processes. On the one hand a sizeable proportion of the working population, by any previous standards, is employed in the advanced industrial societies in communications in their traditionally differentiated form: in the press and publishing, radio and television, advertising, public relations and publicity, cinema, musical publishing, performance and recording, galleries, theatres and entertainment clubs, together with all those who produce machines and equipment for these sectors or are involved in distribution in them. It is then already the case that communications is a very much more significant sector of the economy than it was in periods when (confirming an already established prejudice) it could be seen as, and in the practical economy was, peripheral.

But this visible differentiated area is only part of the change. At every level of the constitution and reproduction of the social order, and most notably in the continually expanding area of administration, communications processes take an increasingly larger share of workers and working time. Further, in direct production of the traditional kinds, in areas well beyond the important sectors of communications manufacturing, not only internal administration but programmes aimed at influencing production and labour relations amount, even in this area, to a significant proportion of workers and working time. Again, within education, which in its primary practices can reasonably be differentiated from communications, though the links between them are obviously close, the use of all kinds of direct communications materials and techniques has rapidly increased.

In all these ways there has been what has to be seen as a qualitative change. All societies depend on communications processes, and in an important sense can be said to be founded on them. But in advanced industrial societies, both in their scale and complexity and in their changes in productive and reproductive techniques, the dependence is central, and the elements of foundation, often in simpler societies in effect dissolved into other social relations, are manifest and crucial. Thus while it has always been necessary to understand a society in terms which include its communications processes and techniques, it is necessary in advanced industrial societies not only to emphasize their importance but to try to think through again, from what they are showing us, the nature of all, and especially of these, social relations.

But then as we enter these problems, necessarily in our own kind of world and in relation to a continually developing technology, we may hear at our side those old and still powerful words:

> Language, and thought like the wind
> And the feelings that make the town
> Man has taught himself . . .

II
LANGUAGE

Ferruccio Rossi-Landi
and Massimo Pesaresi

LANGUAGE

Some theories on the origin of language
from the 18th century to Engels

In Western thought the problem of the origin of language has always been of central importance in the debate on the origins of man. Ever since the concept of a human being began to be worked out, language, in close connection with thought, has always appeared to be a fundamental attribute of the human species.

If we reject that kind of scientific optimism which sees the history of a problem simply as a progressive approximation to some given 'reality', we can see the different ways of stating the question and the different answers given as ways in which the different societies have formed a picture of the origins of man, and thus of human nature – and, in recent centuries, of human history also. In this each society always promotes a quite definite picture of itself.

The need to define the gap between man and the 'animal world' has made itself felt in various forms. In an immobile universe – where the march of time had no place – different forms of life were viewed as the product, not of evolution, but of direct creation. Hence also the idea of the divine origin of language. Inability to explain a phenomenon by research into nature was given metaphorical expression in the shape of an intervention 'from outside'.

This great ideological edifice, most completely and consciously expressed within the feudal world, was confronted with its final crisis by the culture of the Enlightenment. Eighteenth-century anthropology presupposed as its basis the existence of a 'natural' individual, not the product of history but its point of origin. History itself was viewed as the mere unfolding of the two essential human attributes of thought and sociality. The basic problem then became that of the role of language and of society in the emergence of man from the animal world.

To get round the Biblical creation, anthropologies of this kind took as their starting point a human race reduced to animality after the Flood, or supposed a primordial couple who, separated in infancy from any social context, were in a position to recreate the arts and institutions of civilized life on the sole basis of their own human potentialities.

At the beginning of the second part of his *Essai sur l'origine des connoissances humaines* (1746), Condillac sketches a philosophy of the development of language. His description starts with natural signs ('cries expressive of the passions') and implies a naturalistic approach to the origins of society, seen as the interpretation of individual needs and instincts. The discovery of the original nature of man is effected by progressively subtracting whatever seems acquired in the individual mind in order to reach the 'pure potentiality' of human nature.

This procedure was hypothetical, but the possibility of experimental research was opened up by the study of so-called 'wild children' – children or adolescents abandoned in early infancy and rediscovered in a feral state after a longer or shorter period of isolation. Victor, discovered in the forest of Aveyron in 1799, is a typical case. A detailed report on this case has been left us by Itard, the doctor who tried to re-educate him. The doctor's investigations are based on the firm belief that close observation of the human faculties lacking in Victor will enable us to calculate the sum of the knowledge and ideas that men owe to education. Itard's analysis leads him to the conclusion that man has no pre-social nature. Man's sole characteristic is adaptability. Before humanization begins man is devoid both of intelligence and of language. He can develop these two faculties only in a social context, by means of imitation, and the motive for such development is need.

A somewhat similar thesis had been sustained some years before by the Scottish philosopher James Burnett, Lord Monboddo. In his researches, designed to establish 'what kind of animal the Man of God and nature is', he reaches the conclusion that man's erect stature, his fitness for society, his thought, his language – all generally considered *a priori* specific marks of human nature – are rather the *products of a gradual progress*.

And if we rightly consider the matter, we shall find, that our nature is chiefly constituted of acquired habits, and that we are much more creatures of custom and art than of nature ... For it is the capital and distinguishing characteristic of our species, that we can make ourselves, as it were, over again, so that the *original* nature in us can hardly be seen and it is with the greatest difficulty that we can distinguish it from the *acquired*.

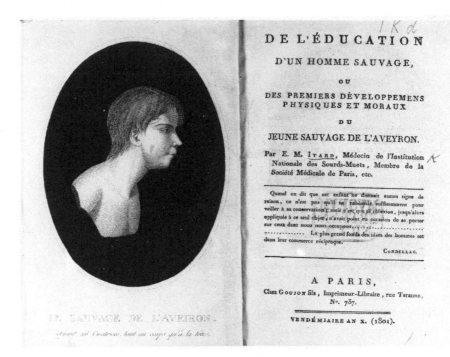

DE L'ÉDUCATION
D'UN HOMME SAUVAGE,
ou
DES PREMIERS DÉVELOPPEMENS
PHYSIQUES ET MORAUX
DU
JEUNE SAUVAGE DE L'AVEYRON.

Par E. M. ITARD, Médecin de l'Institution
Nationale des Sourds-Muets, Membre de la
Société Médicale de Paris, etc.

Quand on dit que cet enfant ne donnait aucun signe de
raison, ce n'est pas qu'il ne raisonnât suffisamment pour
veiller à sa conservation; mais c'est que sa réflexion, jusqu'alors
appliquée à ce seul objet, n'avait point eu occasion de se porter
sur ceux dont nous nous occupons............................
.... Le plus grand fonds des idées des hommes est
dans leur commerce réciproque.
CONDILLAC.

A PARIS,
Chez GOUJON fils, Imprimeur-Libraire, rue Taranne,
N°. 737.
VENDÉMIAIRE AN X. (1801).

LE SAUVAGE DE L'AVEIRON.

The study of 'wild children': was language 'natural' or the product of society? Frontispiece and title page of Itard's book on Victor, discovered in the forest of Aveyron in 1799.

In this process of ·self-production, the chief motive is necessity. The responses to this necessity are made possible not by instinct, which would aim merely at the preservation of the individual, but by association.

Monboddo examines the origin of society in close connection with that of language and has no hesitation in affirming that 'in the order of things' society comes first, since

> though a solitary savage might in process of time acquire the habit of forming ideas, it is impossible to suppose, that he would invent a method of communicating them, for which he had no occasion.

It was a commonplace of 18th-century anthropology to attribute particular importance to society in the development of the linguistic faculty. Monboddo's originality consisted in the fuller conception he had of society as an association for the organization of communal labour. German thinkers of the Enlightenment (Herder, Tetens, *et al.*) ascribe to man a generic sociality which embraces the reciprocal communication of desires, feelings, and needs, to be sure, but not the dimension of organized production which is also to be found within a social organism. The humanizing character of work was confirmed afresh, according to Monboddo, by the social grouping of orang-utans that he read of in Tyson's *Orang-Outang sive Homo silvestris*, published in 1699. These animals lack speech but are intelligent, live in families and small social groups, have affections and feelings similar to those of men, and communicate with one another. Only the relative isolation in which they are found has prevented them from developing language. But that in no way detracts from their *potential humanity*. Monboddo's lengthy treatment of the orang-utan along these lines has a double aim – both to verify his own hypothesis of the connection between language and society and to confirm that these creatures belong to the same species as man. This second point makes it possible to fit the Scottish philosopher's apparent anticipation of evolutionary theory into the framework of his spiritualist metaphysics. Man's progress is due to the development of certain natural potentialities which emerge in an appropriate context. Thus speech can make its appearance only in the particular situation created by the necessity to find a way to work together. The idea that orang-utans, though they have not had the opportunity to develop this potentiality, nonetheless belong to the human race, seemed to be confirmed by other indications (e.g. the use of implements like the walking stick that they are traditionally depicted as carrying). Monboddo gives no answer, however, to the problem of the transition from the inarticulate forms of animal expression to human language. He attributes to certain anthropoid apes the potentiality for speech not *qua* animals but *qua* members of the genus *Homo* who have been assigned to a species different from man only by faulty evaluation. Monboddo, like so many thinkers before and after, remains convinced that the sole barrier between 'man' and 'the animals' is language. As Max Müller puts it, language 'establishes a frontier between man and the brute, which can never be removed'.

The attention paid to the essential continuity between human capacities in general and those of other animals, particularly primates, was an important advance made by the materialists of the Enlightenment. Unfortunately it had no sequel in the 19th century. The last century did, however, see interesting developments in the approach to Monboddo's problem of the origin of man and hence of language. His ideas about the advance from original to acquired nature and about the self-creation of man through work have many analogies with the position of Engels's chapter in *The Dialectic of Nature* on 'the part played by labour in the development of apes into men', though there is probably no question of direct derivation.

Engels rejects spiritualist metaphysics and the conception of human nature as something whose potentialities are gradually realized in and through the environment. He reduces the origin of man to a process of self-creation with the aid of the social environment. The driving force in the production of man is labour, which is 'the prime basic condition for all human existence'. Thus it can be said that 'Labour created man himself'. When the practice of working in association was added to man's natural sociability 'men in the making arrived at the point where they had something to say to one another'. At this stage necessity brought about the development of the requisite organ. 'The undeveloped larynx of the ape was transformed slowly but surely by means of modulation in order to produce constantly more developed modulation, and the organs of the mouth gradually learnt to pronounce one articulate letter after another.' Labour in the first place and language in the second were the two essential stimuli that gradually transformed the simian into the human brain.

A certain Lamarckism betrays Engels's lack of understanding of some fundamental Darwinian concepts. It is almost as if Engels's ideas have been infected by an optimistic belief in providence, whereby evolution will spontaneously produce what a species needs. This optimism was of service to Engels the revolutionary, but it was transformed into a theoretical prejudice and still lingers on in some ethological accounts which make the organism's adaptation to the environment the sole driving force of evolution. In claiming that the brain is produced by labour and by language (i.e. by the social environment), and that language arises spontaneously when men 'have something to say to one another', Engels seems essentially to be saying that speciation itself is due to a necessity imposed by the environment.

At the close of his exposition Engels criticizes the idealism of those who attribute the advance of civilization to the development and activity of the brain, explaining man's behaviour by his thought rather than by his needs. This criticism, aimed as it is at one of the most flagrant explanatory inversions of all time, we can unreservedly echo, but at the same time we must point out the danger of letting the importance of man's work, which must certainly not be denied, obscure the slow and difficult labours of nature in the production of biological structures for organisms intricately involved with the environment.

Modern tendencies

In *Le geste et la parole* the French writer André Leroi-Gourhan gives us a genuinely anti-idealistic and anti-teleological interpretative scheme for the evolutionary processes that led to the emergence of language. He attempts to display in a single panoramic view the principal functional factors operative in the course of this evolution. For ease of exposition these may be reduced to five: (i) the mechanics and organization of the spinal column and the limbs; (ii) the method of suspension of the cranium and the relative position of the occipital foramen (the hole at the base of the skull), whose placing makes it one of the most sensitive points in the whole functional mechanism of the body; (iii) dentition, with its obvious bearing on social life – one need only consider the role of teeth in defence, in predation, and in the preparation of food; (iv) the hand; (v) finally, the brain, whose coordinating role is clearly primary but which from a functional point of view seems to inhabit the whole structure of the body. A careful study of the development of the brain box and the consequent enlargement of the cerebral tissue allows one to say in fact that in the progressive adaptation of the more evolved species 'the part played by the brain is evident but it is that of bringing advantages in the natural selection of types, not that of directly guiding physical adaptation.'

The brain, that is to say, has been able to profit from the progressive adaptation of the means of locomotion. This last, according to Leroi-Gourhan, is where we must look for the determining factor in biological evolution. In the interplay of successive adaptations to the environment, which has given rise to a progressively more efficient and complex nervous system, a basic role is played by the anterior relational field (i.e. the forward-facing ambit of contact with the environment and with other organisms) and its constitution. On higher evolutionary levels this field is divided into two complementary territories defined by the action of the facial organs and of the extremities of the anterior limbs respectively. The facial and the manual poles operate in close collaboration in the most complicated technical operations affecting the capture of prey and the preparation of food. When the hand was released from its locomotive function by the assumption of erect stature, it could become specialized enough to discharge the technical tasks previously carried out by the facial organs: they thus became available for more refined vocal communication. Leroi-Gourhan found an unexpected precursor in the 4th-century theologian Gregory of Nyssa:

> The hands have taken on this task [that of feeding] and have freed the mouth for service through the word.
> (*De creatione hominis*, AD 379)

In an explanatory framework such as we have described the parallel evolution of linguistic and manipulative capacities in the course of the emergence of man can be seen as the last phase of a general tendency with evolutionary roots of great antiquity.

Complex though it is, this essentially palaeontological hypothesis is also supported by precise neuroanatomical or anthropological evidence. Examples are the contiguity in the sensory-motor cortex of the brain areas for the hand and for the face; the close connection between oral and written linguistic dysfunctions (aphasia and agraphia); and the observed inseparability of language and implements in the structure of human society. On this basis Leroi-Gourhan goes so far as to sketch a 'palaeontology of language' by inference from the archaeological evidence of the manufacture of implements. Thus the first hominids reached a technical level which would postulate the existence of a language, not a mere system of signals comparable to the spontaneous vocal communication of the primates. This is because, when implements are being made, their various operations have to exist in advance of actual occasions of use and, furthermore, because the implement is kept with a view to a succession of actions. Thus there has to be a process of abstraction from context akin to that which has permitted the emergence of human language no longer directly tied to environmental stimuli.

The connections between linguistic and manipulative functions, so lucidly picked out by Leroi-Gourhan, have been the object of detailed research in several fields in recent years, and have also prompted new speculations on the origin of language, seen now against the background of a vaster and more complex network of operations and social relations.

In the neurological field the chief subject of observation

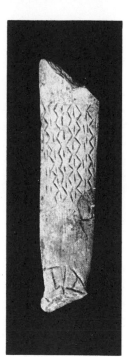

The level of communication between individuals implicit in the making of these prehistoric fine tools (harpoons, *above*, and spatulas, *below*), and the brain development required to plan and use them, offer specific evidence of the existence of language between 10,000 and 20,000 years ago.

has been the phenomenon of cerebral lateralization – the process, that is, by which in the majority of individuals the left hemisphere is dominant for language and manual operations (i.e. they are right-handed). Some have thought the asymmetry of both of these functions sufficient proof of the parallel development of language and of the construction and use of implements. Thus one author, Gordon Hewes, refers to a time sequence in which the lateralization of handedness led on to that of verbal language, the intermediary being gesture language, the closest link between these two complex and asymmetrical functions.

There has been no lack of interesting studies of palaeoneurology aimed at ascertaining the occurrence of lateralization in human fossils. The skulls are studied by means of casts, usually artificial, sometimes natural (when sand has replaced the soft tissues). These show greater development of the frontal and rearward areas of the left hemisphere. Observations on the chipping of stones also confirm the prevalence of right-handedness in earliest man: some students have been led to try to establish precise connections between the evolution of language and that of the technique of chipping. But, first of all, verbal language is not an essential prerequisite of activities like hunting or the manufacture of implements, witness the 'non-verbal' transmission of complex work techniques by artisans in our own day. Secondly, the analogy between the use of tools and the use of language does not imply the existence of a common cognitive mechanism, whereby language would have to be viewed as an elaboration of the 'tool function'. Both are instances of 'planned skilled motor-sequential activity', but that does not enable us to draw inferences about the origin of language or to identify the cognitive characteristics that distinguish language from all the other forms of planned skilled activity. Perhaps the only thing that can be said is that the known complexity of certain operations forces us to assume mental functions of such refinement that the absence of a capacity for linguistic communication would be surprising. Artisans who pass on work techniques to one another are speakers (have *become* speakers) even if at a given moment they keep quiet.

Gesticulation is often identified as the most direct link between manualization and language, as referred to above. The arguments for the priority of gesture over speech are of divers kinds. Gordon Hewes has an experimentally-based theory of the gestural origin of language. As far as neurological data are concerned Hewes takes up not only the complex theme of lateralization but also the two distinct forms of neural control of the voice mechanism to be found respectively in the higher primates and in man. In the

It has been suggested that language evolved from manual gesticulation. A Nemadi tribeswoman from the Sahara reports on the return of her hunter spouse: 'He will return . . . in a day . . . and a night . . . with addax antlers.'

primates vocalization is controlled by what are from an evolutionary point of view more primitive cerebral regions. In primates the cortical control present in man is lacking so that their vocalization is highly stereotyped and scarcely if at all open to learning. Now, while the vocal mechanism of primates, by virtue of its very neural structure, does not lend itself to forms of communication higher than mere signalling, the situation is totally different as regards their front limbs, which are gifted with a vast range of behavioural activities permitting them to act on the environment and be guided by the feedback issuing from it. From all this we might conclude that the complex motor sequences required by any form of language were at an early date carried out by the hand and arms. Here we must also bear in mind the superior degree of manual precision possessed by the hominids, which is again controlled by more advanced regions of the brain than is the case with the other primates. Further confirmation is to be found in the fact that while attempts to teach a vocal language to chimpanzees have always failed (as the Hayeses found with Viki), good results have been obtained from experiments designed to utilize their manual capacities for the learning of special languages.

The hypothesis of a gestural origin for language can thus be based at least in part on differences in the neural control of vocalization in men and animals. It would follow that the verbal language of men was not derived from the vocal responses of the lower primates but was an entirely novel emergent characteristic:

> From a neurological point of view, the evolution of speech must represent the evolution of those mechanisms of the cerebrum located posteriorly in zones of cortex that function to analyze the information of the senses, to establish memories thereof, and to organize voluntary responses which proceed from these analyses of memories.
>
> (Ronald Myers,
> 'Comparative neurology of vocalization and speech')

To reduce the function of language to the mere elaboration of data and preparation of plans can result in a dangerous constriction: the affective and motivational side of human behaviour ought not to be overlooked in a general account of language. We think it useful to place motivational functions within a general scheme of the development of psychical functions (a sketch of the neuropsychological framework referred to is given below). The terms 'affect' or 'feeling' are not applied to knowledge of the external world, but there is development and modification of affect at every level of the cognitive process: 'Affect is like *form* to developing content.

One can say that there is an affective side to every action, perception, or utterance.' (Jason Brown, *Mind, Brain and Consciousness*) Thus, in the dynamic framework, feeling is not seen as energy directed in objects already 'given': in fact the external world and the affective charge corresponding to it are both products of the same activity of construction of reality by the nervous system.

'Language, like consciousness, is brought into being by the demand, the need, for dealings with other men', according to the famous statement of Marx and Engels. (It was important for Marx that need arose in the context of the processes of production and consumption. This is in contrast to the idea that needs are 'natural', so constituting 'the biological foundations of culture' (Malinowski).) We can state definitely that language did not emerge simply from a generic need for communication but arose from the need for a certain level of communication deriving from a particular organization of society and rendered possible by the level of communication already existing. There must have been a new dynamic whole in the form of the social practice of hominids, thrust out from the forest into the savannah and trying to overcome the difficulties of adaptation to their new ecological niche, forced to move over open ground rather than through trees, with more predators around and food not accessible or available quite as before. We can try to isolate some contexts within such a social practice where language may have been of particular evolutionary value.

We must first point out that language cannot be reduced to mere communication. In *Evolution of the Brain and Intelligence* Harry Jerison observes that if the basic evolutionary pressure favouring the development of language had been mere communication, we should expect the response to have consisted in the development of preconstructed linguistic systems with sounds and conventional symbols that had need neither of a long period of learning nor of complex neuronal systems, as had happened with birds, for example. But human language can be thought of as the expression of a further contribution by the nervous system to the formation of mental images analogous to the contributions of the sensory and associative systems of the brain. This means a mind capable of separating image and object, word and thing, reference and thing referred to. Nor can it stop there: there must be the possibility of referring to something not present, or non-existent. So the power of informing entails the power of *mis*informing. One scholar, Umberto Eco, actually defines semiotics as 'the study of whatever can be used to lie'.

The importance of higher symbolic capacities can be adequately judged only against the background of situations

It is supposed that these prehistoric rock drawings from Glen Canyon, Colorado River, had symbolic meanings with the power to motivate men. From the start language has been present in social organization in this role as well as in the role of 'mere' communication.

of conflict such as frequently arise in social groups founded on complex hierarchies and on constant struggles for supremacy as among primates. The study of pre-human rivalry behaviour enables us to understand certain social dimensions which would be lost sight of if our view were fixed too exclusively on economic cooperation. The quest for social prestige as the highest good independent of concrete material advantages shows the enormous weight attaching to affective and symbolic factors in the social process. A paradoxical happening like the destruction of goods in potlatch demonstrates that man does not seek objects and goods simply for use-value. In the production of objects needed by man one important dimension is precisely the production of their affective and symbolic significance.

Society, thought and language

In considering the problem of language in society we need to carry out two preliminary operations. The first is to condemn as inadequate the very phrase 'language *in* society'. It suggests a sort of container in which language is to be found alongside everything else. We prefer to regard language as in its way co-extensive with society, the latter being composed of numerous other institutions but the former being woven into the woof of everything. Still worse would be the phrase 'language *and* society', an absurd though usual contrast, as if we had on the one hand *society* and on the other *language* – a society without language and a language isolated from society. An inquiry such as ours would then consist in the attempt to join together what had thus clumsily been put asunder.

Still, once these matters have been made clear, it is possible to examine *inside* language (and hence also inside human society, given our principle of co-extensiveness) both biological aspects and social aspects. Dissection is useful, when applied to a real totality accepted as such.

The second preliminary operation (to which we shall now turn) is that of enriching or at least rendering more consistent and articulate our too general notion of society. We must translate it into that of social reproduction, following a line of interpretation pursued by Rossi-Landi for a number of years.

Social reproduction and sign systems

Social reproduction is the complex of all the processes by which a community or society survives, whether it grows or simply continues to exist. The notion has strong economic connotations but is not reducible to activities productive of goods. Even when it is a matter of satisfying elementary needs by immediate consumption, human beings have from the start joined together in groups and set in motion complex superindividual procedures, one of these being precisely verbal communication as a particular variety of their total sign system. Indeed, to take quite the opposite approach, it was only when all this had been accomplished that men *began to isolate themselves from one another*. Higher forms of organization were required by the need to 'accumulate' and then distribute material goods not immediately consumed. All the main processes that go on in a society and not simply those that are immediately productive form integral parts of social reproduction.

It should be noted that we have spoken above always of *sign systems*, not of mere *codes*. A sign system comprises at least a code (i.e. materials to work with and tools to work on them) but also the rules for applying the second to the first (these rules have a double location, residing from some points of view in the code, but to a still greater extent in the users of it); a system also includes the channels of, and the circumstances necessary for, communication and, further, the senders and receivers that employ the code. Thus a sign system also includes all the messages exchanged and capable of being exchanged within the universe set up by the system. The fact is that a sign system is a slice of social reality, and certainly not merely a symbolic machine which is at the disposal of anyone (so that its use would be at least half-way a-historical). There is no social reproduction without sign systems, nor do sign systems exist save within the compass of a real historical instance of social reproduction.

Sign systems are an integral part of social reproduction as a whole. They operate within it at every level and along every line of influence, and they are conditioned by, and in turn condition, everything else in it. At the same time it must be admitted that sign systems, large or small, have a relative independence of their own, which permits development in accordance with organizational laws proper to them alone. This is particularly true of verbal sign systems, i.e. of language in general, which in a certain sense is independent of the rest precisely to the extent to which it is a complex self-regulating system. Language is something so powerful that a specialized illusion is generated, that of its *total* independence in relation to social reproduction, of which it is in fact an integral part, being producer, tool and product at the same time. This illusion has been strengthened by the practice of considering language independently of other sign systems or as particularly pre-eminent in comparison with them. It is thus forgotten that not only for language but for every sign system, indeed for every socially effective mechanism historically transmitted, the very fact of forming a whole requires the operation of laws of internal organization. Yet the advent of machines in the literal sense, from the most primitive to

modern self-regulating ones, has been available as an obvious source of comparisons.

Verbal sign systems

Every human action is capable of communicating, i.e. is potentially part of a sign system. Language is only one complex of sign systems out of many that society needs in order to reproduce itself. Calling it the richest and most important is to state the obvious and banal, but from a rigorous point of view can be simplistic. The pre-eminence of language over other sign systems has come about principally for ideological reasons. Language has always been *par excellence* the repository and carrier of power inasmuch as dominant classes or groups have always used it for their own ends. Everywhere in the world the people speak – or would speak spontaneously – in some dialect or other. A national language is like a blanket covering up the enormous variety of dialects because to do so is in the interests of the state power organization. The opposition between intellectual and manual labour has from the start been, *inter alia*, an opposition between verbal and non-verbal sign systems: 'I speak and give you orders: you carry them out by working with your hands.' Nor can the other sign systems be said to *depend* on language. Indeed the opposite is true, for many of them at least; first because the others genetically preceded language and hence condition it; secondly because language is so to speak supported by various sign systems to which it makes reference. Language, of itself, *does not exist in reality*: for reality is always verbal *and* non-verbal, consists indeed of signs *and* non-signs. Saying that language is more important than other sign systems sounds a little like saying that the lungs are more important than the kidneys or digestion less important than breath. The fact is, rather, that if the kidneys cease to function, so will the lungs, if digestion ceases, so will breath.

For some theoretical linguists, on the other hand, the pre-eminence of language consists in certain formal and abstract criteria which to a considerable extent they themselves impose upon their material. Examples of such criteria are Chomsky's universals, the 'rules' of an 'idealized speaker' belonging to a 'homogeneous linguistic community' by which 'deep structures' are transformed into 'surface structures'. The danger of such an approach is that any form of communication that does not satisfy the criteria may be excluded as non-linguistic. The linguistic faculty can then be viewed as responsible for the differences between man and the other animals. Thus it becomes a metaphorical concept analogous to 'reason' among the idealists or the 'soul' in Christian tradition.

Language as a form of social control: dissident linguistic minorities, Catalan (*above*) and Welsh, draw attention to the homogenization of national language in the interests of state power.

A note on 'linguistic relativity'

A good way of securing a frontal examination of the relations between thought and language in general might be via a study of the relations between thought and individual or 'natural' languages. According to the American linguist Benjamin Lee Whorf, the overall structure of each language exercises a differential influence on the way in which a speaker of it (above all, but not only, if it is his mother tongue) perceives and conceives the world, on how he develops and employs his own thought and on how he behaves in the face of reality. No detailed discussion of this complex of propositions is possible here, but, following for convenience in the footsteps of the criticisms directed at it by Rossi-Landi elsewhere, we will advance some observations which will bring us to the threshold of our next topic, that of the relations between language and thought in general. Our discussion may seem too schematic but if we say that the two fundamental terms on which the whole matter turns are 'language' (i.e. particular languages) and 'thought', the shrewd reader will already see where we are going. Two unwarranted restrictions of vast totalities, complicated by other illegitimate operations, are what is involved here. We shall try to list singly, but without pretence of completeness, some of the principal moves into which the thesis can be dissected.

(i) Language, in the sense of the individual languages, gets cut off from language in general and particularly from that complex of social techniques that underlies communication and comprehension and that is best summed up in the idea of a community of speech. Thus a system of tools and materials gets looked at separately from the social processes that have produced it and that bring it into play.

(ii) Not only is the idea of a language frozen and hypostatized in this way, but a simplistic conception of it is put forward, ignoring polysemous and synonymous elements, i.e. not taking account of the multiformity of content that may 'lie behind' each word. Still less account is taken of metaphorical and metonymic elements.

(iii) Also neglected is the fact that different linguistic units can be found with different semantical structures in the course both of historical evolution and of individual human development.

Already at this point we find totally obscured, not only the complexity of the connections between the verbal designation of phenomena and the actual perception of them, but also the intricate network of relations that comes into being between the grammatical structure of a language and the system of concepts that it expresses, represents, or conveys. It will then seem strange, not to say methodologi-

Hindi, Urdu and English on a street vendor's sign in Delhi. Different languages offer different possibilities of expression, but that is far from saying that the mental equipment of a culture is the product of a language with which in some *a priori* way it has been endowed.

cally incorrect, that these very relations and connections have to be, as it were, salvaged *a posteriori*, after the language has been impoverished in this way. But there is more.

(iv) The verbal sign system which a language is is dealt with in isolation from other sign systems, and that in two respects: on the one hand no account is taken of the further developments that any language can be subjected to, i.e. the self-extending power of language is neglected and its power of forming special, technical, or ideal languages, or 'secondary' ones of whatever kind in relation to that normally spoken; on the other hand – and yet more serious – the contemporaneous and undeniable existence of non-verbal sign systems is completely ignored.

(v) Thus a language emerges as something totally isolated from the actual processes of social reproduction. The messages composed or transmitted with or in the language and inside the social reality consequently appear to be the mere product of the reified structures of the language itself, and any other factors acknowledged as contributing to their production would by definition have to be non-linguistic and strictly speaking not even describable in words.

It is perhaps by now clear that, whatever be meant by 'thought', the parallel between, and still more the inter-penetration of, 'language' (a language) and 'thought' is either impossible or seems totally artificial. But if we pass to what the supporters of linguistic relativity understand by the second term of their comparison things become even worse.

(vi) Thought itself, *qua* a complex of activities in one way or another mental, also appears isolated from social repro-duction. It is spoken of as a process which 'goes ahead of its own accord', as a constant independent of the real variables of social life.

(vii) Moreover under the umbrella term 'thought' there have to be included not only the fundamental categories of thought formally considered, but also the contents actually present – images, intuitions, representations, ideas – and, further, collective psychological habits, and finally everything normally meant by 'consciousness' and 'world-view'.

But, it may perhaps be objected, it is always legitimate to make use of abstractions. If I wish to isolate a language, or thought itself, within some vaster whole, it is not clear what edict ought to stand in my way. Even a fairly partial conception of language and/or thought can be useful for concentrating the attention of research. Much might be said here. In part we have already begun it with our discussion of social reproduction in general; but it is pointless to continue that discussion, since the thesis of linguistic relativity ultimately rests on a further operation as to whose illegitimacy no doubts can remain.

(viii) The two separate sub-totalities called 'language' and 'thought' get combined in a *one-way causal relation*: a 'language', isolated by all the operations we have described, is invested with the power of continuously and systematically conditioning a thing called 'thought', likewise isolated in the way described. Not only are two arbitrary and inadequately defined sub-totalities invoked to form an obviously spurious totality with no real existence, but inside that imaginary totality there is even set up a supposedly real dynamic to help us explain the course of events.

The result of all this is that thought is represented as the mere *product of language*. Such a theory can never grasp the contribution of non-verbal sign systems and various other extra-linguistic factors to the formation of every type of state or process that in any way deserves the name 'mental'. Yet it is obvious that all the factors in what is 'mental' are jointly operative in all processes of social reproduction. Language in its turn is the product of a social practice. The inevitable verdict is that the thesis of linguistic relativity represents idealistic favouritism regarding the role of language in social reproduction, and hence also in the genesis of that vast complex normally called 'thought'.

These criticisms are totally negative as regards the theoretical foundation of linguistic relativity and its usefulness in throwing light on our problems, but they should not make us forget the grace and delicacy of some descriptions from the inside of 'remote' languages such as Amerindian ones, nor the fertility of some of the intuitions of Whorf and others in fields that are essentially socio-linguistic. The very fact that every language is the historical product of a certain community of speakers distinct from all others implies that its possibilities of expression will also be unrepeatable. According to Dell Hymes this is 'the irreducible element of truth in what is known as the Whorfian hypothesis. The

means available condition what can be done with them and, in the case of language, condition the meanings that can be created and transmitted.' The English linguist Basil Bernstein offered to extend the concept of relativity to the comparison of uses of the same language (English) by children of different social classes.

The foregoing discussion of the complicated problem of the relations between different languages and thought pushes us on to a different plane, where we can reformulate the much deeper and more unitary problem of the relation between language and thought in general.

How the structures of language and thought are formed

Let us try to locate our problem within the dialectic of 'external' and 'internal world' which has been so fruitful in the tradition of philosophy and can supply suggestive ideas even in the neuro-psychological sphere.

It is possible to interpret the evolution of the brain functions and the relevant structures that have to do with perception and action, and their unfolding in the development of an individual, as the progressive construction of an external space. Jason Brown, *Mind, Brain and Consciousness*, gives a detailed model of cognitive development. At the *sensory-motor* level (reticular formation, mid-brain, tectum and basal ganglia), the perceptual and motor space is concentrated on the body and a very limited area around the body. Then at the *limbic-presentational* level (hypothalamus, cingulate gyrus, hippocampus, and other subcortical groups like the amygdala, the septum, and the dorsomedial nucleus of the thalamus) extrapersonal space begins to be formed, though it is still substantially intrapsychic: objects do not exist in it as independent realities but are of the nature of dream-images or hallucinations. At the *cortical-representational* level (neocortex) the object is completely externalized and placed in an abstract space, and the 'self' too is perceived as an object (as in the case of self-recognition in mirrors by non-human primates). All these levels, therefore, are possessed by man in common with other animals. At the level of the human species we arrive at a further distancing of action from perception, both now being fully externalized – placed in fact in the 'external world'. Meanwhile the emergence of language leads to the construction of an *internal* world and the self is constituted as a conscious subject, no longer merely as an object of awareness on the same footing as other objects in the physical world.

This is the biological basis for a conceptual scheme in which to frame our approach to the problem of reflexivity, the core, perhaps, of any discussion of the relations between thought and language. That an adequate scheme must include social factors is precisely what is meant by calling this basis biological.

We have seen that one fundamental tendency in the evolutionary history of the nervous system is that of withdrawing the organism from immediate dependence on environmental stimuli. One of the most important aspects in the fairly varied phenomenology of this tendency is the gradual construction of an abstract space into which sensations are projected in the form of objects and actions upon them. Externalization involves the emergence of awareness of the external world as 'other' than the perceiving subject.

In *Phenomenology of the Spirit* (1807) Hegel observes that 'Language and labour are outer expressions in which the individual no longer retains possession of himself but lets the inner get right outside him, and surrenders it to something else.' In the light of modern neuro-psychology, Hegel's

Higher animals, like man, have sufficient brain development to make possible the perception of an external space – but not of themselves as objects within it. The possession of language proper makes possible the construction of an internal space and the subjective perception of one's own mental processes. (Cartoons by Steinberg.)

profound insights acquire a yet wider significance. We can locate labour and language within the evolutionary process of externalization in which the nervous system 'is externalized and passes into the condition of permanence', perfectly comprehensible and modern words, but an exact translation of Hegel's own phrase. The result of this process is the constitution of a space and of objects endowed with ever greater perceptual stability.

Material production modifies the natural environment directly, so to speak, while linguistic production (and symbolic production in general) functions in a more indirect and complex manner. In the first place, according to Marx, language projects words into external space not just in the obvious sense of 'layers of air set in motion' but rather by producing meanings that have 'a life of their own' in the external world. This 'life' takes on the character of a 'thing', witness the adhesion of meaning to referent in primitive cultures and the tendency in the early stages of language learning to conceive of the word as a property of the thing; but even at a higher level of conceptual abstraction verbal signs still assume an objective character, conferred on them by constancy of significance or denotation.

Alongside the objective meaning, however, there is the personal *sense* in all its richness, which refers to the private world of an individual's experiences, though without ceasing to be social. This twofold character, so essential to linguistic signs, is perhaps the very feature which makes it possible to construct an internal space – the mind – based on the model of external space. Neither 'space' is metaphysically 'given': both are rather the product of evolution and of the history of mankind.

The central position of language flows from the fact that it is not the origin of consciousness but the form in which consciousness exists. Consciousness is in fact generated by internal reflexion effected through the activity of the nervous system.

The innermost and most delicate aspect of the problem, therefore, concerns the modes of internalization or rather (to use the term employed by the Soviet psychologist Lev Vygotsky) 'transplantation'. What, essentially, does this consist in? Convinced that the study of higher psychical functions cannot be tackled by reductivist methods, Vygotsky stresses the mediate structuring of mental processes (their reliance on intermediate structures), in which sign systems play a basic role.

Particularly important is the specifically human capacity to create artificial stimuli – 'means-stimuli' – i.e., according to Vygotsky, 'language, the various forms of counting and

Language produces meanings that have 'a life of their own' in the external world: Steinberg's cartoon alludes to verbal phrases which individuals may perceive as objective props to their identity and security.

calculating, mnemonic devices, algebraic symbolism, works of art, writing, sketches, diagrams, maps, blueprints, plans of all kinds, and so on.' By such means, and above all by language, man can organize his own behaviour not on the basis of direct stimuli but *via* an internal sign field reflecting environmental influences in a more or less generalized way. With the progressive internalization of intersubjective language (i.e. language used for primary communication) more complex forms of reflexion are attained until, after repeated reorganization of man's psychic processes, whole systems of concepts mediate his reflexion.

Vygotsky collaborated with his pupil Luria in research carried out in the field in Uzbekistan in 1930–2: the results were to be given systematic philosophical form by Luria himself in his *Cognitive Development: its cultural and social foundations*. At the beginning of the thirties that remote district of the USSR was in the process of passing from a feudal agrarian system to a socialist economy. The central thesis is that the processes of abstraction and generalization are 'a product of economic and cultural development'. Language has a fundamental role to play in the evolution from concrete, situational forms of thought to the theoretical operations typical of evolved abstract thought, including precisely the abstraction of the characteristics of things from the things themselves and the assignment of things perceived to logical categories. In other words, even if the passage to new theoretical forms of generalization is caused by changes in the real conditions of life, the means that make it possible are essentially linguistic. Words are already concepts, language is already categorical thought. Teaching better speech is the same as improving the capacity for abstraction.

The only major reservation that we think it necessary to advance against a position like Luria's is that it remains on too general a plane. This is certainly not true of the theories proposed by the historian and classicist George Thomson. In *Studies in Ancient Greek Society* Thomson makes twofold use of the principle that nothing exists in consciousness unless it has previously existed in social reality: on the one hand the formation of ideas and concepts reflects actual social relations, on the other antecedent non-verbal sign situations are given verbal formulation. Along with the formation of a monetary economy, and only then, there emerges in Greece for the first time the Parmenidean conception of a unitary being, which has value simply by existing, quite independently from any internal differentiae observable by the senses and modifiable by manual labour.

The philosopher Alfred Sohn-Rethel extends the analysis to paper currency. The exchange of commodities, he says, like every type of exchange, itself constitutes a non-verbal sign system which gets more and more complicated and reaches a higher level of abstraction with the institution, first of coinage, then of currency. The structures of this non-verbal sign system are reflected in language as the result of super-personal processes that are for the most part unconscious. This is how the possibility of knowledge cut off from manual labour makes its appearance. Abstract and formal concepts begin to be formed inside language, which in the course of time facilitate the construction of an objective natural science such as Galilean physics.

The Hungarian psychoanalyst Melanie Klein gives a remarkably complete and coherent formulation of the role of affective factors in the genesis of symbolic and thought processes, following on a tradition of exhaustive psychoanalytic researches stretching back to Freud. Reflecting both on clinical data and on the ideas of her teachers, Klein fixes on the affective and fantasy values that accompany the initial operations of intelligence and creativity and shows that both content and form in these last are invested with affective significance. Her well-known thesis of separation anxiety, and the attempts of her school to get to the bottom of the complex problem of the earliest object-relations and the defence-mechanisms employed by the child, have revealed the series of operations that bring the child to gradual

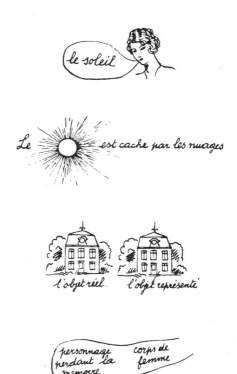

Magritte's paradoxes exposing the equivalence of words and images as graphic representations of objects show how we sometimes think of words not just as tools of reference but as actual properties of the things they describe.

recognition of the difference between self and mother and father. These operations form the affective basis for thought and temporally precede the first rudiments of language. All the complex apparatus, the mechanisms of splitting and denial and so forth, are themselves a sort of emotional grammar and syntax which play a structural role in promoting, or in pathological cases hindering, the genesis of the earliest stages of language. According to Wilfred Bion, for example, the basic mental operations of connecting and differentiation have their origin in the affective experiences of oral contact with the breast, and subsequently of the link between mother and father, not to speak of that of separation from the mother's body. In this connection Riccardo Steiner has no hesitation in seeing the development of the

> capacity to tolerate minimal differentiations between the self and the external world as one of the necessary conditions of that discriminative capacity on which the formation of the distinctive phonemic clusters of language is based and which for Jakobson, as we know, constitutes a primary and fundamental type of logical operation, since it initiates the process that gives rise to the most elaborate forms of thought.
>
> (*Il processo di simbolizzazione nell'opera di Melanie Klein*)

Insisting constantly, as she does, on the importance of early experience (in her last works even that of pre-natal life) for the formation of consciousness, Klein makes clear the partly pre-signific, not to mention pre-verbal, origin of the most important psychic processes. It will be clear that in taking up these themes we by no means intend to make any idealistic or biologistic uprooting of the individual from social reproduction. We wish only to stress the importance of that experience of his own body and of the external world which the child lives through before being exposed to sign systems proper.

We are now arriving at a certain view of the internal articulation and the delicate interweaving present in theoretical constructs such as 'thought' and 'language'. The inner complexity of such constructs and their intricate relationships with other factors in social reproduction are enough to show the shakiness of generalizations made not only by philosophers but also by scientists, who, though they operate experimentally, nonetheless continue to employ obsolete philosophical ideas when explaining or commenting on their results. To repeat: no one would dispute the legitimacy of certain abstractions: what we wish to deny, and emphatically, is the supposedly homogeneous character of the concepts in question, and we wish also to indicate the fertility of alternative approaches. Instead of illegitimately

talking of thought and language as uniform entities, and quite separate from one another at that, we think it more interesting to study individual 'chunks' of social reproduction in the light of various aspects of behaviour – behaviour with signs; verbal, affective, and economic behaviour; fantasy behaviour; and so on.

Ethnocentric prejudice no doubt plays a part in the references still quite frequently made to thought and language as generalized notions. Our native tongue seems to be identical with language, our way of thinking with thought. Ethnocentrism absorbs into itself, so to speak, all the other features of social reproduction: just because it is our own it is left out of account as being simply natural. A sort of mirage then comes into play, whereby we seem to see already present and operating something that is in fact only the goal of more or less conscious social planning. It is in fact undeniable that the worldwide homogenization fostered by state or monopolistic neo-capitalism is leading to the unification of innumerable different non-verbal sign systems and (irrespective of differences of language) to an almost uniform role for verbal sign systems inside different forms of social practice. Early capitalism has burdened us with enormous and horrific examples of 'unification'. We have only to think of the destruction of thousands of different cultures and languages in the two Americas, carried out, chiefly in the last century, by the physical destruction of their depositories or speakers. The more restricted brutality of the forms of homogenization at present in course should not give rise to the illusion of their being less radical in tendency.

Problems of linguistic innateness

The importance of the innateness thesis for those who follow in the footsteps of the renowned North-American linguist Noam Chomsky resides in their conviction that the stock of innate knowledge of a speaker (his competence being the formalization of such knowledge) is describable in biological terms and can be put forward as a *model of the mind*:

> The 'innateness hypothesis', then, can be formulated as follows: Linguistic theory of U.G. [Universal Grammar], construed in the manner just outlined, is an innate property of the human mind. In principle, we should be able to account for it in terms of human biology.
>
> (Chomsky, *Reflections on Language*)

In this way the general notion of language as a 'mirror of the mind' is given precise content. Universal grammar based on the system of conditions which all individual grammars must satisfy, and at the same time on a set of empirical hypotheses concerning linguistic ability, should actually be transformable into a psycho-physiological structure. Even in his latest theoretical work, quoted above, Chomsky is backing up the position of his *Aspects of the Theory of Syntax*, where he stressed the systematic ambiguity of his own use of the phrase 'theory of language' to refer both to 'the child's innate predisposition to learn a language type' and to 'the linguist's account of this'.

In the wake of this almost wilful confusion universal grammar assumes in Chomsky's – or at least in many of his supporters' – eyes all the concreteness of a physical organ. It is no accident that he speaks of a 'mental organ'. Chomsky's fellow-American Eric Lenneberg was convinced that all behaviour was an integral part of an organism's structure. He therefore set about investigating the biological foundation of linguistic behaviour, which is said to distinguish man from all other species. He was also convinced that the relation between structure of the organism and mode of behaviour was not direct or necessary. He was therefore obliged to find the neurological equivalent of language, not in some specific structure, but rather in the brain's mode of functioning, i.e. in the maturation of the encephalon and the lateralization of functions. The central point in the 'explanation' thus arrived at consists in regarding these biological correlations as written into man's genetic code and also as specific to the human race. The unfolding of linguistic competence is therefore viewed as a mechanical type of process, where the linguistic environment of human society plays the part of a *releaser*, i.e. a key-stimulus capable of *activating* but certainly not of shaping a form of behaviour. Given such a point of view it would seem that any research into the evolutionary origin of language is not only useless but cannot even be started. Language gets presented to us as a 'unitary faculty' isolated from other cognitive systems and emerging *de novo* as a result of genetic mutation.

What are the chief elements in this theoretical construction? First of all, the conception of language as a 'faculty of the mind' can easily be criticized in the light of advances made by Soviet psychology. The concept of a functional system or of the global function of several tissues or organs, first applied by Bernstein and Anokhin to the motor and respiratory systems, has been extended by Luria to mental functions, thus superseding both rigid localization and the theory of non-specificity of cerebral tissue. The thesis of functional 'pluripotentialism' means that a single formation can under different conditions be included in different functional systems and contribute to the performance of different tasks. Thus for the 'centres' where functions used to be located it substitutes 'dynamic systems', with quite distinct elements playing highly specialized roles in the execution of a

given function. Such systems are complex and dynamic in a way that does not permit us to conceive of mental activity as a set of simple and independent faculties.

Further confirmation of the 'constellation' character of higher psychical functions is provided by the study of their pathological breakdown. The basic hypothesis of clinical neurology, which views the nervous system as a hierarchical organization of interdependent sub-systems, many of which can be analysed in relative isolation, can be regarded as valid also in the case of language. A study of the syndromes arising from damage to different neural systems allows us to observe from time to time the loss of one or other linguistic function: word-hearing (acoustic agnosia), object-naming (amnestic aphasia), logico-grammatical operations (semantic aphasia), and so on.

Besides, Lenneberg's conviction that language can be learnt only inside a certain critical period (from 2 to 12, before which the maturing brain has not yet acquired, and after which it has lost, the necessary plasticity) has recently been quite precisely falsified. We refer to the case of *Genie*, the Los Angeles girl who was kept in isolation by her psychotic father until the age of 13 and reduced at the time of her liberation (1973) to a state of grave psychic and organic deficiency. After long treatment Genie gained a fair mastery of language at an age clearly outside the so-called critical period. Her case is related to those of the 'wild children' mentioned above.

As Robert Hinde has rightly stressed (*Biological Bases of Human Social Behaviour*), the fundamental error of Chomsky's reasoning consists in transforming the discovery of an innate difference obtaining between two forms of behaviour into an assertion of their own innateness. But actually from the fact that there is *an innate difference* in language-acquiring capacity between man and other animal species it cannot be inferred that *the capacity itself* is innate and therefore not dependent on learning at least one language. This leads to a confusion of perspective: the common structural characteristics of all language – the linguistic universals – come to be attributed to a genetic predisposition without any regard being paid to the constant features of the physical and social environment of the species *Homo*.

Let us for a moment re-examine the cases of 'wild children', taking them together with cases of chimpanzees who have been taught a form of language based on arbitrary symbols. *Washoe* used the gestural language of deaf-mutes, American Sign Language; *Sarah* arranged coloured pieces on a magnetic blackboard in accordance with a syntax; *Lana* is capable of operating an apparatus built specially for her and connected with a computer. These two categories of 'quasi-speakers' plainly contradict all theories of the innateness or species-specificity of human language – the form of the latter here refuted is that which is 'absolute because a biological datum'. When apes begin to 'talk' a part of the territory originally thought to be *purely* human crumbles away, but it does not follow that the fully worked out use of language in its historical social setting ceases to be indeed purely human. Wild children are not alone in showing that in default of a suitable environment linguistic behaviour simply does not take shape, and only in certain cases is it possible to recover it later. When children are brought up by animals such as wolves, bears, goats and gazelles the human adolescent shows a striking degree of adaptation as regards both general and communicative behaviour to the animal species among which he has lived. All this brings out the extraordinary importance of the environment, and particularly the human social environment, for the development of modes of behaviour.

As for the experiments with chimpanzees, these show how unsuspected intellectual powers can be actualized in members of a non-human species once individuals are exposed to the stimuli of an environment as sophisticated as that of a research laboratory. To interpret the phenomenon correctly we must look again at the problem of the relations between structure and function. We note first the impossibility of discovering a structural difference between human brains and those of the great apes. The most recent investigations show that even the anatomical asymmetry of the two hemispheres (lateralization, which Chomsky regards as so important) is also present in non-human higher primates. Marjorie Le May has found that in chimpanzees and orang-utans two anatomical features, the Sylvian fissure and the occipital pole, are both longer in the left hemisphere. There can thus be no difference of localization: we must have recourse again to the functional pluripotentialism of cerebral structures already mentioned. Chimpanzees would be capable of a form of language, only they have never found an environment that would allow it to be realized. This fact will seem 'a remarkable miracle' (Chomsky, *Reflections on Language*) only to those who underestimate the complexity of the structure-function relation. Our intention is not to deny the diversity of the various evolutionary levels, only to stress that for the attainment of the most complex forms of behaviour it is requisite that the *necessary* conditions of structure should be supplemented by functionally *sufficient* conditions furnished by the play of individual interactions with the natural and cultural environment.

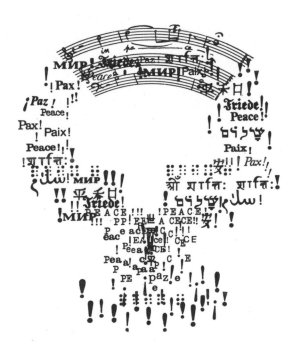

Maurice Roche's ironic soliloquy arranges the word for peace
in many languages in the shape of an H-bomb mushroom cloud.

Face-to-face

Body language and voice are the primary forms of human communication. The language of gesture, though more primitive and limited, continues to co-exist with that of words. In the crises of life, the emotions of sympathy, love, anxiety, grief, anger, fear can sometimes be more adequately expressed without words. The same is true of joy, relief and amusement. These are all cases where 'non-verbal' communication, or 'body language', appears instinctive. At the other end of the scale is the language of specialized and agreed gestures, which are as elaborately structured as words and indeed are learned through verbal explanation.

To a certain degree we share non-verbal communication with animals, but ours can be far more flexible than any animal system. Hand gestures are astonishingly varied, while the human face, with its myriad of tiny muscles, especially round the eyes and mouth, can convey so much in a single glance that any verbal equivalent (say in a novel) will be no more than an approximation. The art of mime, brought to a high pitch in the silent film, relies on this vast range of expression and gesture. Such communication works instantly and powerfully, although it is subject to ambiguity and may be misunderstood. Since it is less conscious than a spoken language, it is less easily used to lie.

Language in this section means spoken language. In our print-conscious culture we tend to think of it as something in books. But all languages were spoken before they were written down; most never were written down. They are nevertheless extremely complex. Because of the antiquity of language (probably more than a million years) no such thing as 'primitive language' survives. How languages originated, why they differ as they do, how deep these differences lie, how far the structure of language depends upon social structures and how far upon the structure of our mental processes, are questions that still exercise scientists.

1 Tender coaxing on the one hand, fearful and yet trusting hesitation on the other, and total mutual absorption are all conveyed in facial expression, gesture and contact in this detail from Bruegel's Peasant Dance **(1568). A young child is being taught to dance. Gaze, closeness and bearing tell the whole story.**

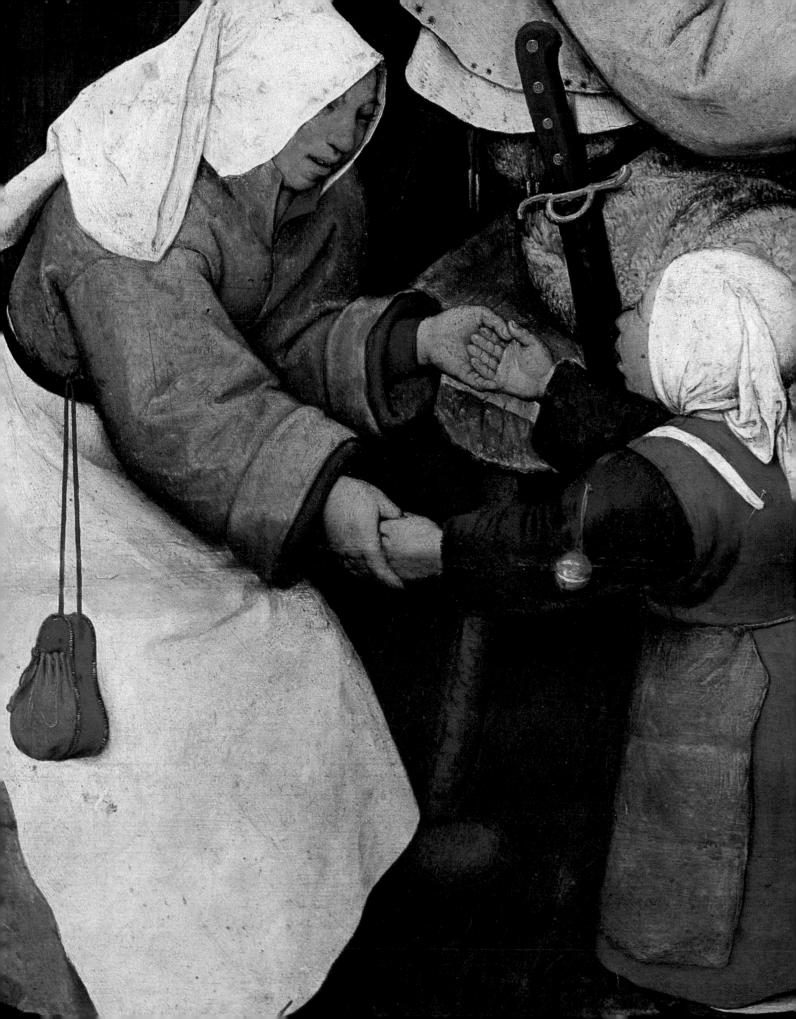

'Nothing in sight'

'Ostriches'

'Antelopes'

'Lots of does'

'Does over here'

'Make camp'

42

'Addax'

'Does'

Sign-language is indeed part of language, and not an aspect of non-verbal communication. The point is that – as in both the examples here – the signals convey definite meanings as part of a more or less elaborate conventional system. That is to say, there is no necessary resemblance between the form of the signs and what they represent: meaning is attached to them only by agreement. (Since in these two specialized examples we are not party to this agreement, we cannot understand them.)

So with language in general. Its complete dependence on conventions, its qualitative separation from the things it refers to, is the key to its potential for complexity and the explanation of its role, not just in communicating elaborate messages, but also in making possible any kind of abstract thought, without which we would have no elaborate messages to convey. But, as the following pages emphasize, this does not mean that it is the only kind of sign system that deserves our attention.

2–9   The sign language of the Nemadi, a hunting tribe of the Mauritanian Sahara.

10–12   A bookie signals the odds to his colleague at the race track.

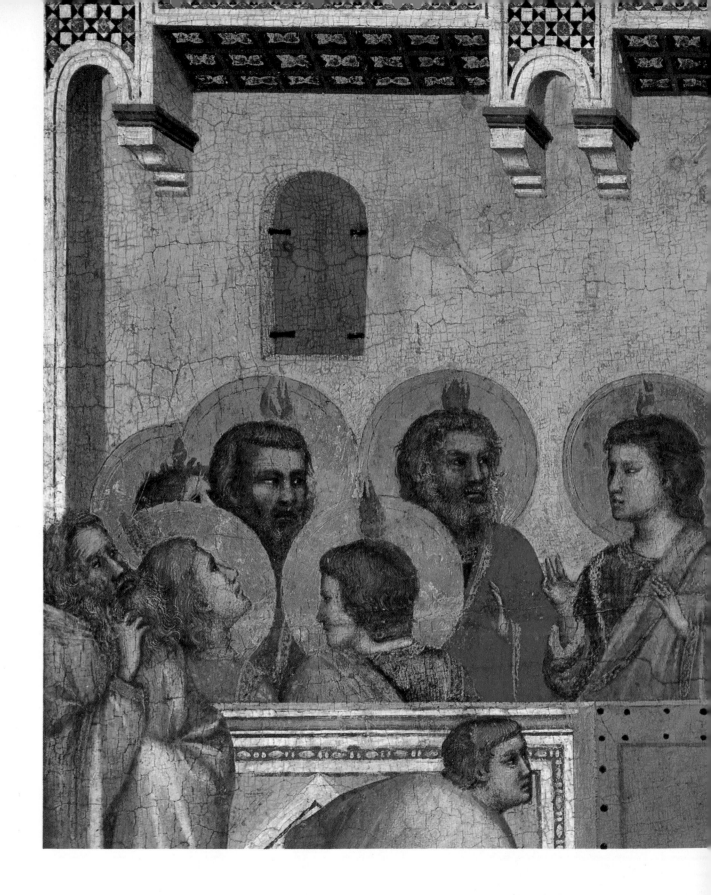

THE ORIGIN OF LANGUAGE: HUMAN OR DIVINE?

In the mythology of many cultures, language has been seen as a divine gift. Only comparatively sophisticated societies could conceive of it, on the contrary, as a skill which they acquired for themselves.

13   Pentecost, **School of Giotto. In the Christian myth of Pentecost,** or Whitsun, divine intervention takes visible shape in the tongues of fire descending on the heads of the twelve Apostles. Here God miraculously undoes his own action in instituting the diversity of languages – babel – as punishment for man's temerity in building a tower on the plain of Shinar that was to reach up to heaven. After the first Whitsun, the Apostles could (it was thought) be understood whatever the language of their hearers.

THE LANGUAGE OF GESTURE

Except for the most basic examples, the meaning of a gesture varies with the context in which it is used. This cultural diversity reflects the fact that non-verbal languages, like verbal ones, are the result of social development.

14 Two smiling West African boys express mutual affection in what is in fact a modified gesture of aggression. This kind of inversion is frequently met with in the study of animal behaviour, where aggressive instincts are diverted into ritualized forms which can become gestures of affiliation (this is one suggested explanation for the origin of human

laughter). Another way of looking at this gesture is to see it as a reflection of social conditioning, whereby these youths would feel inhibited from making more conventional gestures of affection for fear of being thought effeminate.

15   The handshake is a highly formal gesture, communicating greeting. It is also an opportunity for passing other, and perhaps more significant, 'messages': for instance, pressure and duration can indicate intensity of feeling. Here it appears that the status of the participants in relation to each other is being confirmed. Different formal styles of dress and the bearing and facial expressions of both the participants and their 'supporters' seem to reinforce this transaction.

16   Chinese children miming the words of a song in a welcoming committee break into formal hand-waving. It is suggested that this vertical flapping type of wave is a primitive form of the side-to-side waving which is familiar to most people.

17   French farmers arguing in a town street exhibit two different combative hand gestures, one stabbing towards the ground with pointed finger, the other in effect pushing away the arguments of his opponent. In addition the speakers lean towards each other in a threatening and aggressive manner, but not actually moving so close as to escalate the dispute into physical threat.

Intense human emotions, originating far back in the evolution of the human species, are thus manifested in the same way in different ages and cultures. Facial expressions in particular vary little, except insofar as they are modified by cultural conventions about what is permissible.

The observation of the artist seeking to give 'expressive' quality to his subject is as useful as the 'factual' record of the camera in drawing attention to the characteristic features – the mouth drawn down at the corners, the contracted brow, the eyes narrowed in weeping. There are also striking similarities in posture (the head inclined to one side), manual gesture (the manner in which the body of the loved one is held) and gaze (both look obliquely, with distracted glance).

18   Fourteenth-century Pietà from Westphalia.

19   Vietnamese soldier with body of child.

MAKING FACES

The face quite clearly offers the most important and the most subtly expressive way of signalling non-verbally that we have. Its particular usefulness in the human species is in communicating emotions. In higher animals its use is confined to communicating attitudes towards other individuals – dominance, aggression, sub-mission, sexual attraction – and for humans it also has this role. We read faces to inform ourselves about people's personalities – although we can often be misled – and facial signals, like other aspects of non-verbal communication, play an important part in guiding and regulating the inter-change of conversation. Various attempts have been made to discover if there is a complete 'language' of facial expression and if it can be decoded in a systematic manner. A more general interest in the expressive qualities of the human face is represented here.

20–5 Masks used in the courtly Nō drama of Japan.

26–9 Photographs from an exhibition entitled Masks by the Polish-born photo-grapher Krystina Baker.

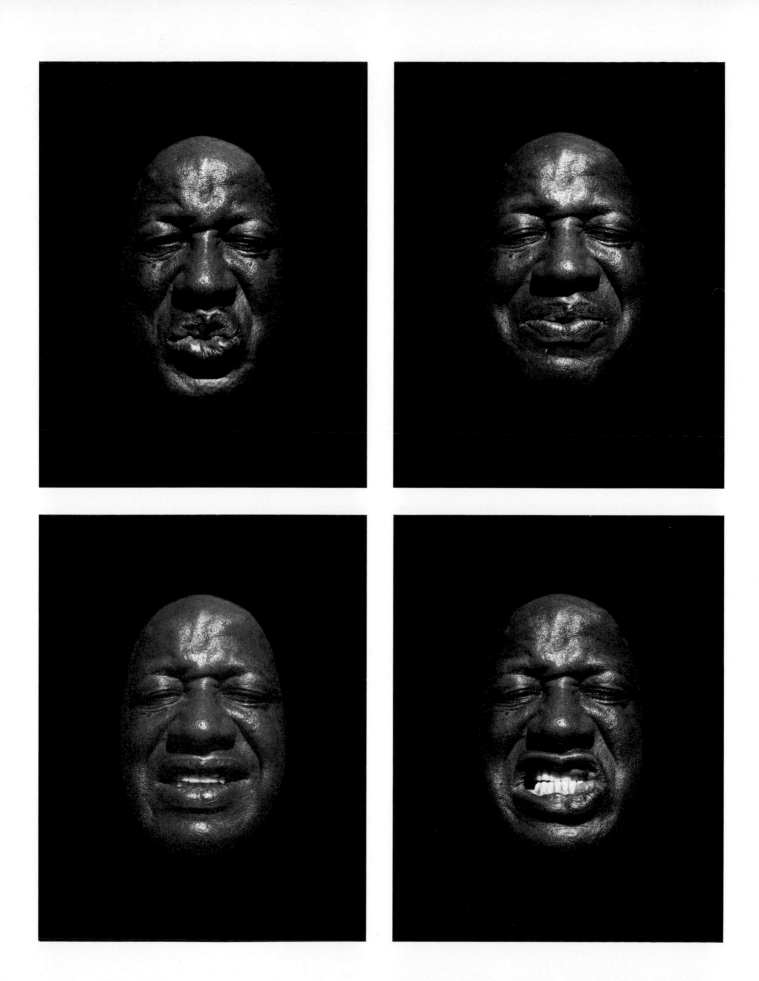

ACTIONS AND WORDS

In ritual and ceremony, the actions performed by the participants are as important as the words they speak, and even the words are formulaic, often couched in archaic language. The symbolic power of such rituals in reinforcing meanings is well attested in history, and remains today.

30 A grant of land on the occasion of a marriage, an illustration from a 13th-century Catalan manuscript known as the Liber Feudorum Maior, which records a number of such feudal grants. The joining of the hands visibly symbolizes the transmission of ownership from the father to the young couple, and the crossing of his arms in this gesture attractively suggests the uniting of their two families.

31 A marriage ceremony depicted in a 15th-century French version of the romance of Alexander, a favourite epic of late-medieval chivalry. Though the costume is everyday courtier's dress of the period we have no difficulty in recognizing what is going on. Despite the secularization of British and American society, the Christian marriage ceremony is still a powerful social ritual. The special status of the partners expressed in their dress, the symbolic actions of a man similarly set apart by his costume, and the surroundings of a special building, do much more than merely convey information to the witnessing congregation and the participants.

32 The coronation of Frederick IV of Germany as Holy Roman Emperor by Pope Nicolas V in 1452, from a painting by an anonymous Flemish master. Coronations were real political events of the utmost importance in the medieval world. Signifying much more than a mere appointment, they enacted the conferring of divine authority and power to rule. The Pope, God's chief representative on earth, identified again by costume and by the papal tiara, crowns the king after anointing him with sacred oil. The placing of a crown upon the head itself powerfully communicates both the relative status of the crowner and the crowned, and the total transformation of the man who now wears the crown.

HANDS UP: DESOLATION, DESPAIR, JUBILATION

The expression of grief – beginning no doubt as a spontaneous outpouring of emotion – was soon 'ritualized' and made into a quasi-dramatic enactment; but forms acceptable to one society are rejected by another. It may be significant that these three examples of very ample mourning gestures are all Mediterranean.

33 A typical representation of mourning women in a funeral procession from the Egyptian XVIIIth Dynasty, 16th to 14th centuries BC.

34 Mourners in a 14th-century Spanish tomb painting.

35 Similarities echo across the centuries in the gestures of bereaved Cypriot women during the troubles of 1974.

But a meaning and its opposite are often expressed in closely analogous ways: consider the baring of teeth in animals which can be a threat display or the equivalent of smiling.

36   It is impossible to know the meaning of this prehistoric cave painting from the Vallée des Merveilles in France, known as 'the Sorcerer', but our own interpretation of it, whether as a gesture of triumph or of horror, tells us something about the non-verbal communication system in which we all participate.

37, 38   The gestures may be similar, but what these express could hardly be more different. In Enrico Baj's collage Fire! Fire!, it is horrified despair; in the British football supporter, triumph.

III
NON-VERBAL COMMUNICATION

Arthur D. Shulman
and Robyn Penman

39   Detail from a Madonna al latte **by the early
15th-century Italian painter Gregorio di Cecco.**
    The experience of the mother's breast in infancy
is said to be the origin of the emotional strength
associated with the sense of touch. In infancy,
touch is of course the most important form of
communication, and touching continues to play
an active role up to adolescence. But between
adults it is very much circumscribed by social
convention, although it remains of primary
importance in sexual relationships.

NON-VERBAL COMMUNICATION

In the days of silent movies, Charlie Chaplin could communicate with his audience without using words. His hands, his face, his funny walk and his clothes all conveyed his messages. Only occasionally was it necessary to insert a frame of writing. In our everyday life we are constantly sending non-verbal messages to other people: we wink, grimace, shake our heads, point with our hands and tap our feet. These non-verbal messages can be much more important in human interaction than we sometimes give them credit for. Spoken language is at the forefront of our consciousness: non-verbal communication embraces, as well as conscious gestures, quite automatic signals like changes in pupil size and things that are only partly under conscious control like facial expression, tone of voice, stance and physical distancing. But 'bodily communication', prior to language in evolutionary terms, is an essential part of the communication system, and the vehicle for many fundamental human transactions which speech alone is unable to deal with. The communication process is more than just the exchange of words: in fact, communication can occur without words at all. Whenever two or more people are together, non-verbal communication always occurs, verbal communication only sometimes.

But it is only recently that various aspects of our non-verbal communication have been given serious scientific attention. One area of study has been concerned with looking at the extent to which certain types of non-verbal behaviour are universal in the human species, with evolutionary parallels in other animal species. For example, postures of dominance and submission in face-to-face encounters between human beings have been shown to be remarkably similar to ritual displays of aggression and appeasement which establish and maintain ranking order among other primates. However, the focus of attention in these studies has been the display of individual features of non-verbal behaviour and not human non-verbal communication as such. It is this that we are concerned with here.

In fact, when we stop to consider what communication is all about there is one thing we would all agree on: it is something which goes on *between* people. Thus, looking at the behaviour (non-verbal and otherwise) of individuals is not necessarily looking at the communication process. To look at this process we must see the individuals in relation to each other. When people are acting in social situations they are not self-sufficient, isolated units but are inextricably involved with others. In such social situations the behaviours of the individuals in them take on a new role: they become messages which are sent and received.

This exchange of messages has to be studied with the aid of quite artificial conceptual constructs, looking at the seamless web of communication in terms of articulated elements of message, encoding, transmission, decoding and so forth. And, since there is no equivalent of writing (in relation to speech) to provide a formal objective record of non-verbal communication, we have to invent systems of notation before we can subject it to organized scrutiny.

Thus the recent literature with reference to which this historically oldest form of communication has to be discussed is obliged, in a further paradox, to consider in quite academic terms what we think of as part of commonplace, everyday experience.

Eyeball-to-eyeball confrontation: there is a lot besides verbal communication to this encounter between umpire and Los Angeles Dodgers manager at a game in Cincinnati.

Verbal and non-verbal communication

But what is the boundary between verbal and non-verbal communication? It is not just a simple matter of the difference between actions and speech, because there are non-verbal elements of speech such as tone – or even silence. Instead of making a distinction based on the 'channels' involved in the communication – the physical apparatus of transmitting and receiving, such as vocal chords or eyes – it may be better to refer to the 'code' which the communication employs. One suggested scheme of distinction relies on the degree of subtlety in the code that is used, defined according to the presence or absence of specific coding rules; so nodding affirmatively in answer to a question would count as verbal communication. Some people have tried to avoid the problem by using alternative terms such as 'body language', 'kinesics' (the science of movements) or, at the most comprehensive level, 'semiotics' (the study of meanings). But these have been objected to on various grounds, and they only reproduce the dilemma between 'channel' (body language and kinesics) and 'code' (semiotics) as alternative bases for defining the phenomenon we are trying to study. The difficulty arises from the very nature of communication, which involves combinations of 'messages' in various codes, transmitted along various channels, and inseparable from the people in the communication. In the end we probably have to accept the somewhat inaccurate 'non-verbal' epithet, and also acknowledge that we cannot be precise about the boundaries between verbal and non-verbal communication.

But we can still make useful distinctions between verbal and non-verbal if we think in terms of typical examples of each. The most typical example of verbal communication is written language, with spoken language coming close behind. Facial expression and body gestures are the most typical examples of non-verbal communication. Somewhere in between these two prototypes lie such things as tone of voice, accent, and so on which potentially belong to either category.

The most general characteristic of our typical non-verbal examples is that they are analogue rather than digital in form. In a digital form of communication there is no necessary resemblance between the elements in the code and the meaning behind it. In contrast, the analogue form preserves at least some characteristics of the meaning in the elements used to express it. Digital coding always consists of discrete units (such as words) whereas the analogue form is continuous (like laughter). The difference is the same as that between a conventional (analogue) watch and a digital one: the former represents time on a continuous dimension (the circular watch face); the latter represents it as discrete numbers.

This difference makes it difficult to translate non-verbal messages into verbal ones, and vice versa. For example, try to explain in words what makes a face look sad, or try to communicate the meaning of the word 'philosophy' by gestures alone. The analogue form is inadequate for expressing logical relationships because it does not use the

Elementary recognition of the role of facial expression in the later masks of Greek drama: bronze mask of tragedy and comic mask in mosaic, 3rd or 2nd centuries BC.

logic of language. It is impossible to express non-verbally a message using 'either...or' or 'if...then' constructions, and it is impossible to express the negation of a proposition. Thus the message 'if you go I will not be angry' cannot be conveyed by exclusively non-verbal means.

Because of the analogue nature of non-verbal communication, it requires less learning to understand. However, at the same time it has far greater potential for ambiguity since there is in general no explicit, clearly-defined set of cultural conventions for interpreting its meaning. For example, the bringing of a gift can be seen either as a token of affection, or as a bribe, or as an act of restitution, depending on the recipient's understanding of his relationship with the giver.

Intention, awareness and meaning

Some writers argue that 'real' communication requires that the sender is conscious of sending a message, and intends to send it, and succeeds in getting it received. However, the particular difficulties of making distinctions between intended and non-intended, successful and unsuccessful, and conscious and unconscious in the case of non-verbal behaviour become clear when we consider the subtleties of our own behaviour with other people. When we are talking to someone, there is usually little doubt that we are conscious of it and intend to do so, or that we are being heard and understood. But when we move our arms as we talk it is more difficult to say whether we are aware of it and intend to do it, and whether the other person sees it and 'understands' it correctly. Furthermore, some behaviour may be planned and acted with a high degree of conscious awareness: some behaviour we design to look unintentional: and some may be so habitual that we are not aware of it. Because of such subtleties it would seem better to think of intent, awareness, or consciousness as varying in degree, rather than as simply either present or absent.

The closely related question of what non-verbal behaviour means is even more problematic. While our behaviour with other people is public, the meaning of it is in a sense private. It comes from the individual's understanding of what seems to be happening. Communication is not simply a matter of the behaviour of two participants: as R. D. Laing has pointed out, we have to consider the meanings people attribute to their own behaviour and to that of the other person (not to mention what I think you think I mean, or even what I think you think I think you mean). Thus there are at least two meanings to any message, the sender's and the receiver's; and communication is possible to the extent that these coincide.

The non-verbal communication system

It does not make strict sense to talk about the non-verbal communication system, since it is only a component (albeit an essential one) of the total communication system. However, for practical purposes we can think of it as such, and break it down into further components. The most common subdivision is by channels, usually defined in terms of the sensory apparatus of the sender. The authors' preference is to define the channels as joint functions of sender and receiver, emphasizing the nature of communication as interrelation between the participants.

The sender has at least four main sets of physical apparatus: face, eyes, body, and voice. The repertoire of the face includes but is not limited to frowning, smiling and grimacing; the eyes can signal by direction of gaze and changes in pupil size; the body offers posture, positions of arms and legs, and distancing and orientation in relation to others; and non-verbal aspects of the voice include tone and speech rhythm. The receiver has five primary senses: vision, hearing, touch, taste and smell.

Out of the twenty theoretically possible combinations which result, we can identify five major channels and at least three minor ones in 'normal' communication. The major channels are (a) face-vision, (b) eye-vision, (c) voice-hearing, (d) body-vision and (e) body-touch. Among the minor channels are (a) body-hearing, (b) body-smell and (c) face-touch. Of course these channels are not used one at a time. In a typical situation, a number of messages is conveyed in different channels both simultaneously and in succession. When we take into account the different meanings that can be attributed to the signals in each channel by sender and receiver, we can appreciate even better the complexity of non-verbal communication. Imagine an encounter between a woman and a man, Ann and Bill. Ann turns her head in Bill's direction (A_1) and raises her eyebrows (A_2), while Bill moves so that he stands in front of Ann (B_1) and gazes at her (B_2). Now, from Ann's point of view, B_1 could be seen as blocking her path or attracting her attention, while B_2 could be seen as a stare or an invitation to speak. On the other hand, Bill could see A_1 as an indication of interest or a chance movement and A_2 as surprise, or as a silent invitation. If we than asked Ann and Bill what they intended, we could find out that Bill wanted to attract Ann's attention and Ann was waiting for Bill to start a conversation. In this instance their desires are compatible and the communication can continue easily. However, if, for example, Ann had turned her head in Bill's direction, smiled and then turned away, Bill would probably have had more difficulty in understanding Ann's message and some further negotiation of meaning would have been necessary.

Studying non-verbal communication

Two general characteristics of the non-verbal communication system, as we have described it so far, that have major implications for studying it are its analogue form and its complexity. Since our normal methods of describing the communication process rely on a digital code, i.e. the written word, some loss of information or distortion when we try to express the meaning of non-verbal behaviour is inevitable. This applies whether it is the originator of the behaviour making the translation or an observer. For the purposes of analysis that translation is usually made by assigning each element of the behaviour to one of a number of pre-established classifications. Some classification schemes refer to structural features, i.e. to the physical description of the behaviour. One such scheme, which deals with only one channel, is the Facial Affect Scoring Technique (FAST) developed by the American writers Ekman and Friesan. Some examples of their classifications are shown below. FAST was designed primarily to measure facial movement relevant to emotion. It is now being superseded by a more complex and comprehensive system called Facial Action Coding System (FACS) which notates all facial movements that can possibly be distinguished visually. This new system will facilitate the study of facial movement in research unrelated to emotion, e.g. facial punctuation in conversations, difficulties with facial expressions indicating brain lesions, and so on. The practical application of schemes of this sort is in quantifying observable features of non-verbal behaviour, so as to make possible statistical analysis. Trained observers watch filmed or videotaped interactions and code the action in accordance with the chosen classification scheme on standard forms. This provides data in a usable form.

A scheme of the same type developed by Ray Birdwhistell attempts to code all aspects of human movement. It divides the body into eight major sections: (a) total head, (b) face, (c) trunk, (d) shoulder, arm, and wrist, (e) hand and finger, (f) hip, leg, and ankle, (g) foot, and (h) neck. Part of the face coding descriptions from this scheme is shown below.

ᴑᴗ	Wide eyed	ᴗ	Set jaw
—ᴏ	Wink	ᴗ	Smile tight — loose o
> <	Lateral squint	⊢	Mouth in repose lax ortense —
>< ><	Full squint	⌐	Droopy mouth
ᴓ ᴓ	Sidewise look	ᴓ	Tongue in cheek
ᴓ ᴓ	Focus on auditor	ᴖ	Pout
● ●	Stare	ᴍ	Clenched teeth
◉◉	Rolled eyes	ᴗ	Toothy smile
ϟ ϟ	Slitted eyes	⊞	Square smile
● ●	Eyes upward	◎	Open mouth
-●●-	Shifty eyes		

Other schemes refer to function. A functional classification makes assumptions about the meaning of different behaviours: usually this is the meaning as understood by the observer.

For example, Ekman and Friesan have developed a scheme with five categories: (a) *emblems* – movements that are substitutes for words; (b) *illustrators* – movements that accompany speech and accent, modify and punctuate it; (c) *regulators* – movements that maintain or signal a change in speaking and listening roles; (d) *adaptors* – movements related to individual need or emotional state; and (e) *affect displays* – particularly the facial expressions showing emotions.

The complexity of non-verbal communication requires that some relatively arbitrary boundaries are imposed in any attempt to understand it: we have already imposed one in distinguishing between verbal and non-verbal communication. In addition, even as participants in the communication process, we do not usually take into account all the aspects of an interaction that could provide information. We select only the aspects we consider relevant or that we notice. Investigators of non-verbal communication select relevant aspects in the same way.

A particularly striking and important example of this kind of selection is the investigator's choice of viewpoint. Three

Attempting to classify facial movements: photographs of brow, eyes and mouth said to be registering surprise, from the FAST system, and some of the eye and mouth notations from the face section of Ray Birdwhistell's scheme for the whole body.

major positions can be differentiated: (a) the sender's, (b) the receiver's and (c) the observer's, which takes both into account simultaneously. As will become apparent, each perspective has its limitations, but each adds to our understanding of the non-verbal communication process as a whole. It is sometimes the case that research findings arrived at from one perspective seem to conflict with those from another. This is usually attributable to the fact that different viewpoints have been employed for different purposes, using different levels of analysis and different units. This being so, we will focus on each of the viewpoints in turn, rather than attempt to give an integrated account of research conclusions.

Sending non-verbal messages

When sending non-verbal messages, we cannot perceive all our behaviour. We can usually hear our voices, but do not usually see our gestures, postures, or expressions. Because these non-verbal behaviours are also typically more ambiguous and more continuous than speech, they are probably less prominent in our consciousness. It has been

suggested that the sender has less direct control of non-verbal behaviour than of speech, and this has led some investigators to study the extent to which our non-verbal behaviour indicates our 'true feelings'. As Marcel Marceau, the mime artist, said, 'Language has always been distrusted because there have always been lies within the truth. People have been misled by words.'

One approach to this question has been to attempt to show that particular types of non-verbal behaviour do reliably and consistently express particular emotions, regardless of period, place, or nationality. Paul Ekman and his colleagues used the FAST technique to compare the facial expressions of American and Japanese viewers watching two films, one unpleasant (dealing with sinus surgery), the other more pleasant (on the subject of autumn leaves). Americans and Japanese displayed the same types of facial expression, varying in accordance with the nature of the film. Expressions of surprise, sadness and disgust (as defined by FAST) were exhibited during the unpleasant film, while the other film produced more expressions of happiness. The Japanese, however, tended to suppress their negative expressions, unless they were led to believe that they were alone and unobserved. A more important finding was the discovery that the facial expressions of the viewers kept on changing, and changed very quickly – so quickly that these 'micro-expressions' showed up only when viewed in slow motion. This multiplicity and rapidity of facial movements provides one explanation of why different people viewing the same face make different judgments about what it conveys. Indeed, differing judgments may reflect equally accurate perceptions of different facial movements. These points are most relevant for understanding the decoding process and will therefore be expanded upon later.

Ethologists such as Eibl-Eibesfeldt have done similar studies in more normal settings. Eibl-Eibesfeldt attempted to determine whether particular facial movements can be found in similar environmental situations in different species of monkey and in man. The evidence he presents illustrates striking similarities, suggesting that there are some inborn, universal expressions of emotions. Some examples are shown opposite.

Such studies of facial expressions of emotions indicate that there are facial movements which are related to the sender's emotional state and that some are the same in different cultures and perhaps even in different species. However, we do have some control over the facial expression of our emotions. In our own culture, and in others, people are aware that facial expressions can reflect feelings. (The tendency for Japanese people to conceal emotions was alluded to above.)

Darwin was a pioneer of the scientific study of the behaviour involved in non-verbal communication. This photograph from his *The Expression of the Emotions in Man and Animals* (1872) is meant to portray disgust.

Since there are often social prohibitions on particular emotional expressions, facial expressions may not always be representative of an individual's true emotions. In contrast, body movements are less subject to prohibitions, since they are normally outside our awareness. So perhaps, when people are deceiving themselves or other people, the body may indicate it more accurately than the face. The information that the body provides in this situation is called 'non-verbal leakage'. Leg and foot movements are the most likely sources of leakage, hands and face being progressively subject to awareness and voluntary control.

As a test of this proposition, Ekman and Friesan filmed an interview with a depressed woman, who was trying to appear well in order to gain discharge from hospital. Films of her head only and her body only were shown to different viewers who were asked to rate their communicative value on an adjective check list. The results showed that the face and head transmitted the patient's intended message of being well, while the less accessible body movements, in particular leg movements, conveyed the information that she was actually still disturbed.

This study exemplifies one method of measuring non-verbal messages in terms of the sender. In general, studies of this type are concerned with how people's personality, attitudes or emotions are related to their non-verbal behaviour. But because psycho-physical emotional states are involved, it is difficult to say which characteristics are the 'cause' of the behaviour. In the study just quoted we do not know how far the depressed woman's leg movements, which were presumed to represent non-verbal leakage revealing her true state of mind, were affected by her general depressed state. Because of this problem, other researchers have asked 'normal' people (e.g., people who are not depressed) to act out roles and have measured the non-verbal behaviour which results.

In a recent series of studies Bob Krauss and his colleagues asked more generally 'Does a person behave differently when telling a lie and when telling the truth?' According to popular belief, a person who is lying is supposed to reveal the fact in a variety of ways: by failure to meet our gaze, by unconsciously holding the hand over the mouth, and so on. In particular the behaviour associated with deception is believed to be

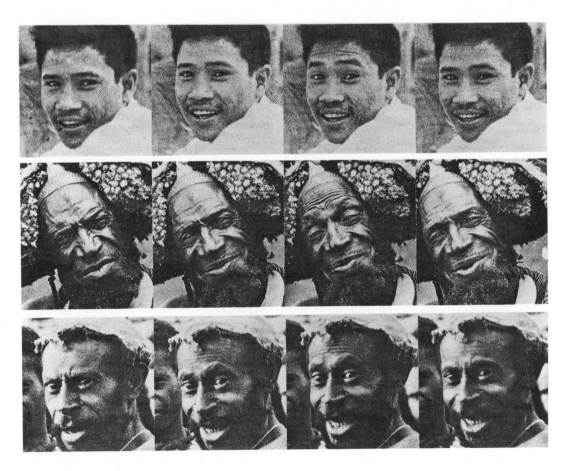

Evidence for the universality of some facial movements expressing emotions: 16-mm film frames recording the quick raising of the eyebrows in greetings from Bali and two different parts of Papua New Guinea, from Irenäus Eibl-Eibesfeldt's *The Biology of Human Behaviour*.

primarily visual, rather than auditory. In order to test this belief, the investigators used two sets of structured interviews, both with the same verbal script. One set of interviews was face-to-face, while the other was over a telephone. The interviews consisted of a number of questions addressed to the deceiver, some of which he responded to with a lie and others with the truth. In both situations the deceiver was filmed and recorded. Careful analysis demonstrated differences in the use of gestures by the deceivers as between the telephone and the face-to-face interviews: they controlled their body movements and facial expressions in the face-to-face interviews but no such holding back was seen in the telephone interviews. Moreover, some deceivers controlled their behaviour better than others. It was also found that the commonly-held belief associating avoidance of the other person's gaze and shielding of the face with lying was erroneous.

Results from such studies consistently show that there are many channels and codes that can be used to send non-verbal messages. While there is some consistency in channel usage and code between individuals for some sorts of messages, there is also a great deal of variability for other messages. It appears that individuals can change the use they make of channels in response to the situation; and people have been found to differ in the degree to which they can monitor and control their non-verbal behaviour. Conclusions of this kind have prompted studies aimed at demonstrating specifically the variability between people in the channels and codes they choose.

Berman and colleagues looked at this variability by asking six actors to behave in a cold manner and then in a warm manner while reading a standard five-minute script. Videotapes of their performance were seen or heard, or both seen and heard, by people who rated the performances on a mood scale. Most interestingly, some actors chose body movement, posture, and facial expression to communicate the differences between warmth and coldness, while others used mainly tone of voice, intonation and other vocal behaviour. But there was considerable overlap between the different channels in the meanings conveyed: in other words, the same message tends to be transmitted in a number of different channels.

One limitation of these studies of message-sending has been the fact that they incorporate the investigator's assumptions about what non-verbal channels are used and why they are selected. For instance, the face has usually been studied in relation to the display of emotion, and yet it can also convey attention, involvement and other things. Senders are rarely asked what information they see themselves as sending on the assumption that they are incapable of giving an objective picture of their own behaviour, free from prejudices about what sorts of things they would and would not communicate. But these prejudices themselves are an important part of the communication process, since they in turn affect the use that is made of different channels and codes, and they ought to be studied as such.

There are many things we as senders can do to help make sure messages get across. For example, we have to be aware

A sequence of emotions, from tranquillity to apprehension to joy, in 'Baptiste's soliloquy' by the 19th-century French caricaturist Grandville. First he anticipates a pleasant night's sleep, then he fears an intruder, who turns out to be his Minette.

of the channels that are inaccessible to the receiver. Obviously, when we are talking on the telephone nothing visual will be received; neither will it be received if the person addressed is not facing us, or is blind, or is too far away to see facial movement. In such instances, we have to use other channels. One way of making sure that the intended message gets across is to increase its physical intensity. In fact we sometimes overdo this, as when talking to someone with a hearing aid. Another possibility is to send the message over multiple channels. For example, to indicate that we are just about to stop talking, we may let our voice tail off, finish gesticulating, relax back into our chair and look expectantly at the other person as if awaiting a reply – all at the same time. This method may require the sender to learn some new skills, for the sending of two messages simultaneously can result in the receiver being overloaded. Non-verbal feedback exercises, as used in sensitivity training groups, are one approach to this. A fourth alternative is to use novel combinations of behaviour. An example of this is standing on a chair or sitting on the floor to attract attention. It has been shown experimentally that such unexpected out-of-role behaviour is perceived by onlookers as providing more truthful information about the person's intent than behaviour which follows the prescribed role. Another alternative is to stimulate the receiver's receptivity. Obviously one way of doing this is to tell him to pay attention directly, although there are often less obvious non-verbal signs which can be used for the same purpose. Another way of demanding attention is to use the channel in which the message can be most specific. For instance, one may be able to communicate ambiguity of feelings more effectively by verbalizing the feeling than by expressing it non-verbally.

The sender bombards the other person with all sorts of messages both simultaneously and in sequence. The receiver selects only a small number of these for attention. Thus, to be effective, the sender needs either to focus the receiver's attention on the desired message, or to control or eliminate non-relevant material.

Receiving non-verbal messages

From the point of view of the receiver, hearing and vision are the most important sources of information. Vision and hearing differ significantly in the degree to which they continuously monitor signals, the degree to which the receiver uses them to focus selectively on incoming messages, and the degree to which they can receive messages simultaneously or in sequence. While we always have our ears 'open', our hearing system is less active than our vision. We can search more readily with our eyes than with our ears. The listening

system generally operates sequentially, while the visual system can more easily receive many stimuli simultaneously. Although we may choose to focus visually on one aspect of the sender, we usually pick up other signals simultaneously that are communicated through the sender's body position, facial expression and physical distance.

The relative importance of vision led many early researchers to focus solely on this aspect of the receiving process, and in particular on how the receiver sees facial movements.

The FAST scheme which we described earlier has been used to find out whether different areas of the face convey information about different emotions to the receiver. In a study in Ekman's laboratory, photographs of faces expressing six different emotions were cut up and the participants asked to rate the parts of the face in terms of the six emotions. In most cases just one part of the face was as useful as the whole face for recognizing the emotion. Fear was best predicted from the eye, eyelid and ear areas. Sadness was judged most accurately from the eye and eyelid areas. Happiness was almost always seen in the cheeks and the mouth, or in the eyes and eyelids and cheek and mouth together. Surprise was detected most accurately from the brows, eyelashes and

Reinforcing a verbal message with a gesture. Already the advocate in this drawing by Daumier has the advantage of being in an elevated position at the centre of attention.

forehead. Anger, however, could not be judged accurately from any one part of the face. They suggested that this was because anger is more ambiguous than other facial expressions of emotion: judgments of anger were not consistent unless the anger was displayed in at least two areas of the face. Ekman and his colleagues have also collected evidence demonstrating consistency in the interpretation of expression in specific facial areas between cultures. There does appear to be sufficient evidence for the claim that facial expressions of particular basic emotions are universal.

However, non-verbal communication involves more than just the expression of emotion and the face-vision channel. As we have already said, visual information is usually received concurrently with aural information and the messages may be inconsistent. The recognition of this has led to a series of studies of the use people make of aural and visual information, and the preference they give to one or the other.

Studies of consistent messages, which is the usual situation in everyday interaction, generally show that reliable judgments of emotions can be obtained from both visual information (e.g. face and body signals) and aural information (e.g. tone of voice), but that visual information allows for a slightly higher degree of reliability and accuracy. Furthermore, most people prefer to be able to see a person when making judgments about his emotional state. However, people do not like to rely on visual information alone. They say then that they do not have enough information and feel they are making their judgments by imagining what the person's emotional state might be. Moreover, not all people attend to the same visual or aural information: different people appear to look to different parts of the face and body for their information. In spite of this they arrive at similar interpretations of what emotion is being expressed. This underlines what we have already noted in discussing message-sending – that the same message tends to be sent in several channels.

Pursuing the point that people vary in the reliance they place on different elements of non-verbal behaviour for interpretation, Robert Rosenthal and his colleagues have developed a test which they call the Profile of Non-verbal Sensitivity, or PONS. This assesses individual differences in the accuracy of judgments from three visual channels (face only, body only, and face and body together), two aural channels (electronically filtered speech, in which the words cannot be distinguished, and randomized speech, which retains only pitch and loudness), and their six aural-visual combinations.

From the use of the PONS test all over the world some general observations about overall skill in interpretation have emerged. For example, women and girls do better than men

and boys, and people who score well have fewer friends but warmer friendships. An interesting finding in the development of the PONS test was that usually almost everyone could provide accurate answers when the test scenes lasted for more than five seconds. For differences between people to show up, the scenes had to be cut down to two seconds. Some individuals could still score better than chance when the exposure time was reduced to one twenty-fourth of a second (equivalent to one frame of film). The greatest increase in accuracy occurred between one frame and three frames: that is, from one still photo to a short scene.

Michael Argyle and his colleagues have confirmed that length of exposure makes a difference in a series of experiments in which they compared the influence of glasses on people's judgment of the intelligence of the wearer over different exposure times. In exposures of fifteen seconds people wearing glasses were judged more intelligent than people not wearing them; but after a five-minute video film of the same people engaged in ordinary conversation the glasses had no influence. First impressions are not always reliable.

The studies described above used situations in which the visual and aural channels were giving similar messages. Other studies have looked at situations where there is a discrepancy between the channels and have been concerned especially with how the receiver deals with the discrepancy. There has been particular interest in this because of the idea that individuals who are constantly bombarded with inconsistent messages will be unable to relate effectively to other people.

The evidence suggests a greater reliance on visual cues in this situation. Albert Mehrabian tested reactions to photographs of pleasant faces accompanied by unpleasant recorded voices and vice versa. He found that 55 per cent of judgments about what feelings lay behind these contradictory indications relied on the face, 38 per cent on the tone of voice, and 7 per cent on the content of what was said.

However, some of the studies from the sender's perspective, described previously, cast doubts on the accuracy of judgments that result from predominantly visual information. In talking about deception, we pointed out that senders appear to have more control over facial expressions than over voice or body movements. So receivers who want to arrive at accurate judgments should attend to these likely sources of leakage. In fact, the studies by Bob Krauss mentioned earlier found that people were better at detecting deception over the telephone than face-to-face: so vision cannot always be the most useful source of information.

Other work suggests that people actually show a preference for aural information in given situations. For instance, it has been found that children (but not adults) are more influenced by tone of voice than by facial expression. Another study, which compared people's reliance on visual and aural information according to whether the two types of information were consistent or inconsistent, found that some people consistently used the aural channel rather than the visual when there was a wide discrepancy between the two. Others appeared not to use either channel with any consistency. The exact pattern was dependent to some degree on the type of emotion or feeling the people were attempting to recognize.

Although a preference for aural information may occur when different channels give inconsistent or ambiguous messages, in more normal situations visual information is preferred: this is particularly so when the choice is between facial information and tone of voice. It has been suggested that the face predominates because it can convey a greater amount of information than body or voice characteristics. However, it is also true that there are particular sorts of messages, such as messages of dominance, for which body and voice information are better.

Despite the recent advances in understanding the complexities of receiving non-verbal messages, we still have to rely mainly on common sense to be a 'good' receiver. It seems that most of us do feel the need to make most use of the visual channel. A possible reason for this preference is that we have more selective control over what we see than over what we hear. Such control helps us to separate out the significant from the less significant, and the intentional from the unintentional, in what we perceive. When deception or ambivalence are suspected in everyday interactions, primary reliance on visual information may not be the best strategy. In this case interpretation can be improved by concentrating on listening rather than on looking. Exclusive reliance on vision in such situations can result in confusion.

It appears that almost everyone recognizes and classifies specific facial features in a similar manner. However, such universal understanding of facial behaviour only appears to apply to conditions where the facial movements are viewed in slow motion, or in still photographs. Under normal conditions, where social rules apply, what we see are ambiguous blends of facial expressions. Regardless of this, we still tend to apply our general ability to what we see, and confusion results. Such confusion is lessened if the cultural conventions become well understood. Obviously, one way of increasing understanding is to check on our initial perceptions by specifically asking the sender what was intended. Another way is to look for confirmation in other channels, or in the same channel, as the conversation progresses.

Non-verbal communication from the observer's viewpoint

Something of what we know about non-verbal messages from the sender's and the receiver's viewpoints has been described. We have been dealing with non-verbal behaviour, not with non-verbal communication – communication being a process which occurs between people over time. In order to perceive the non-verbal communication system itself, we have to look at it not from either end of the exchange process but from the perspective of an observer looking at the process as a whole. From this higher perspective, time becomes of crucial importance. Looking at non-verbal communication as it occurs over time we have to ask how the process is organized, with particular reference to what is taken as meaningful or significant and to the interplay or coordination between the people involved.

The complexity of the behaviour involved in non-verbal communication has become apparent in what has been said up to now. In spite of it, we normally can, and do, make sense of the process as we continually perform it in our daily life. To do this we must be selecting some aspects of the flow of information as significant and neglecting others as insignificant. Otherwise we would be overwhelmed by the sheer number of non-verbal messages in all the different channels and communication would break down.

Adam Kendon has demonstrated that people can be quite confident and consistent about what non-verbal behaviour is significant in communication and what is not. He showed a silent film of a man addressing a group of people in Papua-New Guinea to twenty white Americans. After seeing the film a number of times, they went slowly through it pointing out where they observed body movements of different kinds. Every effort was made to allow them to make their own distinctions and to use their own words. They all identified movements they thought were significant, especially in terms of what they thought the speaker was trying to say. They saw them as deliberate, conscious, and part of the speech. They all also mentioned other movements but described them as 'natural', 'ordinary' or otherwise of no significance.

Kendon draws a number of conclusions from this study. First, not only could all the people who saw the film make clear distinctions between significant movements and others, but they all mentioned the significant movements first. Further, they distinguished significant movements from ordinary movements of no significance without hesitation and with a very high degree of agreement. What is also very interesting is that they were able to distinguish deliberate speech-related movements from others, even though they had no sound to guide them or any knowledge with which to interpret the speaker's lip movements. All the significant movements identified by the viewers were closely related to the actual speech flow and corresponded exactly to what Kendon had previously marked as gestural units.

The main point to be drawn from this study is that people can, and do, recognize deliberate and significant movements related to the thrust of a person's message just by watching body movements. There is evidence which suggests that this recognition occurs even in very young infants.

It is obvious that there is usually some degree of mutual attunement or coordination between people although, of course, we have all experienced failures in this attunement at some time or other. According to Kendon, such failures are often the result of misunderstandings of the social definition or context by which the communication is framed.

Communication is always framed by a set of social definitions which may or may not be agreed upon by the people involved. When it is not agreed upon, then coordination is difficult to achieve.

The social definition also affects what we perceive as significant. For example, if the social situation is mutually (but not necessarily explicitly) defined as an exchange between a 'local' and a 'tourist' seeking directions, then the tourist will find most significance in directional gestures and the local in facial expressions of understanding. Neither the tourist nor the local is likely to treat feet or leg positions as significant. On the other hand, if the tourist has defined the situation as male (tourist) attempting to be friendly with attractive female (local), then he will attribute far more significance to her facial expressions for indications of interest, and to her body and

A gesture of goodwill is included in the pictorial information attached to the American Pioneer F deep space probe launched in 1972. Since non-verbal gestures of this kind, insofar as they are universal, are so only within the terrestrial human species, it may be doubted whether this would make any more sense to intelligent beings outside the solar system than, say, writing in a particular alphabet and language.

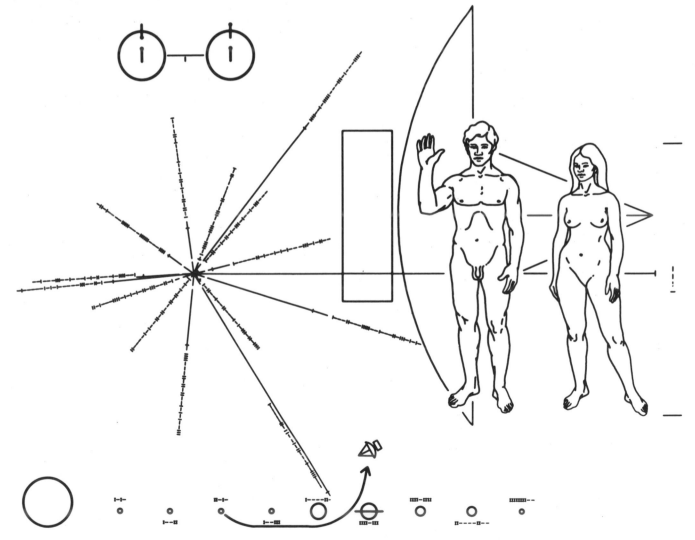

head orientation, than to her arm directions. However, if the local does not share this frame of definition, she may not understand why her arm movements are being ignored!

As can be seen from this example, the nature of the frame also affects the nature of the relationship between sender and receiver. We have available a number of different non-verbal behaviours which can be used to indicate a variety of relationships. In addition, the particular use of such non-verbal indicators can also act to change the frame over time. Thus the definition of the nature of the communication process, and therefore the relationship between the people, can change as the process continues.

Apart from deciding what behaviour is significant out of all the alternatives that we are faced with simultaneously, we have to be able to tune our own behaviour to coordinate with the other person's so that the communication can proceed. Both eye gaze and body gesture have been shown to play a significant role in the initiation of an interaction. Studies of 'natural' interaction indicate that people, in general, look at the region of the eyes more than at any other region. It is at the start of an interaction that gaze direction is crucial: before we start to speak we have to 'catch the eye' of the other person. Avoidance of eye contact (what Goffman has called 'civil inattention') is used to indicate to the other person that conversation is not desired. On crowded trains, when total strangers are packed closely together, one can easily see people striving hard to avoid each other's gaze. Conversely, by continuing to look after the initial eye contact, one can indicate that an encounter is desired without speaking.

We also engage in various movements of face and posture at the start of an encounter. Kendon and A.E. Scheflen have shown that the arrangement of our bodies and faces acts as a frame for the interaction. In particular, they have identified what they refer to as the F (for 'facing') formation, where the people talking face each other, forming a small group or circle, with everyone facing inwards. Participants in the formation cooperate to maintain it. If there is a slight movement by one person, others will move to compensate.

Within the course of the interaction, various definite changes in the shape of the F formation occur. These changes are brought about by joint manoeuvres, and they are associated with major changes in the interaction. Changes occur after the initial greetings, such as the handshake or embrace, are completed. Changes in arrangement also occur with changes in the topic of conversation or with changes in the composition of the group. Although these changes take place, there is a sustained cooperative effort to maintain the formation, which confirms the participants' sense of being a group while the encounter lasts.

At the same time as these major spatial and postural arrangements are occurring, direction of eye gaze continues to regulate the interaction. In particular, gaze direction has been shown to be a major indicator of when a change in speaker is about to occur or is wanted by the group. Starkey Duncan and his colleagues have shown that when the sender turns his head towards the person he is speaking to, this is a major cue to the other person that he is now expected to speak, especially when it occurs at a natural break in what the speaker is saying. In a complementary manner, the other person shifts his head away from the person who has been speaking before starting to speak.

When the speaker's head turns towards the person being spoken to at the end of a sentence, that person often responds with an 'uh-huh' or equivalent non-verbal utterance. This serves to indicate that what has been said is understood but the person indicated does not want to speak then. An interesting finding is that other non-verbal behaviour can serve the same function as the head and eye movements described above. For example, relaxation of the speaker's foot, or finishing a hand gesture, can also indicate that the person being spoken to may now adopt the speaker's role. Duncan argues that these different types of turn-taking indicators function in an additive fashion: that is, the more different indicators there are present, the more the person listening is likely to start speaking.

These turn-taking behaviours are just one of the sets of coordination behaviours that contribute to the communication process. Michael Argyle and his colleagues have looked at how gaze direction interacts with these other behaviours in a larger context. They suggest that one of the major requirements for a continuing exchange among participants is the establishment of a comfortable level of 'intimacy'. They define intimacy as a product of gaze direction, physical distance between the participants, smiling and other behaviour. The point at which the approach and avoidance tendencies of the people involved are in balance is the point of comfortable intimacy. Approach tendencies include the desire for visual feedback, which requires looking at the other person. Avoidance tendencies include the fear of revealing oneself or of being rejected. Because intimacy is the product of a number of different behaviours, a change in any particular behaviour can alter the total intimacy level. However, once a comfortable level of intimacy is reached, variations in any one behaviour lead to compensatory adjustments in another so that the comfortable level is maintained.

There is some support for this intimacy equilibrium theory. Several studies have shown that increased physical closeness between people is related to decreased eye contact. Other studies have shown that eye contact will decrease when people have to respond to increasingly intimate questions. However, some other studies show the opposite pattern: that is, increased eye contact and forward leaning by one person is reciprocated by increased eye contact and forward leaning on the part of the other. It seems that these contradictory findings can be explained (as M.L. Patterson has done) in terms of whether or not each participant finds an increase in intimacy pleasant or unpleasant. If it is found pleasant by both, intimacy goes on increasing; if one person finds it unpleasant, that person will 'back off' by behaving in such a way as to reduce the level of intimacy.

In another study, W.S. Condon and his associates carried out detailed micro-coding of videotaped behaviour and revealed an 'interactional synchrony' in which most of the changes in the behaviour of one participant are related to changes in the behaviour of the other – most frequently to changes in speech behaviour. However, they found no consistency in the spacing of these responses: the process was more like a disjointed dance. Their most recent research suggests that this disjointed dance may be inborn. They played speech recordings in both English and Chinese to babies less than a day old and found that they moved and made noises in time with the speech rhythm in either language. No similar patterns were found with music and random noises. However, this often quoted study has been difficult to reproduce. Doubts about the methods used raise serious questions about whether or not 'interactional synchrony' really does exist, at least at this detailed level.

But there is little doubt that people do coordinate their non-verbal behaviour in other ways. For example, when two people are talking without seeing each other, the loudness of their voices tends to change so that they eventually match each other. Why people do this is not at all clear, though there is some evidence which suggests that it is related to the tendency to act in a socially desirable manner. Generally, however, it seems that the precision with which participants synchronize their behaviour with the behaviour of others is related to their ability to anticipate what the other person is going to do.

Conclusions

We have referred repeatedly to the integral relationship between non-verbal and verbal behaviour in the communication process. However, an exact specification of how they are integrated as the process continues is not yet possible: it still remains one of the thorniest problems for researchers and theorists alike. The difficulty has been increased by the tendency to use theoretical frameworks derived from linguistic studies or theories. Yet, as we pointed out at the beginning, most non-verbal behaviour is coded in a manner substantially different from verbal or written language. Thus, to use a framework oriented towards language for understanding all communication is to distort those crucial elements which are not linguistic in nature.

In this chapter we have hoped to make clear that there is far more to the meaning of our social world than just words. There is at least some overlap between the functions and structure of non-verbal and verbal communication: some ideas, thoughts or feelings can be communicated effectively by words in digital form alone, some by non-verbal behaviour in analogue form alone, and some most effectively by both forms together. But whatever the exact proportions, there can be no doubt of the importance of the non-verbal in the total communication process.

IV
SIGNS AND SYMBOLS

Donis A. Dondis

SIGNS AND SYMBOLS

In the complex topography of contemporary communication, visual signs and symbols hold a special territory. Their application to the expression and interpretation of the relationships between individuals, and of the relation of individuals to primary and secondary reference groups, to culture, to national entities, is vital. They serve as guidelines to actions, responses and acceptable behaviour, and have importance far beyond what their functional use indicates.

Visual symbols are marks with attached meaning that are meant to represent concrete information. Their development and utilization should not be confused with the production of symbolic thought, a separate and distinct process. If symbols and signs are lesser versions of the symbolically enriched metaphor, they are nevertheless not without great power and great importance for human communication.

In the many steps that mark the evolution of form in human communication from the development of spoken language to writing, visual signs and symbols represent the transition from visual perception, via pictures, picture-strip mentation and pictograms to abstract marks – notation systems capable of conveying the meaning of concepts, words or single sounds. Whether as simple gestures, or as pictures, or as abstract marks with prescribed meaning, signs and symbols convey ideas in pre-literate and virtually illiterate cultures. But their usefulness is no less among the verbally literate: on the contrary, it is greater. In the technologically developed society with its demand for instant comprehension, symbols and signs are most effective in procuring a quick response. Their strict attention to visual essentials and their structural simplicity provide easy perception and memorability. Just as they once played an important role in the development of a variety of written languages, they continue to fulfil a unique function in contemporary communication. Whenever, wherever, however a communication transaction takes place, signs and symbols are certain to be part of that process.

Warning and direction signs, ranging from the representational to the abstract:
prohibited categories of road user on a highway in Turkey; a warning to use chains in snowy conditions
in the French Alps; a sign for an anchorage in Greece; and junction and 'no entry' signs in London.

Characteristics of signs and symbols

Signs and symbols, as classifications, are not clear and distinct from one another; rather, they interact and overlap, demonstrating considerable similarity in both use and character. Nevertheless, there are differences. Signs can be understood by animals as well as humans; symbols cannot. Signs signal; they are specific to a task or circumstance. Symbols are broader in meaning, less concrete. Both are surrogates. In the case of representational pictorial signs or symbols, they may appear convincingly like the originals they stand in for and can be understood without explanation. As abstract shapes, with no physical resemblance to the information they represent, signs or symbols possess meaning solely through social agreement. Often this must be arrived at through education, even persuasion. Since they channel information and are connected to that information conventionally, it is necessary to know that signs or symbols are not the object or concept themselves; they hold its meaning.

Signs are less complicated than symbols. Whether as a drawing, a code, or a gesture, signs take a visible form to express an idea. They can be identification for a shop or a service; as a seal show authorship or ownership; as a gesture deliver meaning; as a cue guide actions. As such, signs often play a crucial part in problem-solving, directing the perceiver toward a solution.

The study of signs has burgeoned into an important field of scholarship called semiotics. It deals with both the function of signs in the process of communication and the place of symptoms in medical diagnosis. A grasp of the nature of symptomology can contribute substantially to an awareness of how signs differ from symbols. Symptoms are related or unrelated physiological or neurological signs. A headache, a sore throat, aching muscles, suggest a search for other clues. Is there a fever? Does the patient have a stomach problem or nausea? The signs constitute functional and objective evidence of a disease. But what disease? It is up to the doctor to recognize the symptoms, relate them to one another, and then make of the seemingly unrelated cluster of signals a coherent diagnosis. In other words, the doctor must read the signs and attach meaning to them, which might signal the direction for action.

In communication, signs and signals are often set in similarly illogical structures. They are not always units in a prescribed system with attached and fixed meaning. They sometimes require an intuitive approach to make sense of them, and consequently lend themselves to creative interpretation. In fact, what are often referred to as the 'intuitive overtones and undertones' of mystical intelligence can be seen as nothing more than a special sensitivity to signs and an aptitude for relating them to one another.

Intuition, inspiration, creative problem-solving, whatever we choose to label this special activity, one thing is certain, there is no logic, no predictable pattern inherent in it. Albert Einstein's description of his own thinking aptly describes the process. 'The words or the language, as they are written or spoken, do not seem to play any role in my mechanism of thought. The physical entities which seem to serve as elements in thought are certain signs which are more or less clear images which can be voluntarily reproduced and combined. Taken from a psychological viewpoint this combinatory play seems to be the essential feature in productive thought, before there is any connection with logical construction in words or other kinds of signs which can be communicated with others.' Einstein presents his refreshingly unique method of thinking. As long as our view of intelligence is tied firmly to conventional systems of thought we will find it difficult to understand that the lack of logic implicit in the use of random signs can be the pathway to innovative problem-solving. From the organization of unrelated signs comes release from logic toward the lyric leap of interpretation. Call it inspiration, but, in fact, it is a special kind of intelligence. It is the essential aptitude cultivated by a doctor trained in diagnosis, by an automobile mechanic who must determine the flaw in the operation of a motor, by an architect who has to find the proper site on a parcel of land for a new building – or by anyone who must organize diverse information and make sense of it.

Like signs, symbols can extend meaning to a number of levels of interpretation. The king can stand for the country; the nurse, for health care; the judge, for justice. The depiction of a mother and child can signify a specific and basic human relationship or can extend the message to a more general meaning of mother love. In art, thousands of paintings, drawings and sculptures of mother and child are surrogates for the Virgin Mary and the Christ Child. As such they hold many layers of meaning: the powerful force represented by motherhood and its importance to individuals and society; the mystery of the Virgin Birth as a demonstration of the existence of God in human form on earth; the purity of the love of God. Each individual layer of meaning is consonant with all the others, extending and intensifying the message.

Symbols can be composed of realistic, representational pictorial information drawn from the environment, easy to recognize and easier yet to invest with meaning. They can also be composed of shapes, tones, colours, textures – basic visual elements which bear no resemblance to objects in the natural environment. These abstract symbols hold no meaning except that which is assigned to them. There are many classifications and combinations of these two distinct categories. The form they take depends primarily on what they are intended to identify and in what way. They can be simple or complicated, obvious or obscure, effective or useless. In the final analysis, their value can be measured by how far they penetrate the public mind towards recognition and memorability. The measure of their success lies as much in the eye and mind of the viewer as in the conception and craft of their creator.

To understand how signs and symbols make their meaning accessible, we must examine their source and evolution as well as the ways they are used at present.

Cave paintings and totems

One of the oldest symbols still preserved for examination and evaluation is a box-like mark that appears with some frequency in the cave paintings of Altamira and Lascaux. This mark is a perfect demonstration of the limitations of an abstract symbol whose meanings, both conventional and attached, are arrived at arbitrarily. It bears no resemblance to any natural form. It is impossible, in the present, to decode this symbol, even to guess what meaning its creators intended. The individual or social group that created it, used it, and understood it is dead. No clues have been left behind to guide us. The animals in the drawings in whose company this abstract symbol can be seen are easy to recognize and identify. But the purpose for which the cave drawings were artfully executed is equally mysterious. We can only conjecture about why they were drawn on the cave walls and how they served the society that created them.

The most educated explanation of the purpose for which these cave paintings were created must rely on a later creation in human history that seems connected, even similar. As in the cave paintings, animals, together with other visual images drawn from nature, are the most important component of totems. The primary use of totems as objects or marks is to clarify family and social connections. Primitive people understood their place in society, the significance of their names, all through the animal or natural-object symbols

The undeciphered box-like mark that appears repeatedly in the caves of Altamira and Lascaux.

Totemistic association in advertising: Standard Oil have succeeded in appropriating to themselves the tiger as a symbol of power and energy, now without the specific allusion to 'a tiger in your tank'.

that identified their families and, perhaps, their tribes. Implicit in these totems and their wider purpose as reference lay guidelines for the rights and responsibilities of all members of a related grouping, as well as rules for acceptable interactions between members of different groups. The use of totems in less sophisticated societies can be viewed as the first glimmering of a system of laws as well. Totems defined affiliations and made clear what the nature of those affiliations could and could not be. It is in the context of prohibition, or taboo, that their power is most recognized and studied in sociology and psychology. Totems provided an indication as to what was socially acceptable behaviour. Totems are also typical of many of the artefacts created in a primitive society which have special powers attributed to them. Magic is a special quality of these already useful devices. Long life, success, good health, fertility, protection against disaster are some of the promises of the powers associated with totems. For the vulnerable and ignorant member of a pre-literate culture, the importance of these mystical properties and the assurance they offered is easy to understand.

Totems remain lively components of contemporary communication. The brave are still identified as 'lion-hearted', the stubborn are seen as 'bull-headed'. Many commercial products are marketed through the extension of their value by totemistic association: automobile tyres with the ability of a cat's paw to hold the ground in speedy motion; petrol or gasoline with power in the dramatic fantasy of 'a tiger in the tank'. Totems survive in family names like Wolf, Ash, Rose, all examples of the persistent link between individual and tribal connections and objects and animals drawn from the environment, familiar to participants in their symbolic meaning.

The stars

It is not surprising that animals as support and means of survival – or as mortal threat – dominated the consciousness of prehistoric and primitive man. They are not only dominant in the visual records and in the symbol-making of totems, they are also a key ingredient in the first faltering attempts to recognize, record and predict the passage of time. Lancelot Hogben observed the process in his book *From Cave Painting to Comic Strip*: 'Preliterate man maps the heavens as a guide to his seasonal pursuits. He associates the rising or setting of the sun with a particular star cluster as a favourable signal for hunting the unforbidden or for the sacrificial ceremony for his tutelary.' The main means of recognizing these star clusters was by relating them to pictorial information, to life forms such as animals, fish, flowers, the human figure. It is a method for reading the heavens still very much in currency.

The patterns do not always resemble their references. Some do. The Big Dipper, Ursa Major, is easy to recognize as an object, but looks little like its designation of the Great Bear. Whatever their names and pictorial interpretation, the configurations of the constellations are patterns that can be learned and recognized as easily as they were by the ancient star-gazers who first charted and named them, although the ancients had little or no understanding of the true construction of the universe.

Finding visual clues, visual signs, suggested by the position of stars in the night sky and investing them with names, figurative patterns and time sequences provided early societies with the means to predict changes in seasons, the possible occurrence of natural disasters, the most desirable time to plant and harvest crops. The living history of this first calendar system is with us still in the signs of the zodiac and the calendar time frames they represent. From its Mesopotamian and Babylonian origins, the zodiac brings into our modern and technologically advanced lives the ancient traditions and distant times of its source. In their beginnings astrology and astronomy were viewed as one activity of singular, scientific importance. But the true scientific astronomical discoveries of Copernicus in the 15th and 16th centuries left astrology the traditions of predicting individual destinies in what are called horoscopes. Each birth sign with a constellation of stars as a calendar designation is represented by an organism or object drawn from the environment. Among them are a bull, a fish, a lion, a crab, each endowed with characteristics shared by those born under them. The twelve categories are also identified by abstract symbols. How many of us know the astrological sign we were born under, its purported significance, and the symbol that identifies it?

Rituals, myths and legends

Rituals are patterns of action that are intended to communicate a wide variety of messages of varying importance among many classes of living creatures, not just humans. Animal and insect ritual is innate, while human ritual is created and learned. Human rituals stretched from the spiritual significance of worship to more superficial behaviour associated with manners. The rituals of lower organisms are most frequently part of courtship and mating activities. In most cases, the rituals are firmly based on visual cues, gestures and conventions. Whether they are learned in a social context or imprinted and exercised automatically, the symbolic meaning implicit in ritual must be recognized and responded to knowledgeably to be effective.

Myth reduces its characterizations and themes to distilled essentials and then projects them, larger than life, achieving a symbolic form designed to capture the attention and imagination. The result is sometimes entertaining, but the interest they attract is their potential for education and inspiration. Through story-telling and image-making, myths can encapsulate and make available information by which the vulnerable and illiterate people of a primitive society can explain to themselves the complex phenomena of the world. But myths have equal value to the sophisticated and educated. To them their themes can support increased understanding of self. Always, in the making of myths, the message and meaning is tied to images that represent basic dilemmas and concepts and encourage increased perception of the environment and understanding of human relationships.

Just as the intended purpose of totems and the signs of the zodiac is to extend meaning far beyond the visual figures that serve as their basic referents, myths are designed to be guidelines for living. The mythology of Greece (and its echoing Roman versions) typifies all myths that tend to endow an individual with specific and symbolic form or forms. Many of the characteristics of the mythical figures are presented visually through particular objects or exaggerated physiological features signifying power. In their narrative, myths can be understood and interpreted in many layers of meaning from simple to highly complex, none of them necessarily exclusive.

The visual cues of mythical characterizations support and reinforce the power of the message: the wings at the heels of Hermes underline his role as messenger of the gods; the lyre of Apollo designates his poetic and mystical talents; the helmet and spear of Athena emphasize her wisdom as a prudent warrior; the cornucopia of Demeter identifies her as goddess of agriculture and is not inconsistent with her power as protector of marriage and the social order. The stories peopled by these gods are concerned with the homely dilemmas of life, the nature of society, the demands on the individuals living within it, and the significance of the natural world and its phenomena. Myths, the world over, tend to have many similarities and predictable outcomes, since they grow out of basic, human situations which are universally shared. Their guidance goes far beyond the obvious in the direction of explaining the inexplicable.

Everywhere in their structure the myths and their archetypal characters are dominated by images, whether in verbal or iconic form. Mountains dominate the landscape, expressing monumental power in symbolic terms and forming the perfect visual setting for the habitat of the gods. Trees and their fruits are frequently used as figures in myths representing the source of life and knowledge. The most commonly-used symbol with assigned meaning for power over life is the sun, to which many forms are given, most of which move, like the Greek Helios, his chariot drawn across the sky, or the Egyptian solar bark sailing eternally across the heavens. Lightning and thunderbolts are hurled by Zeus to destroy whole cities. Rituals, myths, legends, folk tales, are rich with characters that serve as symbols or models that explain how the world works and the relationship of the individual to the world, and in the end have profound influence on customs and behaviour.

Ritual and myth overlap in the early stages of the development of tragedy, the unique Athenian contribution to literature. Its roots are ascribed variously to the ritual worship of Dionysus and to choral songs performed at religious festivals. Whatever its source, in its Greek beginnings drama was almost ritualistic in its rigid structure. It consisted of a series of narrative odes about divine and heroic characters, alternating with an actor who exchanged dialogue with the chorus. As Greek drama evolved from one actor with chorus to a larger number of characters, it moved closer to theatre as we think of it today. Like myths, it presented a segment of life objectively as an opportunity for the audience to interpret the action as a subjective learning experience. By relating to the characters, symbols of life's universal difficulties, members of the audience could experience their own emotions as they were acted out by others. Furthermore, the drama provided the audience with the opportunity to identify specific problems, to observe potential solutions, and, most important, to experience catharsis.

This tradition of archetypal dramatic story-telling still makes the remarkable tragedies of the 5th and 6th centuries BC a rich reference for a course in symbolic characterization and plot. The nature of the characters revealing their complex problems through dramatic action has remained remarkably stable while the vehicles of drama have evolved and changed over the centuries. Contemporary society can choose between viewing theatre, film and video, each with its own conventions: theatre, the modern version of the Greek drama with its acts and scenes; film, with its exaggerated scale presenting people and objects larger than life; video, with its immediacy, accessibility and pervasiveness. The purposes of presentation are the same. It is the technology and visual techniques that facilitate control of the signs and symbols as they are presented.

In the development of his theory of psychoanalysis Sigmund Freud used the mythical Greek god Eros to illustrate the force of sexuality in conscious and unconscious behaviour. The symbolic manifestation of this instinct for close union is given the name 'libido' by Freud. The conflict evoked in a child by sexual needs and feelings directed toward a parent was characterized through the symbolic meaning of Oedipus, who in his dramatic role acts out the most profound and profane desires of the child as well as the deep fears of punishment. In giving the name 'Oedipus complex' to the psychological syndrome, Freud brings a symbolic dimension to the human problem which transcends medical description. The name holds the meaning and the power of the original drama and, in the process, promises catharsis and cure.

In these instances, Sigmund Freud was influenced by symbolic characterizations already in place. In his courageous exploration of the unconscious mind through his analysis of dreams and their meaning he is original. Interpretation of dreams was certainly not unknown. The Bible is filled with prophetic dreams. Joseph served as analyst in his interpretation of Pharaoh's dreams recounted in the Old Testament. Freud was concerned not with prophetic meaning but with relating the content of the dream to the life and problems of the person who had it. In his work *The Interpretation of Dreams*, first published in German in 1900, he sought the symbolic clues for the desires, fears and urges of the dreamer. Like a physician seeking diagnosis of an ailment through symptoms, Freud regarded dreams as the means of discovering the hidden motives of the patient. By pursuing the missing connections that fleshed out what the patient remembered, he sought the underlying, frequently repressed, meaning. Like a detective seeking a solution, Freud encouraged his patients to explore the associations of the dream symbols and attempted to strip away the disguises and rationalizations that emerged in order to reveal the true meaning.

From personal and subjective reactions to the content of dreams, Freud constructed a more universal and standardized account of the symbols that appeared. This fixed dream symbolism has been highly controversial. The unqualified interpretation of a snake or a gun as a phallic symbol is no longer generally accepted in psychological or psychoanalytic

The sun as a symbol of power. *Above* Sun and lion in the ancient emblem of Persia on a 13th-century lustre tile. *Below* Helios rides his chariot on the helmet of the Sun King, Louis XIV, in an ivory portrait relief.

practice. The particular significance of the symbol to the dreamer is preferred. But, despite the reservations that have appeared, Freud certainly developed a productive approach to using dreams in the revelation of hidden or aberrant mental activity. Human potential has been expanded and stimulated by these techniques, not only in psychology, but also in art. Through the symbolism of the dream, the individual and collective unconscious can be viewed with deeper insights and greater scope.

Religious symbols

Throughout history belief has been tied to a series of significant symbols. The role of the symbol-maker in any culture is beautifully expressed in the example cited by Keith Albarn and Jenny Miall Smith in their book *Diagram: the instrument of thought*:

> Among the Dogon people of Africa, for example, the key figure in society is the blacksmith, a man who can capture and/or illuminate the inner existence. His products (prized by the West as Art) are strictly functional and act as release mechanisms for specific responses by the social group towards a joint understanding. This 'alchemical' (in the sense of 'transforming') knowledge is passed from father to son. The blacksmith cannot own or till land but holds an honoured place as intermediary between God and Man.

This description demonstrates the importance of the role of the interpreter in the presentation of religious and mystical thought in symbolic form. In primitive societies the tokens and totems serve to express the essential qualities of belief. The Moslem and Hebrew religions alone prohibit the making of images to be used in worship. Instead they emphasize the word and the need for literacy for participation in prayer. It was in this verbally-dominated context that Christianity emerged. Christ preached to the literate Hebrews: but his disciples were missionaries to a substantially illiterate population, and therefore depended heavily on visual symbols together with symbolic ritual to attract and involve their followers. The success of their efforts testifies to the effectiveness of symbols as tools of communication and persuasion.

A symbol is a mark that holds and expresses a whole idea. In terms of style it must be graphically simple, easy to recognize quickly, and, most important, memorable. A well-designed symbol must offer direct access to a constellation of meaning enriched by details that contribute to the whole. And all these attributes must combine in a symbol that can be learned and understood with ease, independent of a complex system of codes. Add to this one last measure of the viability of any symbol: it must be simple enough to be drawn by anyone. The same simplicity that makes a good symbol easy to read makes it easy to replicate.

In the spread of Christianity throughout the western world we find one of the most fascinating symbols ever designed, exemplary of all the desirable characteristics just described. With two simple strokes, it could be drawn anywhere: scrawled on a wall, scratched on to wood, marked in the dust with a finger. The symbol is a fish, ⋉. And what is its significance? It derives from an acronym for the Greek words for 'Jesus Christ, Son of God, saviour', *ichthus*, which means 'fish'. This simple mark not only meets the criteria of simplicity of form, ease of reproduction and memorability, but also dramatically demonstrates the intrinsic power of the symbol to communicate through the ripple effect of extended meaning. Most of Christ's disciples were fishermen. The charge he made to them was 'Go forth and be fishers of men'. In the form of the fish, the first and most effective symbol of Christianity captures much of the feeling of the mission of the group it represents, and expresses it persuasively.

Christianity is rich with symbols. The lamb and the lion are used to characterize opposite qualities of the personality of Christ. The cross carries the reminder of his crucifixion. The Virgin Mary epitomizes the purest form of motherhood reinforced by association with the calming and celestial colour blue. The horned and tailed figure, which is the most common symbolic representation of the Devil, is usually intensified by the provoking colour red.

The making of icons was considered an important part of worship. They pictured the Holy Family, saints and Biblical

The early Christian symbol of a fish in a 4th- to 5th-century Coptic stone-carving.

figures. This activity was questioned in the 8th and 9th centuries by iconoclastic emperors who reverted to the Moslem and Hebrew bias against figurative art. Even though this period was short-lived, it preceded the development of the expressionistic style of Byzantine art, which is a compromise between the realistic and rational visual art of Greece and Rome and the Hebrew and Moslem orientation towards the word. The pictorial content was recognizable but exaggerated towards intensified meaning, devised to provoke maximum emotional response. The same crude but powerful style is used in the illustrations of medieval manuscripts, painstakingly drawn and hand-lettered by monks to preserve and make available to the literate their religious beliefs.

Architectural symbolism

The design and construction of buildings serve two purposes for society: utility and communication. Clearly, the primary and dominant function of architecture is the design of enclosures that respond to concrete needs and practical use. The crude hut evokes little meaning beyond the necessity it was constructed to fulfil. There are many versions of this simplest of habitats made of readily-available materials and practical in their solutions that relate to geographical realities. The tropical hut is very different in form from the Arctic igloo. Their similarity lies mostly in the fact that they use local materials, but there are other subtle connections – the simplicity of shared space that attempts no privacy; the rounded form, a psychologically warm delineation of space; and the one-storey plan. All these design characteristics do not venture far from the natural habitation of the cave that antedated them in human history. The content and form of architecture which communicates with more conscious intention evolved more slowly in the development of technical skills in building.

But whether we are considering a crude hut or a magnificent cathedral, the subject matter of architecture, its content and form, communicate the meaning of the building symbolically. We can understand that symbolism through learning and association or through more direct and unconscious intuition. Learned response to architectural form stems from historical tradition and recognition of what buildings represented in the past. Their design can be stylistically related to a culture, a timespan, a geographical location, the materials available, the state of structural knowledge or the variable influences of taste. They can carry symbolic meaning in floor plan, elevation or choice of decorative detail. For example, the choice of the circle as a mystical form emerged from pagan construction into the dome, symbolic of the heavens, and was often decorated and coloured to simulate the sky.

Greek architecture is cool and rational, expressing the intellectual and philosophical bent of Greek culture: a seeking after order, balance and resolution. In architecture, as in many other things, the Romans added grandeur, constructing buildings Greek in form and content, but larger in scale and more dominant in decoration, effectively expressing the power of Rome.

From the 12th century on, Gothic church architecture slowly evolved structurally towards more and more raised arches with powerful buttressing, raising the height of the interior space to express symbolically the faithful's yearning for heaven. The technical accomplishment was achieved by the master-builders who designed and supervised the construction of cathedrals that frequently took centuries. The grandeur of these edifices reflects the motivation and the mood of the people who contributed money and labour to their construction. The magnificent scale of the cathedrals, the enormous height of their walls supported by flying buttresses, dwarfs the human figure. The soaring effect of the pronounced verticality of the vaulting creates a sense of levitation, of being lifted upward. Beyond the symbolic meaning of the use of the cross in the floor plan, the entire psychological, even physical, effect is a convincing and powerful message. Contribution to or participation in the construction of a cathedral was a way of assuring a place in heaven. Standing in one of the most beautiful Gothic churches, Chartres, gives one a convincing sensation of that movement heavenward that served as an earthly reward to those who helped to build it, and is still convincing to those who experience it hundreds of years later.

The vaulting and buttressing of the walls of the Gothic cathedrals opened them to the addition of stained glass windows. Following the style of the illuminated manuscripts, the pictorial quality of the stained glass windows is unrealistic and exaggerated. The medium imposes a need for simplicity and boldness in detail and colour. The stories depicted in stained glass windows are simple and direct. Form and content complement each other. The natural demands of working in glass and the distance from which the windows were viewed necessitated the adoption of the design characteristics of good symbols: distillation of visual information and intensification of meaning. In this regard, they match their Gothic setting. The exaggeration and distortion is designed to intensify the emotional response on the part of the viewer. In technique and style they represent the polar opposite of the content and form of Greek art and architecture.

Heraldry

When true heraldry emerged in Western Europe, the emblems carried by knights on their shields and banners bore strong vestiges of the totemistic marks by which warriors were identified. Heraldic symbols are not unique to Western Europe: they have been adopted by kings, chieftains, churches, warriors, armies and countries over the ages throughout most of the world. Roman soldiers carried shields decorated with identifying symbols. Despite the religious prohibition of idol-making, the Hebrew tribes are reputed to have carried standards that exhibited figures referring to the ravening wolf for Benjamin, the lion's whelp for Judah, and the ship of Zebulon. In the East, both country and families were represented by such ancient symbols as the five-clawed dragon of China and the chrysanthemum of Japan.

Perhaps most important of all, heraldry reflects the supportive quality of symbols and the way in which they can serve the need for identification of family affiliation, social status or political alliances, as well as individual self-image.

The ancient traditions of displaying badges and seals were particularly urgent in the faceless world of armoured warriors who needed a palpable symbol for others to see and recognize.

The original use of heraldic seals was a proud display of family affiliation in battle. These armorial bearings took on a broader signification as signs of family relationships used in genealogy. The arms were inherited by all the heirs of its holder. Female heirs combined their arms with those of their husbands. Illegitimacy was designated by the baton sinister.

The design of heraldic symbols is almost endlessly varied. The use of abstract shapes is common: squares; circles; triangles; stars; shields; multiple shields; horizontal, vertical and diagonal stripes. Naturalistic animals and flowers as well as fabulous beasts like the unicorn or griffin are common among armorial symbols. These are often combined with the abstract configurations as background. Further distinction is achieved through the use of colour. The result is identification of group affiliation whether family, regiment or country.

Heraldry's rich variety of design and symbolism exemplified in arms of the Holy Roman Empire: a woodcut by Hans Burgkmair, 1510.

Trade marks

Contemporary versions of symbol-making respond to similar needs. The first and most compelling function is to identify an organization or group; the second, to present an easily-understood guideline for some activity, as in a road sign. Symbolism for individual identification has faded away and blended into the broader categories of secondary reference – group affiliations with political parties, clubs, religions, universities and the like. In this context, people take on the roles of receivers and senders of messages, roles that are essentially tied to the demands of communication. The symbol, then, is involved in the interaction between the signifier and the signified. It holds meaning only if it is understood. And in this simple observation lies the most vital fact about symbols. They are only effective if the group to which they are directed is educated to recognize and understand them. This is an imposing argument for continuity in the use of symbols: the older, the better.

Identification marks have existed for as long as individual craftsmen have wanted to identify their work. But the underlying reason for developing these marks was not pride alone, but control. Medieval guilds used trade marks as a way of limiting production in the manner of a monopoly. Many guilds representing different groups such as masons, silversmiths, and paper-makers used the same criteria for the design of their trade marks as those current today: simplicity of rendering, legibility, and high potential for viewer recognition. The use of these marks was not and is not optional, but mandatory. In some instances, such marks are purely proprietary, signifying ownership, as in the case of ranchers who brand their cattle to prevent losses through theft. One of the dangers in the design and use of guild marks or any version of trade marks is the possibility of close similarities, making comparison and differentiation necessary.

The evolution from guild marks to the organizational and corporate symbols of the 20th century can be characterized by the move away from natural objects and animals towards the more abstract devices we think of as contemporary. What does abstraction mean? In visual design, the process of abstracting is one in which unnecessary detail is stripped away, leaving only the essential information. The result is simplicity and boldness. Increasing economy of form is demonstrated in the change from the figurative quality of ancient Chinese characters to the totally abstract version written today. But the process of abstraction is not absolute; it is a step-by-step evolution in which elements of visual representation still survive. This is usually what happens when an illustrative company trade mark is revised into a simpler and less representational version.

Progress from realism to abstraction in successive British railway insignia: North Western Railway, 1870; early post-nationalization British Railways, 1940s and 50s; British Rail, 1965.

Corporate symbols

It appears that the development of writing has come full circle when we consider the increasing use of the symbol as an identifying mark by governments, corporations, and a variety of organizations. In road signs or in the symbols used by meetings attended by populations with many differing languages, the display of symbols is merely a way to communicate concrete information with clarity and directness. This functional approach is tied to fundamental needs. But the use of symbols by manufacturers of products, by organizations who provide services to specialized audiences, by political and governmental groups, in every case reveals a need to extend meaning beyond the single dimension of mere identification. These symbols must, of course, first identify the group or organization they represent. This is no small task.

Every organization is identified by its name. Contemporary American vernacular has appropriated the name of one of the signers of the Declaration of Independence, John Hancock, to stand for any individual's signature. The expression 'Put your John Hancock right there' carries a suggestion of the weighty importance of the act of signing a contract. The use of the same name by the John Hancock Insurance Company carries with it all the implications of signatures on insurance policies as binding on the individuals who sign them. Their slogan is 'Put your John Hancock on a John Hancock'.

For most companies and organizations, the name is designed in type or hand lettering as the most immediate and effective identification. This primary corporate seal is called a 'signature cut' or 'sig cut'. Sometimes the signature cut is integrated with the organizational symbol; sometimes it is used to complement and strengthen the symbol. In either case, it is necessary to know how to read to understand it. Of course, there are some signature cuts that can be recognized by the illiterate. One such, the Coca-Cola signature cut, can be seen as an abstract design and recognized anywhere in the world, so complete is its international currency. But this name identification is an exception. Most company names are not so easily recognized, and need to be read to be understood.

One of the most common methods for short-circuiting the inertia of language is to replace the full name of the organization with its initials: Trans World Airlines becomes TWA; the British Broadcasting Corporation is recognized the world over as the BBC; Canadian National Railways is CN. This alphabet soup of identification came into vogue in the hurry-up mood of the technological revolution with the need for speed in getting a message across to its audience. The Union of Soviet Socialist Republics is not only represented in headlines as the USSR, but is referred to by its initials verbally

as well. The same has happened with individuals, like Franklin Delano Roosevelt, who was more familiarly known as FDR. Reducing names to initials is a kind of headline system, a way of collapsing the maximum information into the minimum space and, consequently, reducing the time needed to communicate.

In becoming identifying symbols, the initials of many corporations have become more recognizable than their names. 'International Business Machines' has little of the familiarity or impact of the sight and sound of the initials IBM. This is true in varying degrees of many organizations – UNESCO, the UK, ITT, to name a few. But for the most part symbols made from initials are recognized only visually. Initial symbols, like all visual symbols, require a vast educational effort to penetrate the public mind. To convey the identity and character of the group they represent effectively, they must be strong designs which can be understood and translated into recognition with ease. But there is an even more demanding quality with which every symbol must be invested, and that is the requirement of a visual association with the basic character of the organization it represents.

A symbol must capture and display the spirit of the company, activity, or group to which it refers. The basic design of the symbol is where that character is established. If the structure underlying the design is in perfect balance, then it would be fair to assume the organization it represents is

Three corporate symbols that enjoy widespread recognition: the Michelin man; the Coca-Cola signature cut which is recognized without reading it (here deliberately mis-spelt to demonstrate this effect); and the three-pointed Mercedes star in an advertising photograph.

solid, dependable, steady. Such an effect is appropriate for a bank.

The very resolution offered by a composition in perfect balance also expresses predictability and, not far behind this effect, may lie implications of stasis, lack of action, maybe even stodginess – hardly an appeal to the young who are attracted to excitement and innovation. Axial balance, with the meaning in structure it extends, would hardly be the best design strategy for a symbol identifying a discothèque. Imbalance, angles and fragmentation would increase stress in the viewer's perception and activate the response that the discothèque's proprietor might desire.

Identification alone is not enough for an effective symbol. A careful analysis of the sponsoring organization has to be accompanied by an understanding of the natural constituency to which the symbol is intended to appeal. And last, and possibly most important, the response hoped for when the symbol is seen must be taken into account. The basic design decision must be educated, and then reinforced by choice of colours, textures, scale and other elements.

National flags

At one end of the visual design continuum lies pure abstraction. Can a symbol of this kind which holds no visual relationship to any information drawn from the environment be an effective and dynamic symbol for a group or organization? The easiest answer is to cite the example of national flags. With very few exceptions, flags are pure, elemental visual designs which resemble nothing in the environment. Yet they evoke strong emotional response. Do we respond to the visual design of the flag, its colours, shapes and size? Or is it that learning about a flag is a nearly unconscious process, in which with little or no thought we accept a device as a surrogate for what it represents?

In fact there is no more dynamic example of the impact of pure visual abstraction than a national flag. It rarely bears any concrete connection with that for which it stands. After all, is the flag of France any more appropriate a design for the French than the Swiss flag for its people? One possible approach to the 'meaning' of flags is to look at the composition and understructure, the abstract design (another is to study their historical origins). In representational pictorial data the pure structural aspects of the composition are often obscured by the recognizable information. In an abstract design, there are no distractions; the elemental forces of the pure message are revealed.

The implications of this rather simple statement focus the fact that there is an enormous meaning potential in abstract visual expression. These dramatic effects must be considered in the process of designing a symbol and must reflect the intention of the individual or group for which it has been created. More simply, the visual conception is crucially influenced by the abstract composition. The structure is revealed in the abstract design of a flag that may represent to the world the character of the country for which it stands.

Let us look at the flag of the United Kingdom. At first glance it appears complex. But in terms of human perception it closely relates to the psycho-physiological orientation of the human organism, which strives constantly for equilibrium. Initially, it visually defines the universal relationship of all things, including the human body, to the earth. Stability and uprightness are expressed by a balanced figure on a firm horizontal plane. Balance, then, the most vital internalized reference of well-being, is represented by a right angle vertical to a horizontal base. This powerful reference is not only the *sine qua non* of successful upright negotiation on *terra firma*, it is also the constant measure of safety in the environment. Consciously or not, we are all agitated by a variation, no matter how minor, in perpendicularity. A picture slightly tilted will provoke an irresistible desire to straighten it.

Set in a rectangle, the vertical in the British flag bisects the field. This is another match with the inner human perceptual process. Not only is there a strong force toward establishing perpendicular balance in the psycho-physiological human system, there is also a need to impose a felt axis that bisects the field so that the units on each side of the axis are balanced. In some instances, as in the British flag, the axis falls on the mid-line and every unit on one side of the centre line is replicated on the other side, producing symmetry. But balance need not always be symmetrical. Just as we are capable of automatically shifting the weight of our bodies in response to a need for balance, so, too, are we capable of automatically shifting the compositional axis of a visual field in order to put what we see into relative balance. This visual shift is the counterpart in perception of the need to maintain relative balance in the physical world. Another strong perceptual need is to impose a similar bisection of the field of vision between top and bottom. The natural sense of balance generates an imposed measurement of any visual data as a way of establishing an inner check on vertical and horizontal stability. The British flag does that, too. The final structural definition in a field of forces is given by the diagonals that connect the corners through the centre point.

Each of these designations maps the forces of design in any field, establishing where, on the field, points of minimum and maximum stress lie. The field of forces is merely an inner check on the environment for relative balance. The maximum stress would be off the horizontal, vertical and diagonal stripes. From this we can infer that the flag of Great Britain presents to the viewer a design that is as close as possible to the internalized visual references that produce a sense of balance in human perception and the least stress.

The colours of the Union Jack are equally clear and balanced. The red cross of St George is superimposed on the white cross of St Andrew with its blue field, and both of them are imposed on the diagonal red cross of St Patrick. The crosses are distinguishable because of the variation in the width of the white fields. The final result is seemingly complicated but, in fact, very stable and, in a sense, very sophisticated in its compositional strategy. The red component most effectively states boldness and dominance, contrasting with the recessive character of the blue field.

The abstract design of the flag captures the meaning of sharpness: variety, activeness, but most of all firm stability. Whether this was the intention of the designers who organized the detail of the flag, or merely the result of natural evolution with no attempt to control structure toward message, it is impossible to say. Considering the unique character established throughout the design of the flag, it remains to ask two questions. First: is there meaning of a universal nature which can be understood in the abstract configuration? Second: does the meaning expressed reflect the essential character of the organization or group it represents?

These questions can be applied equally to the analysis of the meaning in structure and successful symbolization of the flags that represent Switzerland and France.

The flag of France abandons all directional reference except the vertical in its three panels. In contrast with the resolution and repose implicit in the horizontal, its vertical motifs emphasize vigour and activity. The colours of the three panels derive from two sources. The red and blue come from the cockade worn for identification and protection by the revolutionaries who overthrew the royal house of Bourbon. The white panel set in the centre is appropriated from the banner of the opposition, the 'cornette blanche' of the deposed royal family, a fleur-de-lis on a field of white. The combination is a philosophical confusion unless the heraldic tradition of using elements drawn from the past banner as part of the new to secure continuity is considered.

But one of the most striking facts about the French flag in terms of meaning in structure has to do with the departure from axial balance, the emphatic reinforcement of stress in its basic design. The vertical panels are of uneven proportion and in conflict with the implicit perceptual need marked by the map of forces in the field, thus increasing the stress.

Strange to say, the official flag of France is not divided into three equal panels. The blue in the hoist position covers 30 per cent of the field, the white, 33 per cent, the red, 37 per cent. The reason for this apportionment is not apparent except, possibly, as an aesthetic decision, but the effect must be unconsciously unsettling to the viewer. Whether by intention or accident the tricolor is, by this exceptional design, simple, direct, and active because of the differing size of its panels. These design strategies express a number of national characteristics: respect for the past, intensity, alertness, and an intellectual preoccupation with subtle modification.

The flag of Switzerland has its own strong design meaning. It is only one colour; two, if you count the white cross as a colour. The simple cross is centred both vertically and horizontally on a field of red. Analysis of the field of forces in human vision places the exact centre horizontally and vertically as the point of zero stress.

It is as a complement to that minimum visual stress that the vertical and horizontal extensions of the centre point contribute a great deal of meaning as it is used in the structure in the basic composition. What is that meaning? The flag is minimal in colour and elements. The figure is especially rational and reflective of the perceptual balance in the eye and the mind of the viewer. In its abstract configuration, the flag expresses economy, simplicity, monochromatic colour, and, most especially, stasis.

International symbols

It makes perfect communication sense that the International Red Cross chose a reflection of the Swiss flag as its symbol. One might say that the choice was based primarily on the variation of the flag of a country that has been neutral in the wars of the modern era. But visual theorists can pronounce the simplicity and stability in the design totally appropriate to the character of an international organization dedicated to health and care in war or national disaster. Without doubt there is no organizational symbol as widely recognized anywhere on earth, although in Moslem countries it is replaced by the Red Crescent; in Israel, by the Red Star of

 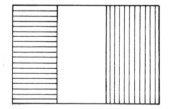 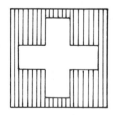

The national flags of Great Britain, France and Switzerland.

David, a response to the possible association with the cross that is the primary symbol of Christianity.

Representational visual information incorporated into symbols short-circuits the international barriers to clear communication. With negligible exceptions, it is universal in meaning. Nowhere is this fact utilized more than in circumstances under which groups that speak many languages are brought together, presenting an enormous challenge to comprehension. World Fairs, Olympic Games, airports and international political meetings are but a few of the venues that inspire the design of a whole lexicon of visual symbols for easy identification of activities and services. Long before plans are in place for an Olympic meeting, a new set of pictorial symbols identifying the games is designed. As well as the symbols for the games themselves, there are complete sets of visual symbols to facilitate rapid recognition of restaurants, first-aid stations, ticket offices, and the like. There is no need to 'learn' the meaning of such symbols. They are intended to be understood on sight by everyone.

The instant and universal meaning of the successful representational symbol is paralleled by the development of a universal system of road signs that uses all levels of visual data, representational and abstract, sometimes in combination with units of symbol systems such as the alphabet. Despite the recognition factor implicit in pictorial symbols, the international road-sign symbol system must be learned. The difference between learning road-sign symbols and coded language is apparent. The road-sign system is composed of symbols that incorporate whole meanings as ideograms representing thought independent of sounds. This is a subtle difference, but one that most dramatically demonstrates the effectiveness of symbols over language. A sign reading 'NO PARKING' requires fluency in the language in which the sign is written. Even if the motorist knows the language in which the sign is written, there is inbuilt delay from the time it takes to decipher the message. The crossed 'P' in the road sign compresses the meaning. Symbols, even those with attached meaning, once learned, deliver the message with a speed that is enormously valuable to activities under time constraints, such as those involving travel. Speed and ease are especially comforting to someone who does not speak the language, or is unfamiliar with the environment, and needs to get somewhere in a hurry. Under these circumstances, it is the symbol that works most effectively to deliver the information. Margaret Mead, the cultural anthropologist, stated the need for 'a set of clear unambiguous signs that can be understood by the speakers of many languages, and by members of any culture, however primitive. These signs will enable mankind to use the great

Luggage trolleys

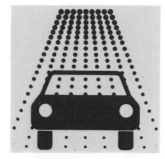
Car wash

Masseur

Indoor pool

Waiter service

Dancing

'Pictograms unite the world.' *Above* Part of a series of direction signs for the 1972 Munich Olympics by the designer Otl Aicher. *Below* An exceptionally effective Japanese design for an emergency exit symbol.

絵ことばは、世界をむすぶ。
Pictogram Units the World | 日本タイポグラフィ協会サイン・シンボル研究部会 | ピクトリアル研究所

非常口 Emergency Exit

new freedom of worldwide travel. Without them, hungry, frightened, confused people will continue to clog the travel lanes, come to grief on the roads, return disenchanted to their small provincial worlds, and contribute to the isolation and hostility in which many communities live today.' What Dr Mead was suggesting was the development of a kind of visual Esperanto, a sign language that could be understood on a global scale.

The task does not seem impossible for those of us that have grown up in a world filled with visual signs and symbols: the three balls of the pawnbroker; the red-and-white striped pole of the barber's shop; the four-leaf clover for good luck. In the 17th century the philosopher Leibnitz hoped to invent a system of universal pictorial symbols to represent the fundamental propositions of logic and reduce knowledge to a quasi-mathematical calculus. The Australian scientist Charles K. Bliss some twenty years ago attempted to invent a symbolic language of about one hundred symbols which, in combination with one another, could achieve thousands of meanings in the mode of the Chinese pictographic writing system. Jean Effel, a Frenchman, attempted the same thing, but instead of inventing signs he drew on the vast reservoir of symbols in use in many specialized systems of notation. Perhaps the most elaborate attempt to achieve a system of universal symbols was that of an Austrian, Otto Neurath, whose International System of Typographic Picture Education, or ISOTYPE, used a kind of 'pictionary' approach to standardizing information presented in pictorial detail. While none of these efforts has quite succeeded, the first steps have been taken towards meeting the challenge of devising an international symbol language.

Conclusion

Signs and symbols have been in use since the beginning of the recorded history of mankind. Although they have been described as transitional between visual perception and the written word, they have never been totally displaced by written language. As a means of communication, they have maintained their own varied functions throughout the centuries. Indeed, their usefulness has increased with the passage of time and the demand for instant communication.

Signs and symbols have helped us to define and identify ourselves in our various roles as individuals and group members, past, present, and future; they have helped us to identify feelings and to seek emotional release in that knowledge; they have helped us to determine appropriate actions and acceptable behaviour; they have influenced the design of buildings and other artefacts so that they become meaningful to us; they have served to identify small companies and large corporations for the business community; they have represented nations in the abstract; and they have helped us to cross national boundaries to represent people, places and things throughout the world. Even now, there are signs and symbols representing us in outer space – our representatives in the galaxy.

As we move from the print- and literacy-oriented 20th century towards an increasingly dominant video environment of sight and sound, the ground rules of communication shift and change. Information proliferates in an exponential curve. Access to it increases. But time limits that access. Symbols and signs will serve the future of communication as they have the past, in distilling information and extending it with intelligence and minimum delay.

Universal Meanings?

In 'Face-to-face' we looked at 'body language' and speech. In the next two picture sections we are concerned with their visual equivalents — symbolic signs and writing. Between the two pairs there are significant parallels. Signs, for instance, can be as widely understandable as gestures, and often derive from them, so that in many cases they are more useful than words (e.g. at airports, on roads, and increasingly in technical institutions; the most universal of all such signs are the Arabic numerals). Like gestures and facial expressions, too, those signs that we call symbols often carry more powerful emotional charges than words, making direct physical impressions in a way that the intellectual medium of language often fails to do. And because they operate at this level, we easily forget how many areas of life are affected by them — religion, art, sport, social standing, commerce, advertising, politics and even self-identity.

40 A wayside Calvary at Roccamandolfi in Italy bears witness to the living power of religious symbols. The Cross itself is a literal and obvious symbol of the Passion of Christ, but is also now a universal symbol of the Christian Church. Highly literal representations of the instruments of the Passion — pincers, sponge, spear, ladder (for the descent from the Cross), whip and hammer — accompany a more stylized crown of thorns (a secondary symbolism deriving from the crown of roses of a Roman emperor) and a chalice, representative both of the acceptance of suffering and of the Last Supper. The letters INRI have become a further symbol of the Passion, not always with the words they stand for consciously in mind. The cock is, by association with Peter's denial, a symbol of human weakness, which the Cross redeems, and, by association with the dawn, a symbol of the Resurrection. The rosaries are mnemonic devices rather than symbols, though the celestial blue is a symbolic colour associated with the Virgin Mary.

A HUMAN SYMBOL

We may speculate on the reasons for the mute eloquence of the hand employed as a symbol. The upheld hand already has forceful significance as a gesture; and offers the best and most obviously purposeful method of imprinting an image of the human presence. In three of the four examples shown here the handprint clearly signifies in a general way human involvement and intention. In the fourth, where it appears with other symbols in a carefully contrived structure, it has the kind of far-reaching, and emotive, reference to a broad constellation of meanings which characterizes many of the most effective symbols.

41 Handprints in cave art, like this negative impression of a hand from Pech Merle in southern France, are even more mysterious than other prehistoric images. Sometimes they accompany drawings of animals and other symbolic marks, and one suggestion is that they were added at a later date to indicate renewed human involvement in the older images.

42 Handprints of condemned prisoners impressed in still-wet plaster on the wall of a Gestapo prison in Paris, a silent testimony of personal expression in the face of annihilation.

43 In a montage by El Lissitzky, illustrating Ilya Ehrenburg's short story The Boat Ticket, the raised hand represents the past that an old Jewish man is leaving behind him, in conjunction with the letters it bears, the plan of the Temple in Jerusalem beneath and the six-pointed star. In poignant contrast are the emblems of impending transition to a strange new world – the liner, the boat ticket and the American flag. The hand indicates the past generally by virtue of the fact that it is a traditional Hebrew symbol (standing for a blessing). The Hebrew letters, standing for 'here lies', are commonly inscribed on Jewish tombstones: perhaps also the hand represents the identity the man is laying to rest.

44 A grim handprint daubed in blood on a wall in Teheran during anti-Shah riots in 1978 speaks inescapably of defiance and vengeance. It also no doubt indicates the significance of the hand as a specifically Islamic symbol, representing either the prophet Muhammad and his four followers, or the five moral pillars of Islam.

HERALDRY

Symbols of individual and group identification have both practical and psychological functions: they are signs as well as symbols. They indicated lineal descent as a guide to who could marry who for North-western American Indians, or distinguished friend from foe for crusading European knights. But also in these and other contexts they could serve as a valuable external focus for feelings of loyalty to a group and so contribute to a sense of identity.

45 The so-called Hole-Through-the-Sky totem pole which belonged to the household of a Tsimshian Indian called Haidzemerhs, in the area of the Skeena River on the Pacific coast north of Vancouver. The figures on the pole are a combination of family crests and representations of ancestors. The crests correspond to myths describing an ancestor's encounter with a supernatural being in some animal form.

46 Heraldry proper is a highly organized use of symbols with an almost infinite repertoire. Instead of attaching one naturalistic symbol to a family or clan, it deals in combinations of symbols (or 'charges'), abstract or representing man-made or natural objects, with colour differentiations elaborated by geometrical divisions. The possibilities of variation are further extended by the practice of combining arms. In the arms of Henry VIII, reproduced here from a writing desk he used, made about 1525, the gold lions on a red ground used as the English royal arms from the time of Richard I are quartered with the gold fleur-de-lis on a blue background, representing Edward III's claim to the throne of France.

47 Jousting and other ceremonial mock-military events represent a late, less serious, manifestation of heraldry. A contemporary manuscript illumination shows Rudolf II's army swearing fealty to him as Holy Roman Emperor in 1611.

48 Liverpool football club supporters rally their enthusiasm beneath red and white scarf-banners and rosettes, in a modern display of group identification analogous to the earlier use of heraldry.

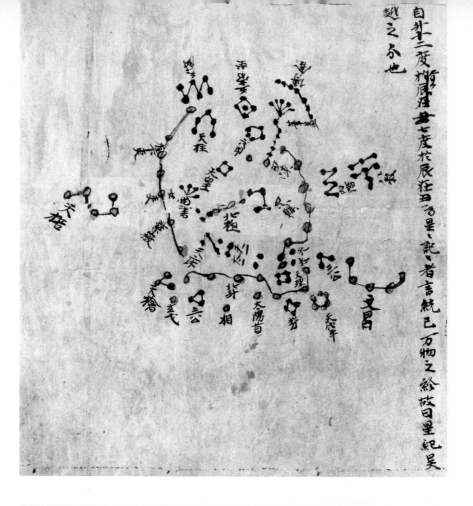

SIGNS FROM THE STARS

The signs of the zodiac represent the constellations that lie in the path of the sun as it moves through the heavens in an approximately yearly cycle. They are only twelve of the 48 constellations named by the ancient astronomer Ptolemy of Alexandria in his star catalogue, called the Almagest, in about AD 137, the basis of the grouping of stars into constellations that we use today. Drawing on traditions stretching in some cases at least back to the Babylonians (c. 2000 BC), he named the constellations according to shapes which only by a considerable effort of the imagination they could be made to resemble. In fact, the designations were just as much useful homes in the sky for the figures of Greek mythology, allusions to the seasons, or aids to memorization and recognition when these were of great practical importance in navigating and predicting the weather.

49 Chinese astronomers followed a system entirely different from that used by the inheritors of Mesopotamian astronomy. As in this example, believed to be the oldest surviving star chart from any civilization, dated C. 940 AD, they drew lines between stars to form constellations, much like modern star maps do – and here the Great Bear or Big Dipper is easily recognizable at the lower centre. But the constellations into which the stars are grouped are not the same, and their names were a direct projection of life on earth – the State Umbrella, the Higher Minister, Un-ostentatious Virtue – unlike the indirect projection of Greek astronomy via the legends of the gods.

50 A characteristic late-17th-century star chart in which the constellations of the northern celestial hemisphere are shown as highly finished and naturalistic representations.

51 In this 6th-century mosaic from an excavated synagogue at Beth-Alpha in Israel, the zodiac is transplanted from its context as a map of the heavens into a more abstract circle, though the correspondence is still recognizable.

Six different versions of Gemini exemplify the way in which the repertoire of the zodiac has been drawn on as a convenient source of inspiration in widely different cultures.

52 From a set of zodiacal coins of the early-17th-century Mughul emperor, Jahangir I.

53 From a 16th-century Persian ceramic plate.

54 From a 14th-century English astronomical manuscript.

55 From a 14th-century German screen showing the figures of the zodiac juxtaposed with representations of the months.

56 From a 15th-century Italian astrological manuscript.

57 The insignia of the American Gemini space programme. The late 20th century prefers the abstract symbol, and even the subsidiary reference to the twins presents them in abstract form as the twin stars, Castor and Pollux.

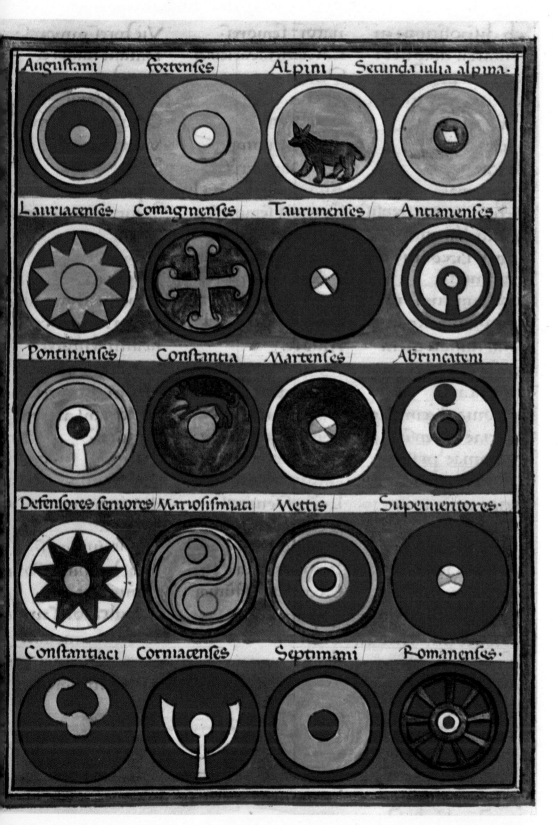

INSIGNIA

Insignia are non-personal symbols of rank or affiliation. Though in some respects akin to heraldry, they nevertheless say nothing about family lineage or personal identity, but are part of organizational structures – social, political, ecclesiastical or military – which are unaffected by the coming and going of the individuals who are temporarily attached to them. But like the symbols of heraldry, insignia have power to focus loyalty, respect or obedience as well as carrying mere information.

58 Decorated shields distinguishing different military units in late Roman Britain, illustrated in a medieval copy of an original administrative document, known as the Notitia Dignitatum.

Headgear is often a badge of rank, class or personality. It can also represent the person of the wearer for the time being in his absence.

59 A 16th-century roof boss at the University of Salamanca portrays papal tiaras and cardinals' hats in conjunction with heraldic emblems and the keys which are another mark of the papal office.

60–2 Turbans of rank of the Turkish empire on tombstones denoting the status of the dead man: a Dervish of the Mevlevi order, a Vizier and a Keeper of the Sultan's Palace.

SHOP SIGNS,
LITERAL AND FORMAL

The symbols with which tradesmen signify their skills and services testify to the speed and effectiveness with which symbols can communicate, whether or not the people they are intended for can read.

63, 64 The first of these signs for places of liquid refreshment could not be more literal. The establishment in Brick Lane, Spitalfields, in London's inner East End, would have been referred to simply as 'At the sign of the dish of coffee boy', after its blue-and-white tile sign dating from the late 18th century. The second, a contemporary African example, is at one remove from reality with its elephants engaged in the tasks of a waiter.

65, 66 The red-and-white striped barber's pole (outside 'Andrew's Gentlemen's Hair Artistes' in Covent Garden in London), immediately familiar to European and American people, works as a totally abstract symbol, whatever its precise origins in the practice of barber-surgeons displaying a red blood-letting pole twisted round with bandages. Less familiar but equally clear in meaning is the literal representation of razor, scissors and comb noticed on the window of an Uzbek barber's establishment at Andkhoy in Afghanistan.

67, 68 The juxtaposition of the house sign of an 18th-century Dutch moneylender in Maastricht with the traditional pawnbroker's three golden balls points to what is likely to be the true representational origin of this now effectively abstract sign. It is commonly believed to be associated with the three disks in the coat of arms of the great Renaissance Florentine banking family of the Medici, but an explanation relating to the spherical shapes of moneybags seems more likely.

BROKE—CALL ON UNCLE

ROTHMAN'S

STORAGE
LOANS MADE ON CLOTHING AND FURS
STORED DURING THE SUMMER MONTHS
HOLMES ELECTRIC PROTECTION

BARGAINS IN LUGGAGE
TRUNKS
CAMP·PACKING ·WARDROBE·
SPORTING GOODS

MAN'S LOANS

LUGGAGE   JEWELRY REPAIRED   LOANS

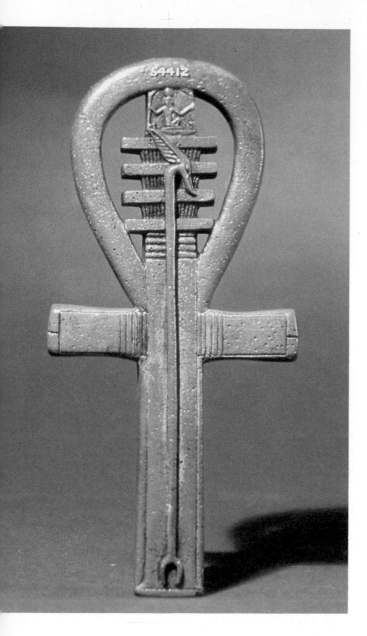

MYSTICAL MONOGRAMS

In an attractive paradox symbolism often borrows back from writing some of its signs and invests them with a meaning drawn from their written context. Added power seems to be given to the symbolic letters when they are combined or interwoven in monograms. In other cases actual words come to operate as visually recognized symbols and no longer function only as 'writing'.

69   In this faience amulet from Gebel Barksh, Egyptian XXVth dynasty, c. 700 BC, the word-picture for 'life', ankh (☥), is combined with stability (djed:) and power (was:).

70   The chi-rho represented the first two letters of the name Christ (chi χ, and rho ρ). This example, further embellished with the letters alpha and omega, referring to the biblical dictum 'I am the Alpha and the Omega, the beginning and the end', is part of a 4th-century AD Romano-British hoard, the Water-Newton Treasure.

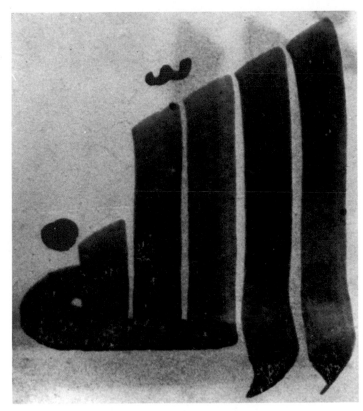

71 A Buddhist mystical formula embodying the 10 sacred characters, the so-called Lau-tsa, painted as a monogram on silk, from Tibet.

72 Because of Islam's prohibition of zoomorphic images, the word 'Allah' itself takes on the character of a sacred image or symbol. It can immediately be recognized even by Muslims who cannot 'read' it.

73–5 Just the same process of quick and resounding communication with letters is demonstrated in these contemporary examples. They are widely recognized as standing for Rolls Royce, Volkswagen and Westinghouse.

HAWKS AND DOVES

The eagle everywhere conveys power and the dove, perhaps not quite so universally, peace and reconciliation. As with all effective symbols, the person interpreting them does not need to know how they came to mean what they do, and by now they seem like instinctive symbols of what they represent.

76　The eagle, a symbol of victory, became the symbol of Rome itself after Marius surmounted the standards of the Roman legions with a silver eagle in 104 BC. This onyx cameo relief of the Roman eagle dates from shortly thereafter.

77　A double-headed eagle on a North American Indian ceremonial robe.

78　The double-headed Romanov eagle, from a Fabergé enamel plate, c. 1900.

79　The choice of the eagle for the Great Seal of the newly-independent United States was an obvious allusion to the status of the eagle as a political symbol in Europe. The fact that it was used symbolically among North American Indians conveniently gave it some added geographical relevance.

80　A giant papier-mâché eagle erected for the Nuremberg Rally in September 1936, a symbolic reinforcement of the physical might more tangibly demonstrated by the thousands of Hitler's storm troopers.

81, 82 The association of the dove with peace in Christian tradition goes back to the story of Noah. 'And the dove came to him in the evening; and, lo, in her mouth was an olive leaf pluckt off; so Noah knew that the waters were abated from off the earth.' (Genesis, 8:11.) In a detail from the Creation mosaic in St Mark's, Venice, Noah is shown putting forth the dove. It is only when it returns with the olive leaf (or 'branch'), as shown in this incised drawing on an early Roman Christian tomb, that it becomes the symbol of peace.

83 John Heartfield's photomontage 'The Meaning of Geneva' (1932) heightens the effectiveness of the dove as a symbol of peace by showing it violently butchered. The montage was made as a protest against the suppression by the Swiss authorities of an anti-Fascist demonstration, seen as an ironic underlining of the failure of the League of Nations.

84 The dove with olive branch in a peace movement poster produced by Picasso for a communist disarmament conference in May 1960.

V
ALPHABETS AND WRITING

Jack Goody

85 Statements of faith: among the badges this person is wearing, two – the Nuclear Disarmament symbol, later taken on by the anti Vietnam War movement, and the Olympic symbol – are instantly and widely understood. Among the other badges here which may need more interpretation are the heart, a rather non-specific declaration of love; the radiant sun, advocating solar energy; the symbol of Expo '67, the Montreal World Fair, which is an abstract rendering of two human figures representing 'humanity'; the seal, in protest against the slaughter of seals by fishing interests; the combined male/female symbol, for sexual equality; a quite obscure 'Ban the bomb' sign which looks like a crossed out 'cancel' road sign; the tree, another ecology symbol; and the inanely smiling face from the recently popular 'Have a nice day' movement in America.

ALPHABETS AND WRITING

The physical basis of writing is clearly the same as drawing, engraving and painting, the so-called graphic arts. It depends ultimately on man's ability to manipulate tools by means of his unique hand with its opposable thumb. There is little evidence of such activities in the early phases of man's history, during the Early and Middle Old Stone Age. But with the coming of the later Old Stone Age (Upper Palaeolithic) we find an outburst of graphic forms – in the caves of south-western France (c. 30,000–10,000 BC), in the rock shelters of southern Africa and on the birch-bark scrolls of the North American Indian tribe of the Ojibway.

It is presumably not by accident that the emergence of *Homo sapiens* with a greatly increased brain capacity coincides with the first appearance of graphic art and what have been called the 'striking innovations ... in the psychic sphere', as evidenced by the careful burial of the dead, clothed and wearing personal ornaments. The larger brain size, which may be directly connected with the dominance man achieved, may also indicate the emergence, for the first time, of a language-using animal. Although graphics and language are often viewed as alternative modes of communication (and so in some ways they are), any elaborate use of visual 'representations' requires the advanced conceptual system intrinsic to language use. The simplest painting on pebbles (such as are found in the earlier Azilian cultures), or the imprinting of hands and feet on cavern walls, probably do not involve a high degree of conceptual elaboration. Even such elementary graphic signs as these are thought by some authors to be part of a more elaborate system of signs, a true semiotic, but this degree of structure seems unlikely; their 'communicative' or 'expressive' aspects appear to be general rather than specific, loosely rather than tightly structured. Nor did they develop into any formal semiotic that could be described as embryonic writing. It is generally agreed that this

gap is filled by the so-called 'picture-writing' of the North American Indians.

Even when found singly or in small groups, early graphic forms, pictorial or conventional, are sometimes taken to be communicating 'messages', implicitly or explicitly, and as such are assumed to be forerunners of writing. At the explicit level of interpretation, there may be as much 'message' in a representation of a hand with pointed finger as in a bison with an arrow in its flank, though one may be a standardized index (a grapheme), the other a unique picture. In North America single indices, depicting a man's 'totem', the emblem of his clan or of himself, are sometimes found located in quarries or water holes to show that a particular group or person has visited the place. Similar designs are commonly used as signs of the owners or makers of property, like the marks of Middle Eastern potters or the five arrows of the brothers Rothschild.

An important step is taken when these pictures, or signa, are strung together in sequential form, as most notably in the great scrolls of the Ojibway Midéwewin society, since the possibility of syntax, as distinct from a 'path expression', now arises. André Leroi-Gourhan in *Le Geste et la parole* comments that all true pictography is recent, mostly dating from after the period of contact with literate societies. This certainly applies to many graphic systems, many of which have been subjected to direct or to stimulus diffusion. But for America the achievements of the Maya and other societies suggest that pictographs, as distinct from pictograms, may well have been present earlier. While such picture-writing is often placed in contrast to later systems of writing because of its reliance on visual communication largely 'independent of the spoken language' (Gelb, *Encyclopaedia Britannica*, 15th edition), the assumption of a direct link between cue and brain seems misleading. Language is involved and linguistic translations are made of the graphic sequences.

Painted pebbles from Mas d'Azil in south-western France: it is unlikely that they reflect any system of meanings that could be called proto-writing.

Among the Ojibway, the use of 'pictographs' inscribed on birch-bark scrolls centred upon the cult of the Midéwewin, a type of 'tutorial shamanism' which in many areas replaced the earlier form of 'visionary shamanism'. Tutorial shamanism depended upon an individual becoming a pupil of a senior member of the society and handing over a large amount of wealth in exchange for instruction by means of the scrolls. It was by means of these birch-bark scrolls that 'the complex rituals and oral traditions of the southern Ojibway were transmitted by the Midé shamans to their disciples or candidates for initiation' (S. Dewdney, *Scrolls of the Southern Ojibway*). Consequently the scrolls were secret documents, meant to act as a mnemonic for the initiate but not as a means of communicating information to the world at large. 'Should the secrecy of his information be uppermost in his mind he might employ condensation, abstraction, atrophy, or even *amputation*. Or he might go further, using symbolic conversion or the ultimate device for misleading the uninitiated: substitution of the significant form by another completely irrelevant one.' The function was always mnemonic: 'It was not the written word, merely a means of recalling the oral tradition and the details of the Midé master's instruction ... even the oral tradition was not transmitted in any rigid way from one generation to another. ... it must be kept in mind that behind the instruction scrolls were individuals for whom the dream spoke with an authority equal to, and sometimes exceeding that of the oral tradition. Interaction between the dream, the sacred lore, and the mnemonic device of the scrolls produced, by a sort of cross-fertilization, a richer and richer body of rites, variations on the traditional themes, and birch-bark pictography.'

The Ojibway scrolls analysed by Dewdney dealt with the main features of Midé concern, that is, the creation of the world and of man, the origin of death, the introduction of the Midéwewin, and the ancestral origins of the Ojibway people. 'For each and all of these purposes a scroll could be devised as a mnemonic aid.' But in fact the same scroll could form the basis of very different interpretations by the selfsame person. Their function is close to that ascribed to the Australian *churinga*, plaques of wood or stone engraved with abstract designs, spirals, straight lines, groups of dots, that indicate the content of myth or the location of sacred places. It is the same function of 'mythogram' that Leroi-Gourhan has attributed to some paintings and engravings of the Late Old Stone Age in France, where 'mytho-graphy' is the visual equivalent of the verbal 'mytho-logy'. While this is not the only function of North American pictographs – Mallery, who worked on them in the late 19th century, mentions mnemonic recording of chants, calendars and chronology as well as the use of

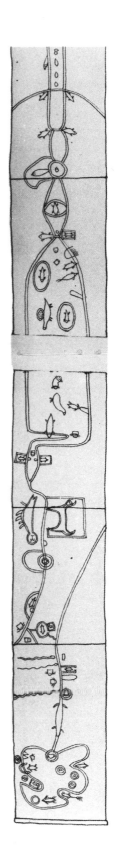
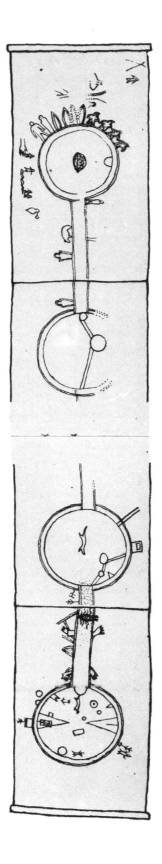

North American Ojibway birch-bark scrolls, redrawn by Mallery. Mnemonic devices recalling tales of the origins of the Ojibway people (*left*) and the creation of the world: the link with language is tenuous.

graphemes for notices of visits, indications of direction, warning signs, simple maps and especially for the identification of individuals and clans by 'totemic' designs – it was clearly one of the main uses of sequential pictographs in general.

The scrolls then consist of origin tales, or Midé migration charts, and of ritual charts showing the stages through which the neophyte progressed. Each of these takes the form of a visual narrative, a more formalized version of the kind of picture sequence used in the popular paintings of the Ethiopian myth. Each implies the idea of a journey, a coming, of movement over space, although in fact the passage of an initiate going through the stages of initiation does not necessarily imply any physical movement. The journey is the way in which time or passage is envisaged. Hence the importance of narrative, of the journey through time and space. One's eye moves from one part of the scroll to the next, unwinding the creation of the world or the origin of death, a quite different type of scanning from that involved in reading, that is, in reading a text.

What is the nature of this proto-writing, often called pictographic, and seen as being a precursor of writing systems that use arbitrary signs? Clearly there is a strong pictorial element in the Ojibway scrolls. But the presence of this component does not result from any inability to use or invent arbitrary signs. As F. Boas, author of *Primitive Art*, has insisted, there is no evidence that 'representative' (pictorial) forms preceded 'formal' (arbitrary) ones, or vice versa. The pictorial element dominates because of the mnemonic (or, better, suggestive) relationship between sign (or index) and signified (or signifieds, since there may be a considerable number of ways of interpreting a given text and even a given sign).

Ignace Gelb of the University of Chicago analyses the forerunners of writing under two heads, descriptive-representational devices and identifying-mnemonic ones. The categories (let us call them descriptive and memory devices) are not exclusive, but they will serve to emphasize the point about the pictorial element in these mnemonic systems.

The first type of device was used by American Indians in making the peace treaties of wampum bead work where an Indian may be represented as embracing or shaking hands with a white; in theory, understanding such signs does not depend upon understanding a particular language. Descriptive devices of this kind are basically natural indices of a static kind.

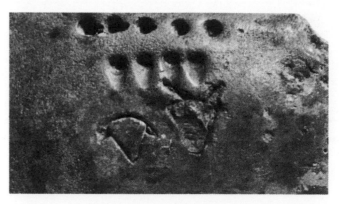

The first systematic link between sign and sound: a sign for 'fifty-four' and representational signs for 'cow' and 'bull' read 'fifty-four cows and bulls'. (From Uruk (level IV), c. 3200–3100 BC.)

The memory devices are used not to describe an event, but to record or identify the words of a song, the actions of an individual, the events of a year. They may be abstract or pictorial, and are 'signs' of a sequential kind. However, they are not transcriptions of language, but rather a figurative shorthand, a mnemonic, which attempts to recall or prompt linguistic statements rather than to reproduce them.

There is no systematic link between sign and sound until we reach true writing systems using word signs (logograms), where the shorthand disappears in favour of an exact transcription of a linguistic statement. For example, three cows are represented by two word signs, one for 'three', one for 'cow', rather than by three similar signs (pictographic or abstract) for 'cow'. In some early systems of writing the use of such transcription is limited, for example, to simple administrative records among the Mycenaeans or the early Sumerians. Nevertheless, there is a definite attempt to transcribe linguistic terms rather than simply to employ graphic signs as markers for recall. Because of the large number of signs needed, both transcription and recall may be facilitated if word signs contain a pictorial element, since an understanding of the graphic code is assisted by visual cues. The representational character of the referential system is thus a matter of its own logic rather than of the constitution of the 'primitive' mind. Indeed, Chinese, the only major logographic system still in use today, contains just such a pictorial element, though some of this has been lost over time.

A 'descriptive' device with no relation to any language: the well-known Penn wampum, recording the treaty between William Penn and the Iroquois.

Early writing systems

It follows from what we have said about 'picture-writing' that the principles behind writing proper are not of a totally different kind. Objects, actions and persons cannot readily be separated from their linguistic symbols, so that even pictorial signs or symbols operate through a linguistic channel as well as a visual one. The main development lies in the degree to which the graphic system succeeds in duplicating the linguistic one, that is, in the extent, firstly, of word-to-sign (semantic) correspondence and, secondly, of phonetic correspondence.

Forms of writing with many pictorial elements were well developed in the Mayan empire of Central America (1st century AD), a society with a pronounced urban character. This writing achieved a considerable measure of elaboration, especially in the area of mathematical, calendrical and astronomical work which require the invention of graphic equivalents of a number system. There is no doubt that the positive achievements of the Mayan calendar were due to the development of a system of graphic signs for the representation of numbers. The emphasis was on numeracy rather than literacy; as far as more extensive linguistic representation was concerned, there is no evidence as yet that the Mayans developed a complete writing system, although the exact nature of their graphic code awaits decipherment, and it certainly appears to have been used for the recording of historical events.

The Mayans were followed first by the Toltecs and then by the Aztecs (14th century), who developed a different script,

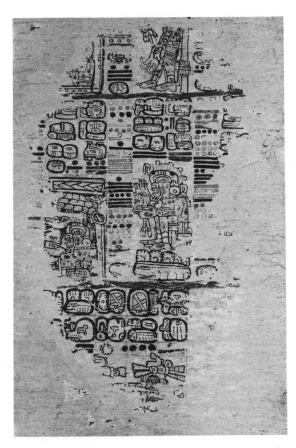

Word signs for numbers, and calendrical signs, combined with pictorial representation: an example of the Mayan script in the so-called Codex Peresianus, 9th century AD.

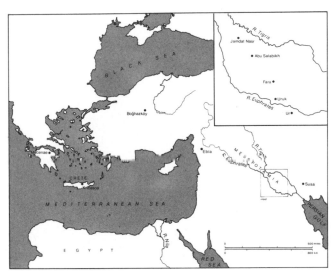

Early writing systems in the Middle East: archaeological sites mentioned in the text.

A more restricted system of pictorial signs: the Dakota Indians recorded the passage of time by counting winters, using a sign which referred to an event of the year that had passed.

stimulated by their predecessors. We have some evidence of the use of phonetic elements (as we have with the Mayan script), but as a system of writing it too was definitely incomplete and was almost always in need of 'supplementary oral description' (David Diringer, *Writing*). The script appears to have been used to record genealogies and political events, though once again it was extensively used for mathematics and astronomy; indeed the inspiration and knowledge was certainly Mayan in origin. This use of writing in the development of calendrical systems can be seen as an extension of the use of pictorial signs for the same purpose in the famous Winter Counts of the Dakota (see page 109).

It is clear that pictorial signs were incorporated into all early writing systems. But they were certainly not the only source either of the signs themselves or of the developed system of graphic-linguistic correspondence that we call writing, as distinct from proto-writing. Before the development of writing, conventional signs clearly had meaning, just as isolated graphic signs do in non-literate societies today. Signs for numerical quantities are central to the development of any elaborate calendrical system, or system of calculation, so that it is not surprising to find the recurrent use of numbers as distinct from letters in early graphic systems such as the Mayan. Indeed, the use of so-called pictographs and arbitrary signs was combined in many early writing systems, as when a pictorial sign for a container is accompanied by a number of marks or impressions to indicate the quantity of the containers involved.

Such a system of calculation involving record keeping by means of objects and graphemes has been proposed as the basis of the oldest form of writing, namely cuneiform, in a recent article in *Scientific American* by the French archaeologist Denise Schmandt-Besserat. A re-examination of the records of archaeological excavations in the Near East covering the 9th to the 6th millennia BC has pointed to the wide distribution of clay 'tokens' (in effect, hand-made pebbles), consisting of fifteen basic shapes further divided into some 200 sub-classes on the basis of size, marking or fractional variation (e.g. half-spheres). The meaning of some of these tokens, whose distribution and frequency vary over time and space, can be discovered by comparing them with the earliest writing on the tablets from Uruk in Mesopotamia (c. 3100 BC), with which the tokens found at Susa (in the Khuzistan region of Iran) were roughly contemporary. Some of the early Uruk signs reproduce in two dimensions almost the exact form of the tokens.

The distribution of these tokens around the Fertile Crescent running between Mesopotamia and Egypt, and their appearance at the beginning of the Neolithic period, provide a clue to their use. The shift to agricultural production based on cereals involved the storage of grain for use throughout the year and the possibility of a surplus over immediate nutritional and consumption needs, a surplus that could then be exchanged with other producers, of animals, crafts, or of other products. Equally, primary produce could then be collected as tribute or 'gift' in order to maintain a hierarchical political or religious organization of kings or priests.

A significant change in this recording system, for such it appears to be, occurred early in the Bronze Age, between 3500 and 3100 BC. This was also the period that saw the creation of cities whose economy was rooted in trade. Craft specialization and the beginnings of manufacture had already made their appearance; smithying in bronze developed; the invention of the wheel by the end of the 5th millennium

Correspondence between some of the shapes of clay tokens from Susa and the earliest writing inscribed on clay tablets from Uruk.

meant a great potential increase in the production of pottery. Later, bronze metallurgy developed; trade expanded; cities came into being.

The increase both in production and in trade encouraged the elaboration of the recording system which was required for inventories, shipments, payments of wages, the calculation of profit and loss. The system of tokens became more elaborate, particularly the graphic component of them, deep grooves being made with the end of a stylus. About one-third of these new tokens are perforated, apparently so that they could be strung together to record a particular transaction. At the same time we begin to find clay envelopes or *bullae*, which also appear to have been used to separate off the records of a particular transaction. The envelopes could then be marked with the seals of the individuals involved. It has been suggested that the envelopes found at Susa were used as bills of lading; a rural producer of textiles might send a consignment of goods to the city merchant, together with an envelope containing the tokens indicating the kind and quantity of the goods.

Such a system could clearly open up the possibility that instead of sending three-dimensional tokens in an envelope on which seals had been stamped, the objects themselves should be omitted and the outside of the envelope marked with the shape of the tokens, either by impressing the token in the clay or by using a stylus. The envelope becomes the writing tablet, the shapes become signs, tokens become writing, thus developing a system that was rapidly adopted throughout the area in which the tokens had been found. The problem of reducing three-dimensional objects to two dimensions is of course a central problem of the graphic arts and one that must lead to some measure of stylization.

That writing developed in such a way is certainly suggested by the history of writing in Crete, where the Minoan civilization began to reach a complex level around the 20th century BC when the first signs of a script appear. Pictorial signs for commodities and a decimal number system were accompanied by the carving of seal-stones with patterns made up of a few, usually three or four, related pictorial signs. J. Chadwick in an article in the *Journal of the Royal Asiatic Society* thinks these were not a true script but rather a 'symbolic system' like the medieval craft of heraldry, that used pictorial and other elements (such as colours) to designate individuals, their status and their pedigree. The association of a numerical notation, signs for commodities and inscribed seals is what one would anticipate in the shift from tokens to script. The tablets in the early Cretan script known as Linear A, though the script is undeciphered, seem to be a series of records of quantities of commodities (mainly agricultural, but including textiles) listed against names.

In this way, it is suggested, the first complete writing systems arose in West Asia around 3100 BC in the period that saw the development of the first urban civilization. They are known as logographic (or logo-syllabic) because they did succeed in representing language by means of signs in a systematic way.

Logographic writing

Logographic systems of writing clearly develop from simpler uses of graphic signs. Initially pictorial representation was used for some signs. But the full writing that developed incorporated the systematic representation of words (and their referents) by graphic signs. Clearly many words have referents which are linked to 'the world outside', so that the written sign X, which we will take to signify 'cross', refers to the concept, to the object or to the action as well as to the sound. But the more immediate reference is to the word, that is to the sound, whereas in the pictorial devices of proto-writing – none of which, as we have seen, can be dissociated from the linguistic channel – the more immediate reference is to the object or incident itself.

Systems which represent every word by a separate sign are unknown, although Chinese constitutes the closest approximation. Every developed type of writing possesses some signs that represent syllables as well as words and hence economizes on the number of signs needed. For example, the sign of 'man' plus the sign for 'drake' could read 'mandrake'. Because of this feature, these first complete systems are known as *logo-syllabic* since they use signs to express both words and syllables.

Their invention seems to have been confined to parts of the African and Asiatic continents, excluding the areas where the use of 'pictographs' was most developed. We know of seven such systems of writing in early society:

(i) Sumerian-Akkadian in Mesopotamia, 3100 BC to AD 75.
(ii) Proto-Elamite in Elam, Mesopotamia, 3000 BC to 2200 BC.
(iii) Egyptian in Egypt, 3100 BC to 2nd century AD.
(iv) Proto-Indic (or Proto-Indian) in the Indus Basin, Indian subcontinent, around 2200 to 1000 BC.
(v) Cretan in Crete and Greece, 2000 BC to 12th century BC (hieroglyphic, Linear A and Linear B).
(vi) Hittite and Luwian in Anatolia and Syria, 1500 BC to 700 BC (Anatolian hieroglyphic).
(vii) Chinese in China, 1500–1400 BC to the present day.

Of these systems, it is generally agreed that three, viz. Proto-Elamite, Proto-Indic (or Proto-Indian) and Cretan Linear A (Linear B is Greek) remain undeciphered, despite many proposals.

The earliest elaborated system of writing is the cuneiform (wedge-shaped) script which appears at the end of the 4th millennium BC. This script was used to write down the language of the Sumerian people who inhabited the lower part of Mesopotamia, 'the land between the two rivers', of the Tigris and Euphrates, where they flowed into the Persian Gulf, and was later taken over by another people of this area, the Akkadians. It was written on moistened clay tablets on which the scribe stamped the triangular end of a reed to produce various combinations of the basic impression. The clay dried and the tablet was either stored away or dispatched to its recipient.

The shape of these characters was at least partly non-pictorial, 'abstract', arbitrary, though some displayed evidence of a pictorial origin. There is evidence of a contemporary cuneiform script, used to write down the language of the Proto-Elamites of Susa, in which the abstract element was stronger from the beginning, and with the development of the form of writing known as Linear Elamite (Script B) we see the emergence of a script composed of syllables with periodic word signs. Both the Sumerian and the Elamite traditions of writing existed side by side and may have had a common progenitor, though the languages appear to be different. But of this we know nothing and it is clear that the origins of Mesopotamian writing include the non-pictorial signs used on earlier tokens.

Whatever the morphological similarities between the more developed graphic systems of North America and early writing in the Near East, the context was vastly different. The former were primarily mnemonic and therefore elaborated for purposes where memory was considered important, namely in recalling mythico-ritual processes (as in the Ojibway scrolls). A related use is the calendrical one found in the Dakota Winter Counts. Other uses are relatively minor, but few if any concern what we would usually describe as the economic life.

How different was the situation in Mesopotamia. According to G. R. Driver in his *Semitic Writing*, the development of the cuneiform script was the result of 'economic necessity'. The earliest Elamite and Sumerian records are not concerned with 'communication' in the usual sense of that word, and certainly not with writing down oral myth or composing poetry, that is, with 'literary' purposes. They were 'mere lists of objects pictorially jotted down on clay-tablets with the numbers of each beside them, indicated by a simple system of strokes, circles and semi-circles'. Usually associated with ancient centres of cult or court, the records mainly refer to the property and accounts of temples; they are 'purely economic and administrative, never religious or historical.' Such a situation appears to have continued for the first 500 years of the history of writing; the only exceptions were scholastic texts, which were also 'mere lists of signs and words, required for the training of scribes.'

The same was true of Egypt, though the economic context was different; it was the need to keep a calendar for calculating the annual flood of the Nile and 'to give a permanent form to the spells and prayers necessary to ensure a plentiful harvest year after year and to transmit them in the correct form to future generations.' While the motivation may have been 'economic' in both countries, it was priests and administrators who devoted themselves to the leisured

Uruk IV c. 3100	Sumerian c. 2500	Old Babylonian c. 1800	Neo-Babylonian c. 600 BC	SUMERIAN *Babylonian*
				APIN *epinnu* plough
				ŠE *še'u* grain
				ŠAR *kirū* orchard
				KUR *šadū* mountain
				GUD *alpu* ox
				KU(A) *nunu* fish
				DUG *karpatu* jar

Some cuneiform signs display evidence of pictorial origins. The plough in the top line can be recognized in the clay tablet from Uruk, *c.* 3000 BC (*opposite, above*).

exploitation of this complex system of writing. It was the complexity of the writing that confined its systematic use to a well-trained set of 'scribes', whose position in Egypt also rested upon the fact that the training was carried out largely by priests.

The earliest Mesopotamian tablets come from a few sites in Southern Mesopotamia, the most important of which are Uruk (modern Warka; level IV, c. 3200–3100 BC) and Jamdat Nasr (c. 3000 BC). These are inscribed in a pictorial script, partly 'deciphered', either thanks to the nature of the picture or through the relation with later cuneiform. The language of the script has not yet been agreed (it may be Sumerian). They are essentially 'lists of commodities, business transactions and land sales', according to Joan Oates in the *Cambridge Encyclopaedia of Archaeology*. Next come a few hundred tablets from archaic Ur (probably Early Dynastic I, 2900–2800 BC), underlying the Royal Cemetery, which are still very difficult to read, consisting mostly of lists but containing a few descriptive phrases. The Royal Cemetery is probably some 300 years later (2600–2500 BC) and in the following century we have approximately 1000 tablets from Fara (Shuruppak) in a form that enables us to see more clearly that we are dealing with an early form of Sumerian writing. The texts themselves consist almost exclusively of numbers, followed by depicted objects. But those from archaic Ur also deal with matters such as land and its products, agricultural implements and cattle, and in addition we find a certain number of school texts. More recent finds from Abu Salabikh, of the same period as Fara, even include some fragments of literary works as well as lists of words. The fundamental discoveries at Ebla (Tell Mardikh, in North Syria) have produced an extraordinary library from approximately the same period. Here the cuneiform script was used to write not only Sumerian and Akkadian but a language which appears to be West Semitic and, possibly, a form of proto-Canaanite – which was later to be used for the first alphabets. These unpublished texts include legends, state treaties and other written documents.

In terms of form, the earliest texts from Uruk (level IV) consist solely of numbers and pictured objects; those from Jamdat Nasr include the first sign with a determinative value (i.e. an indicator of semantic category), while the texts from archaic Ur have a few syllabic signs to indicate the cases of nouns and other grammatical features; and at Fara these same syllabic signs also come to be used to indicate the phonetic value of certain words (i.e. phonetic indicators).

At about the same time, and possibly under some kind of stimulation from Sumer, the Egyptians developed a 'hieroglyphic' system for writing their own language. Egyptian

The way in which cuneiform signs were formed with the triangular end of a reed in moistened clay can clearly be seen in this legal document and its envelope, bearing seals, from Atchana in southeast Turkey, c. 1700 BC.

One of the earliest surviving examples of Egyptian hieroglyphic writing: a fragment from a wine jar bearing the name of the owner, c. 3100 BC, from Abydos.

hieroglyphic writing, so called by the Greeks because they saw its main use as religious, was, with Sumerian-Akkadian cuneiform, the main script in the Near East for the first 2000 years of writing, and the one that provided the point of departure for many later systems. The script appears in a fairly advanced state of development at the time of the First Dynasty (c. 3000 BC), the finest example being the well-known Narmer Palette. Soon afterwards the Egyptians added to their pictorial signs a set of phonograms (or phonetic indicators), which showed the way the word should sound, and determinatives (or semantic indicators), which showed the category of the object or action. While additions were often needed to remove the ambiguity of polyphonic words, many were simply redundant, reflecting the elaborations of scribal practitioners working on the complexities of logographic decoding. Simpler forms of Egyptian writing emerged over the centuries, first hieratic, then demotic, which were preferred for profane purposes. Nevertheless, until Coptic (i.e. Egyptian in Greek letters) took over in the 2nd century AD (an inscription from the Island of Philae dated 394 is a 'fossil'), the principles remained unchanged: the simplifications were in style (i.e. in becoming more cursive) rather than in structure.

Another major civilization of the 2nd and 3rd millennia BC, that of the Indus Basin, in the north of the Indian subcontinent, also saw the development of writing (c. 2200 BC). The Indus Basin script, in which the inscriptions are all very short, may have had some connection with Sumer; there were certainly links in the trade in semi-precious stones such as carnelian and lapis lazuli from Afghanistan. And it has been suggested by one authority that the language itself may also be related to Sumerian, though others have thought it to be an early form of Dravidian, now spoken mainly in South India. Both suggestions as to the language are at present highly conjectural. The seals on which the inscriptions are mainly found do appear to have been used in trading operations, and are similar to those from the Persian Gulf, an area of trade with the Indus Basin, while others have been found in Mesopotamia itself. Most of these seals appear to indicate the owners' names (in early Sumeria usually scribes) and to have been used for stamping goods, and making tokens and amulets, while others may have served a dedicatory purpose.

In the East Mediterranean, another important system of writing developed about the same time. Cretan scripts begin with pictorial devices on seals dating from 2800 BC, apparently showing some Egyptian influence. Subsequently, around 2000–1850 BC, these devices develop into pictorial (hieroglyphic) inscriptions, which lead through a cursive form into Minoan (Linear A), a linear script dating from c. 1700–1550 BC, which has not yet been satisfactorily

Hieroglyphic writing from the pyramid of King Chios, Egyptian Vth Dynasty. The cartouche contains the king's name.

deciphered, though the American scholar Cyrus Gordon has recently claimed that both Linear A and Eteo-Cretan (written in the Greek alphabet, 600–300 BC) are in a north-west Semitic language. This script contained a limited number of signs, between seventy-six and ninety, presumably constituting a simple syllabary, nearly half of which were derived from earlier pictorial forms. Linear B, consisting of some eighty-nine characters partly derived from Linear A, appears to have been associated with the mainland Mycenaean civilization that took over from the Minoans about 1400 BC. Brilliantly deciphered by Michael Ventris, who was an architect by profession, it was shown to be a form of Greek, used mainly for economic and military account books and continuing in use until the invasions of the later Dorian Greeks around 1100 BC. From then until c. 750 BC, runs the traditional account, Greece passed through the Dark Ages and had to re-import writing, this time in alphabetic form from the Phoenicians.

The Hittite script developed somewhat later in the middle of the 2nd millennium BC. The Hittite empire occupied much of the area of present-day Turkey lying between the Black Sea and the land under Assyrian rule. It was the discovery of the royal archive of Hatti (Boğhazköy) that brought to light the way in which this kindgom used the cuneiform script of Mesopotamia, borrowed from a north Syrian tribal school, to write down its Indo-European language (1650–1200 BC). In addition to the extensive series of cuneiform texts, there exist a number of inscriptions, as well as other writing, in a hieroglyphic type of script with pictorial signs (c. 1500 BC) and including some semantic indicators. This was clearly stimulated in a general way by an acquaintance with Egyptian forms. Both cuneiform and hieroglyphic scripts were used for writing Luwian, a related Indo-European language (1400–1200 BC and 1350–8th century BC), as well as Hittite.

The Chinese script is the most recent of the major logo-syllabic systems, both in its invention and in its use. The first evidence consists of divinatory records dating from the 15th century BC. This use of writing appears at a time when Indo-Europeans were controlling the steppe area between West Asia and Northern China, which has suggested to some the possibility of stimulation from that direction. Not only is it the most recent, it is also the most clearly pictorial in its logographic characters. It is the most conservative of contemporary writing systems; there are some 8000 characters in current use, although a basic Chinese for popular literature needs a range of only 1000–1500 characters. Although the problem is eased because of the predominantly monosyllabic nature of the language, the complexity of the script clearly limits access to knowledge, and helped promote and maintain a mandarin type of culture.

Clay tablet bearing inscription in Cretan Linear B.

A very early example of the Chinese script in a divinatory inscription on bone of the later Shang dynasty (c. 1000 BC).

The development of phonetic transcription

In theory, individual word signs can provide a relatively exact equivalence of sign and sound, of image and speech. However, a repertoire that included a different sign for every word would be enormously cumbrous and difficult to work. As we have seen in the three West Asian scripts, Mesopotamian cuneiform, Egyptian and Anatolian hieroglyphic, there developed a type of semantic indicator that was not pronounced and that was originally used to distinguish between signs that had more than one meaning. For example, in cuneiform the sign *Assur* stands for both the city and the patron god; an additional determinative may be added to the initial sign to indicate the class to which the intended meaning belongs, either the sign for 'city' or the sign for 'deity'. In the course of time these determinatives were used for all members of a particular class, whether or not there was any danger of ambiguity.

The use of such determinatives added to the complexity of writing, though in other ways it limited the number of different signs and aided the interpretation of the existing ones. However, the most important development, which opened the way to the modern alphabet, via the introduction of syllabic writing, was the systematic use of the phonetic principle. By the use of the 'rebus' device, signs need no longer distinguish separate meanings of a specific sound (e.g. *Assur*) but could rather denote the sound itself, irrespective of the meaning. In this way the Sumerian word *ti*, 'life', a concept which is in any case not easy to put in pictorial form, can be expressed by means of the sign for arrow, which is also *ti*. This shift represents a neglect of semantic equivalence in favour of phonetic equivalence, the latter involving a more abstract method of transcribing language and one that enabled powerful economies to take place.

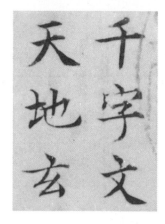

The multiplicity of characters in the Chinese script: part of the Thousand Character Essay, a school exercise consisting of a summary of Chinese history in which no character is repeated (*top*). The enlarged details show the six characters at the top right-hand corner from four 16th-century versions of the Essay in different styles of writing.

The rebus device is the key to the shift from sign representing meaning to sign representing sound – the first step towards the complete versatility of the alphabet. This 16th-century example comes from Abbot Islip's chapel in Westminster Abbey in London. Apart from the eye for I, there is a man slipping from a tree.

Phonetic indicators were frequently used with word signs (as were semantic indicators) to specify the way the sign should be pronounced. The phonetic principle was particularly important in rendering proper names. Such words could be broken down into their constituent syllables (i.e. various combinations of consonant and vowel, of stop and breath) by using word signs already in the language, as in the use of the word sign for 'man' as a syllabic sign in the transcription of names such as 'Manfred'. Such syllabic signs might then be used in other words, as in the case of 'mandrake'. In this way the various systems that combined the use of word and syllable signs gave birth to syllabaries working on the phonetic principle, which could work with much reduced sets of signs. In general this development took place on the fringes of the major civilizations; the Japanese developed a syllabary using Chinese signs, which included some phonetic ones; the Elamites and Hurrians did the same with Sumerian; various minor syllabic scripts of Cyprus and the surrounding Aegean area were derived from neighbouring forms; and Egyptian can be seen as the parent (though jointly with Akkadian) of the West Semitic 'syllabaries' which are the progenitors of the alphabet: indeed, many scholars would count these West Semitic systems as true alphabets, though limited to the transcription of consonants.

Complete systems of syllabic writing need only employ a limited set of signs and are relatively easy to learn and to work. There have been a number of recent inventions of syllabaries, again in 'peripheral' areas, by individuals or small groups who have made deliberate efforts to introduce writing to their own peoples. Two well-known instances of this process took place among the Vai of West Africa and the Cherokee of North America in the first half of the 19th century. In both cases we know the names of the individuals concerned and some of the background to their invention. The Cherokee syllabary was invented by Sequoyah as the result of twelve frustrating years of trial and error. Obsessed with his vision that Indians, like the more educated of the white people, might learn to communicate with 'talking leaves', he neglected his farm, defied his family, and was ultimately tried for witchcraft as the consequence of his behaviour. However, by 1819 he had perfected the syllabary and had taught his daughter to read. He was asked to demonstrate his discovery before a group of Cherokee elders and so successful was his innovation that, within a few years, thousands of Cherokee became literate in their native language. Subsequently a printing press was set up and by 1880 the Cherokee had a higher level of literacy than the neighbouring whites.

A similar series of events occurred among the Vai of Liberia where Bukele developed a syllabary of some 226 signs at about the same time. This invention arose in a similarly competitive context of European and Arabic writing but the script is still widely used by Vai speakers. As with the Cherokee, individuals often learn to read as adults, since literacy is not of much use in childhood and it is relatively easy to learn to write down one's maternal language by this means. A number of other syllabic scripts have been invented in West Africa during the present century, many of them being clearly stimulated by the achievement of the Vai.

But in the Mediterranean and the Near East, syllabaries were swept aside by the further simplification of phonetic transcription brought about by the alphabet.

The alphabet

There are two views about the invention of the alphabet. The first holds that it was invented in Greece around 750 BC, in the period immediately before the great Ionian and Athenian achievements; the second that it was invented by Western Semites, some 750 years earlier, about 1500 BC.

a	e	i	o	u
ga	ge	gi	go	gu
ha	he	hi	ho	hu
la	le	li	lo	lu
ma	me	mi	mo	mu
na	ne	ni	no	nu
gwa	gwe	gwi	gwo	gwu
sa	se	si	so	su
da	de	di	do	du
dla	dle	dli	dlo	dlu
dza	dze	dzi	dzo	dzu
wa	we	wi	wo	wu
ya	ye	yi	yo	yu
ö	gö	hö	lö	nö
gwö	sö	dö	dlö	dzö
wö	yö	ka	hna	nah
s	ta	te	ti	tla

The Cherokee syllabary. It is immediately obvious that a syllabary, though more economical than a logographic writing system such as Chinese, requires many more signs than the alphabet.

In certain respects both views are correct. However, the importance of the Greek achievement for the subsequent history of Western Europe has been over-emphasized, by classicists and others, too much weight being placed on the addition of specific vowel signs to the set of consonantal ones that had been developed much earlier in Western Asia. The consonantal structure itself, and even the order and shape of the signs, was invented by speakers of Canaanite, a Semitic language. At one time it was thought that this latter invention had taken place among the workers in the turquoise mines of the Sinai peninsula, whose Proto-Canaanite script was said to have derived from ownership marks on livestock and pots. Now the proposed location has shifted to northern Canaan, that is, to contemporary Syria, which formed a bridge between the socio-cultural systems of Egypt and Mesopotamia.

An important early step forward in the work on the origin of the alphabet began with the discovery by the archaeologist Sir William Flinders Petrie of a series of inscriptions at the turquoise mines of Serābît el-Khâdem in Sinai in the spring of 1905, inscriptions that he dated to the 15th century BC, though his contemporary, A. H. Gardiner, placed them two centuries earlier. The signs resembled Egyptian hieroglyphic writing, but there were so few characters that an alphabet was indicated. The decipherment of the script was suggested by Gardiner in 1917. He noted a recurrent series of pictorial signs, 'oxgoad (or shepherd's crook)-house-eye-oxgoad-cross', and saw that, if the signs stood for the initials of their names (on the acrophonic principle), their Canaanite value would be 'for the Lady'. This was a favourite epithet of the Canaanite goddess Asherah (or Ba'alat), identified with the Egyptian goddess Hathor, whose temple dominated the site

worked by the labourers (or slaves). This Proto-Canaanite script was finally deciphered by the American W. F. Albright in 1948, by which time additional inscriptions had become available.

These inscriptions consist of three groups, the most important of which came from Ugarit in the very north of the Canaanite area. There, beginning in 1929, the French archaeologist Claude Schaeffer had made a series of very significant discoveries. The main group of materials relating to the development of writing consisted of epic and mythological texts inscribed in a cuneiform consonantal alphabet in an early Canaanite dialect of the 14th century BC. This cuneiform alphabet of thirty-two letters, written from left to right, was developed under the inspiration of the pictorial system of Proto-Canaanite on the one hand, and of Babylonian on the other. The latter was the form of cuneiform used in the Late Bronze Age for diplomatic and commercial communication throughout the Near East. The same alphabet seems to have been used by the Canaanites throughout Syria-Palestine, and specimens include a commercial tablet from Ta'anach from the late 12th century. There are indications that this cuneiform alphabet followed upon the invention of a linear script in the area of North Semitic languages. Scribes who were accustomed to write by impressing a stylus in wet clay may have wished to continue to write in this way even when they had perceived the advantages of an alphabetic script: this would explain the invention of a cuneiform alphabet deriving from a linear one.

The second group of discoveries comes from Byblos but from a later period, the 11th century: they are no longer written in a cuneiform but in a linear script. The third group comes from Palestine and is fragmentary. Nevertheless it includes two important finds, the Gezer Sherd (c. 1600?) and the Lachish Prism (late 15th century) which are roughly contemporary with the later, 15th-century, date given for the Sinai script. And they are written in the standard alphabet.

The alphabet: archaeological sites mentioned in the text.

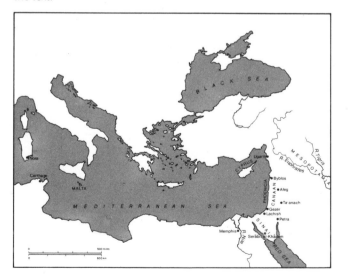

The cuneiform alphabet from Ugarit, displayed in what is the earliest complete ABC extant (although it seems to have followed the invention of a linear alphabetic script).

Proto-Canaanite inscription from Lachish, 13th century BC.

Thus the consonantal alphabet developed in an area situated between the early written civilizations of Egypt and Mesopotamia, among a people known as the Canaanites, Semitic-speaking inhabitants of Syria and Palestine before the 'coming' of the Israelites, from whom they are difficult to distinguish. The land of Canaan, with its rich western slopes covered with the cedars of Lebanon, and its dry eastern ones leading down to the desert, was the entrepôt for trade in the metals of Anatolia and copper from Cyprus as well as itself producing wine, olive oil, wood and the purple dye which later gave the coastal lands the name of Phoenicia. This region of small kingdoms and rich merchant princes was the meeting place of invaders and cultural influences not only from Egypt and Mesopotamia, but also from the north, where the Hurrians and their Mitanni rulers, probably originating in central Asia, spoke an Indo-European language. It was these latter who 'revolutionized society with the introduction of the horse and chariot and the feudal order which that involved' (J. Gray, *The Canaanites*). From the 16th century, the region had strong contacts with the Aegean; there appears to have been a Mycenaean quarter in the port of Ugarit itself, but the movement was mainly in the westerly direction.

In Mesopotamia, Sumerian was replaced as a spoken language by its contemporary, Akkadian, though it continued as a written language, especially for religious texts; in this way the scribal monopoly was maintained. Akkadian was a Semitic language in which some early texts had been compiled; scribes of the Fara period had Semitic names. But now it became the medium of international diplomacy throughout Western Asia, even in the Hittite empire, where Indo-European was the language of the rulers. Under this

empire, local scribes were trained to employ both the Akkadian language and the cuneiform script for the purposes of administration. Trade with Egypt, and the Egyptian conquests of Canaan, made its inhabitants familiar too with hieroglyphic writing, which appears to have had a considerable influence on the development of the alphabet. Both Akkadian cuneiform and Egyptian hieroglyphics were elaborate scripts, with logographic and syllabic elements complicated by determinatives which indicated the semantic category and the pronunciation. Thus their direct use was largely limited to specialists, to the scribes serving the temple and city estates of Mesopotamia and the priestly bureaucracy and administrators of Egypt, though these cultures also produced literary works. Such scripts were less well adapted to the business of Mediterranean merchants in Canaan, the region that saw the beginning of the experiments that resulted in the alphabet.

Between 2000 and 1500 BC other attempts were made to invent a simpler script based upon hieroglyphics as well as upon geometric signs and proprietary marks. One such example is the pseudo-hieroglyphic script used in the texts from Byblos believed to date from between 1800 and 1500 BC; the script appears to be a syllabic system for writing an archaic dialect of Canaanite, in an area which had slightly earlier (2400 BC) used logographic cuneiform for a similar purpose. While the Proto-Canaanite script probably arose under the influence of Egyptian hieroglyphics, this influence may have been mediated by the pseudo-hieroglyphic syllabary.

Helped by the morphological structure of their language, in which consonants, rather than vowels, constitute the morphemes that carry fundamental semantic notions, the Canaanites were able to develop consonantal alphabets, one based upon the cuneiform characters and the other linear. This linear script, known as Proto-Canaanite, was found widely spread in the Late Bronze Age from South Sinai to the coastal Canaanite town of Byblos, and appears to have been more practical for writing on papyrus, leather and similar materials.

Despite the reference in the Wenamon Papyrus (c. 1100) to the importation of papyrus rolls from Egypt to Byblos, and despite the records of commercial transactions on the same medium, little remains of the Canaanite writings on this material. Contrary to what happened in Egypt, the humid climate of the coastal areas has destroyed documents of this kind, so that our knowledge of Canaan is dependent upon the more cumbrous cuneiform texts from Ugarit, in which were preserved literary forms such as the Baal myth and the legends of Krt and Aqht. The new script adapted to the new

A fine example of later cuneiform writing: a sandstone *stele* of the early 7th century BC commemorating King Assurbanipal's rebuilding of the important temple of Esaglia.

materials seems to have led to a considerable extension of literate activity. Quite apart from its appearance in the ledgers of the merchant princes of Canaan, its successor alphabets were widely used throughout the Mediterranean by Phoenician merchants, while immediately to the south it was the script used for the annals of the kingdoms of Israel and Judah. It was in this alphabet that Baruch, the friend of Jeremiah, wrote down the prophet's oracles (Jeremiah 36) and it was this that developed into the script used in the scrolls of the community, thought to have been of the Essene sect, on the shores of the Dead Sea, as well as for all the later manuscripts of the Hebrew Old Testament.

The Hebrews apparently adopted the Canaanite alphabet in the 12th or 11th century BC. It was certainly being used in Palestine before their arrival, but, apart from the recently discovered Afeg Tablet (11th century), there is only one Hebrew inscription that antedates the 8th century, the Gezer Calendar, probably of the late 10th century, the time of Saul and David. The Aramaeans established their small kingdoms and tribal states in Mesopotamia and Syria respectively during the 12th and 11th centuries; they appear to have adopted the script slightly later than the Hebrews and passed on their written language to the Arabic-speaking Nabataeans living in Northern Arabia, South Jordan, South Israel and Sinai.

The Phoenicians emerge in the Late Bronze Age (about 1400 BC) as the inhabitants of the coastal belt of Canaan from Tartus in the north (situated in the south of present-day Syria) to Dor or Jaffa in the south. There they created a special brand of Canaanite culture, which they carried, by trade and conquest, throughout the Mediterranean.

The Proto-Canaanite script is the common ancestor of the Phoenician, Hebrew and Aramaic scripts. In about 1500 BC, it seems to have consisted of twenty-seven pictorial letters, which were reduced to twenty-two in the 13th century; by this time most of the letters had dropped their earlier form and taken on a linear one.

It was this consonantal alphabet that the Greeks in turn adopted, adding their own five characters to represent vowels. The earliest known Greek inscriptions date from about 750 BC and it is generally believed that, following the disappearance of the Mycenaean script in the 12th century, there was a Dark Age of some 300 years at the end of the Late Helladic period. For some time scholars of Semitic languages have tried to date the Greek alphabet to the previous century on the grounds that the Phoenician alphabet was widely diffused through the Mediterranean at this time. In Cyprus, a Phoenician tomb inscription dates from the first half of the 9th century. The earliest Punic text in Carthage, the great Mediterranean base of the Phoenicians founded c. 814 BC,

The earliest extant Hebrew inscription, the Gezer Calendar, consisting of a list of agricultural operations arranged by months.

An example of the Punic or Carthaginian form of the Phoenician script, from Malta, 3rd to 2nd centuries BC.

The earliest known Greek inscription, from the Dipylon Vase, 750–700 BC.

An early Greek monumental inscription, the Euthykartides dedication from Delos, c. 625 BC.

dates from about 600 BC, and in Sardinia we find a stele fragment from Nora which is said to date from the 11th century. It was from the Phoenicians that the Greeks claimed to have borrowed their script, which spread through the Mediterranean; and the Phoenician script also gave rise to the alphabet used in Italy for writing Etruscan and the Italic dialects, having been borrowed possibly from the Cumaean or Ischian Greek colonists. More recently, Semitic scholars such as F.M. Cross, F.D. Harvey and Aaron Demsky have pointed out that the forms of the archaic Greek script are in many ways more consistent with the idea that an earlier form of Canaanite served as a model, the one current around 1100 BC. It is therefore suggested that the Greeks adopted their alphabet at about the same time as the Hebrews and Aramaeans, possibly from Canaanite merchants visiting the Aegean islands, or from the Sea Peoples (or Philistines).

The argument for the earlier invention of the Greek alphabet is not archaeological (as we have seen, the earliest inscriptions are from the 8th century BC) but epigraphical. An American archaeologist, J. Naveh, has argued for the earlier date, around 1100 BC, on the basis of the similarity between the writing of the 8th century in Greece and the Proto-Canaanite script from the Late Bronze Age. In both these scripts, writing went from left to right, then turning in the other direction, in a form known as *boustrophedon*, like the movement of the plough over a field. One objection to the idea of early diffusion has been the absence of a particular letter in Proto-Canaanite, the long-legged *kaf*, which could have served as a model for the Greeks. Light on this matter is shed by the 'Izbet Sartah Abecedary' (a Canaanite ABC for an alphabet with twenty-two letters), discovered in 1976 in the Sharan Valley in Palestine, near Afeg, site of battles around 1050 BC between Israelites and Philistines. This new find provides an example of this letter, and the form of a number of others is closer to Greek than to the script of 10th-century Byblos, which had previously been thought to provide the model for the Greek alphabet; hence it supports the suggestion of earlier borrowing, implying that the so-called Dark Age of Greece was not so dark as had been believed.

If the Greeks did borrow the alphabet at an earlier period, then the Homeric poems may well have been written down earlier than is commonly supposed. Certainly the structure and style, despite the so-called 'oral' elements (such as the formulaic phrases), are unlike those of cultures without writing. From the standpoint of their accepted date of composition parts are archaic in content. Many have supposed the poems to be an oral composition written down at a later date. Are they not more likely to have been a written composition of an earlier date?

The unity and diversity of alphabets

The consonantal alphabet descended from Proto-Canaanite divided then into three main branches, the Phoenician, the Hebrew and the Aramaic, during the course of the 8th century, though some would identify the first two scripts even at this late date. If we accept the hypothesis of the earlier derivation of the Greek alphabet, it split off, not from Phoenician (as the Greeks themselves claimed), but from Early Canaanite writing itself. In addition, there is a more loosely connected branch, known as the South Semitic, used until today in Ethiopia. The spread of the alphabet was extensive and rapid. The Phoenician alphabet, as we have seen, dispersed rapidly throughout the Mediterranean, wherever their merchants and settlers travelled, to Malta, Sardinia, Cyprus and to Carthage, where it gave birth to scripts among previously non-literate peoples, in Italy, North Africa and Spain.

The Early Hebrew alphabet, which is usually seen as acquiring its distinctive character in the 8th century, continued in use until the re-establishment of Assyrian rule in Palestine and the exile of the Jews to Babylon, at which time they took over the language and script of the Aramaeans, though the Square Hebrew which resulted was partly influenced by the earlier form. Early Hebrew writing virtually died out, though it was used on coins in the Hasmonean period; it left as its only descendant in the present day the script used by the Samaritans of Nablus (Shechem) in Palestine, a small band of co-religionists now numbered in hundreds rather than thousands – a remnant of a branch of the Judaic religion that was once as significant as the southern offshoot, based on Jerusalem, that gave birth both to Christianity and to Islam.

The Aramaeans, benefitting from the collapse of the great empires, moved into the regions of the Canaanites and Phoenicians and adopted their script possibly as early as the 11th century. Early inscriptions are few, though important, but from the 7th century we find a large number of texts throughout the Near East, demonstrating the spread both of the script and of the language. Many Aramaic papyri and *ostraca* (inscribed potsherds) have been found preserved in the drier conditions of Egypt. The earliest evidence from the ancient capital of Memphis possibly dates from the 7th century. A well-known example is the Elephantine Papyri which provide details of the religious and economic life of a 5th-century military colony of Jews in Egypt.

The very wide distribution of Aramaic writing shows how, despite the collapse of the kingdoms following the recovery of the Assyrians in the late 9th century, their language and script became the *lingua franca* of the Near East, through its

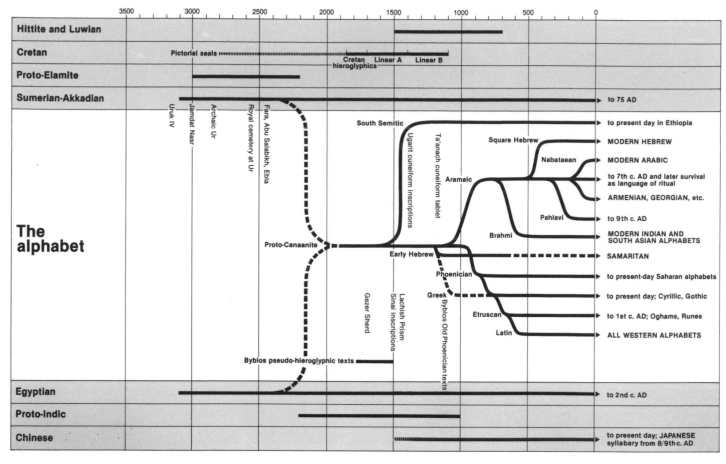

The alphabet

	3500	3000	2500	2000	1500	1000	500	0	
Hittite and Luwian									
Cretan		Pictorial seals			Cretan hieroglyphics	Linear A	Linear B		
Proto-Elamite									
Sumerian-Akkadian									to 75 AD

South Semitic — to present day in Ethiopia
Square Hebrew — MODERN HEBREW
Nabataean — MODERN ARABIC
Aramaic — to 7th c. AD and later survival as language of ritual
ARMENIAN, GEORGIAN, etc.
Pahlavi — to 9th c. AD
Brahmi — MODERN INDIAN AND SOUTH ASIAN ALPHABETS
Proto-Canaanite
Early Hebrew — SAMARITAN
Phoenician — to present-day Saharan alphabets
Greek — to present day; Cyrillic, Gothic
Etruscan — to 1st c. AD; Oghams, Runes
Latin — ALL WESTERN ALPHABETS
Byblos pseudo-hieroglyphic texts

Uruk IV · Jamdat Nasr · Archaic Ur · Royal cemetery at Ur · Fara, Abu Salabikh, Ebla · Ugarit cuneiform inscriptions · Ta'anach cuneiform tablet · Gezer Sherd · Lachish Prism / Sinai inscriptions · Byblos Old Phoenician texts

Egyptian									to 2nd c. AD
Proto-Indic									
Chinese									to present day; JAPANESE syllabary from 8/9th c. AD

Chronology of the seven major early writing systems and the emergence and diversification of the alphabet under the inspiration of two of them, Sumerian-Akkadian cuneiform and Egyptian. Some of the key archaeological discoveries mentioned in the text are also placed on the time-scale.

use as the administrative and diplomatic language in the Assyrian empire (cf. 2 Kings 18:26 and Isaiah 36:11) and later in the Achaemenid empire. Under the Achaemenid rulers of Persia, Aramaic became the diplomatic language, replacing cuneiform with this more democratic script, which was used by traders all the way from Egypt to India. The language became the vernacular of the Jews and was therefore used by the early Christians, only disappearing in the Near East with the advance of Islam after the 7th century AD, though it remains the language of ritual in many Jewish communities.

Just as the Phoenician alphabet spread far to the west along the sea lanes, so did the Aramaic variant to the east along the land routes. It was adopted by the kingdom of Nabataea, with its capital at Petra in modern Jordan, and from there it travelled into Sinai and the Arabic peninsula to become the

An early Aramaic inscription of the 9th or 8th century BC, a memorial to Kilamuwa, king of Yadi.

progenitor of the script used for writing down the Koran. As a result it was widely used throughout Africa and the Old World to transcribe many non-Semitic languages. So, too, was the earlier Aramaic. For it appears to have been carried to India in the 7th century BC by Semitic merchants. There it became the prototype of the Brahmi script of India, the first writing system used there since the early decay of the undeciphered script of the Indus Basin civilization and the one that gave birth to the numerous alphabetic systems of India and South Asia. The Indo-Aryan migration to Ceylon in the 5th century BC took the script to the south, while at a later date the North Indian version was adopted in Eastern (or Chinese) Turkestan and strongly influenced the invention of the Tibetan script in AD 639.

One of the major factors in the further spread of the alphabet outside India was the rise of Buddhism in the 3rd century AD, a religion that was more easily accepted outside the subcontinent than Hinduism. Buddhist monks travelled widely, converting the masses and helping to develop varieties of the South Indian scripts over a vast area that included Burma, Thailand, Cambodia, Laos, Vietnam, Malaya and Indonesia and as far as Tagalog in the Philippines. However, the Korean alphabet, *Han'gul*, dating from the 15th century AD and connected with the use of movable type, was possibly the result of stimulus diffusion from the West during the *Pax Tartarica*.

Apart from its influence on Arabic and the Indian scripts, Aramaic writing was also adapted for the Iranian (Persian) script known as Pahlavi, for Armenian and Georgian writing of the 5th century AD and for a range of alphabets used by early Turkish and Mongol tribes in Siberia, Mongolia and Turkestan.

The more distant branch of the scripts developing from Early Canaanite (c. 1400 BC) was the South Semitic branch, which was confined to the Arabian peninsula and to the adjacent African shore and the mountains of Ethiopia. These are the scripts that flourished in the kingdoms of southern Arabia, the best known of which is the kingdom of the Sabaeans (the land of the Queen of Sheba). All of these were swept away by the rise of Islam and the consequent spread of the Arabic script derived from Aramaic. Today the South Semitic branch survives only in the alphabets of Ethiopia, used for transcribing Amharic and the other major languages of that country.

We discussed earlier the derivation of the Greek alphabet from the Phoenician, possibly from Early Canaanite. Given that the Greek alphabet was the first systematically to transcribe both consonants and vowels, and given that it provided the basis for all subsequent European writing, we need to look at its development in slightly greater detail.

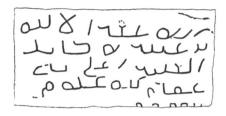

Sixth-century Nabataean inscription from Umm al-Jimāl, beginning (top line, right to left) *Allah ghafran*, 'may God forgive . . .'.

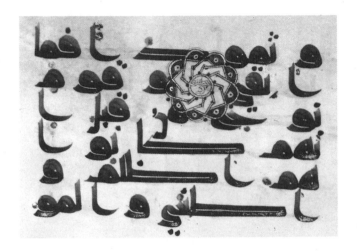

Detail from an illuminated Koran of the 9th century AD, in the Kufic script, descended from the Aramaic.

One of the styles of Arabic script known as Thulith, incorporated in a richly ornamented stucco wall decoration from a building called the school of perfume-makers in Fez, AD 1323–5.

An example of a 13th-century script from Western India: part of a Jain sacred text painted on palm-leaf.

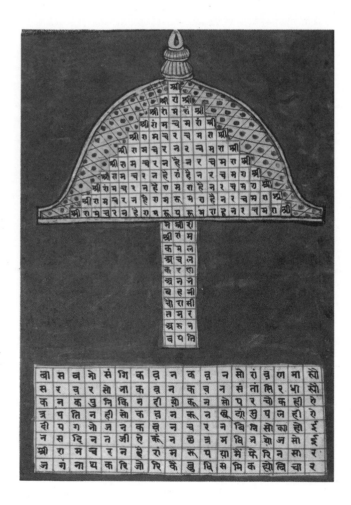

The first adaptation of the Greek alphabet was to transcribe the language of non-Hellenic peoples of Asia Minor, in the coastal areas of what is now Turkey. In Africa, it was used by the Copts of Egypt for a script which included some elements of Egyptian demotic writing. As in the Near East generally, the alphabet quickly replaced earlier systems of writing, emphasizing its greater economy.

In Europe, the Greek alphabet was adapted at a very early stage by the Etruscans of Central Italy; it is laid out as early as the end of the 8th century or the early 7th century BC in the Marsiliana Tablet, which was probably used for teaching the alphabet, and it continued in use until long after Latin became commoner as the result of the dominance of Rome. At a much later date, the Greek alphabet was adapted by Bishop Wulfila for translating the Bible into Gothic. Then, in the 9th century AD, St Cyril and St Methodius utilized the Greek letters for transcribing Slavonic languages, and a modified version of this alphabet became the script of all those Slavonic peoples whose religion was derived from the Eastern Christian Church of Byzantium. It was subsequently adapted, under Russian influence, for the writing of a number of other languages spoken by peoples who were incorporated into what is now the Soviet Union.

Just as the Greek alphabet was early on adapted by the Etruscans, so the Etruscan script was soon borrowed by neighbouring peoples. It is possible that the Runic writing of northern Europe and the Oghamic characters used by some of the Celts were descendants of Etruscan or Venetic writing. But by far the most important offshoot was Latin, first written down in the 7th century BC. Certain changes were made in the script, especially after the conquest of Greece by the Romans in the 1st century BC, but substantially the alphabet has remained much the same in form down to the present day. Its subsequent history has been, first, one of adaptation to the languages of Western Europe following the conquests of the Roman Empire, and then to languages throughout the world following the European conquests of America, Africa and Oceania and the spread of European trade and religion in much of what remained independent. Secondly, the script itself has been continuously transformed by varieties of cursive style required for everyday purposes as well as by the development of printing and the use of movable type. Of the cursive forms the most influential was the Carolingian script introduced throughout the Frankish empire at the time of Charlemagne. This provided the basis of the national varieties of writing that developed from the 12th century, out of which emerged the contemporary types of handwriting that use the Latin alphabet, and of the letters that appear on the printed page.

The letters of the Indian Devanāgarī alphabet, the writing of Sanskrit, arranged as a sacred meditation (19th-century).

The implications of writing

I have discussed the origin and history of writing and the alphabet, but what of their significance? The general implications of introducing a means of recording speech are revolutionary, in its potentiality if not always in its actuality. In the first place it permits the transmission of cultural (non-genetic) information across the generations. So too does speech itself, but writing enables this transfer to take place without face-to-face contact (indeed, independently of direct human intermediaries), and without the continual transformation of the earlier statement that is the characteristic of the purely oral situation. For example, it meant that it became possible to reconstruct the past in a radically different way, so that (to use an unconvincing dichotomy) 'myth' was supplemented and even replaced by 'history'. The kind of transformation this wrought can be understood when we think of how visual recording on film and audio recording on tape have augmented our contact with and understanding of our predecessors. But such understanding is perhaps the least important of its implications. Preservation leads to accumulation, and accumulation to the increased possibility of incremental knowledge. Writing, being in effect the first stage of this process of preserving the past in the present, had the most far-reaching effects. For not only did it create a possibility, but the realization of that possibility changed the world of man, internally as well as externally, in a remarkable way. The process of course is neither immediate nor yet inevitable. The social organization can, and often does, delay its impact. But the possibility is there.

How did it change the world of man? Let me first touch upon the organizational changes. Writing, in the full sense, appeared with the growth of urban civilizations. Nor was it simply a consequence but also a condition of that development, though the complex mnemonic of knotted cords (*quipu*) took the Inca some way along this path. In Mesopotamia, the first written word appears to be that of the merchant and the accountant, sometimes as part of the ecclesiastical organization of the temple city.

What did writing facilitate? Clearly the identification of merchandise, the recording of types and quantities of goods, the calculation of input and output, were much helped by the development of a script. None of these activities is impossible in oral societies. But the scale and complexity of the operation were limited without the written word. Apart from mercantile operations themselves, the organization of the temple city was carried out by means of writing, which permitted the elaboration of bureaucratic arrangements related to tax and tribute, as well as playing an important part

The earliest extant Latin lapidary inscription, in a *cippus* – in effect a funerary urn – of the 6th century BC, from the Forum in Rome.

The codification of laws was one of the ways in which writing was used to change the world of man. The law-giver in the frontispiece to a late-8th-century Visigothic legal code.

in the conduct of external affairs and the administration of provinces. Law was organized around the written code rather than in the more flexible 'custom' of oral society which could react to changing social situations without having to be deliberately set aside. While early writing was employed in the service of the political economy, the training of scribes was intimately connected with the religious sphere. Moreover, the comparative complexity of logographic systems, combined with the desire of scribes to control education, meant that literacy was restricted to a small proportion of the population, and to some extent limited in the tasks it could perform. One of the tasks that cuneiform did perform, however, was the recording of information about the movements of heavenly bodies that formed the basis of subsequent advances in astronomy and mathematics. The possibility of preservation led to accumulation and then to incremental knowledge. Such a process was not seriously inhibited by the nature of the system of linguistic notation, since mathematics was a logographic rather than an alphabetic system.

The invention of the alphabet, and to some extent that of the syllabary, led to an enormous reduction in the number of signs, and to a writing system which was potentially unrestricted both in its capacity to transcribe speech and in its availability to the general population. The descendants of the Canaanite alphabet spread widely through Europe and Asia, and later the remaining continents, making available a script that was easy to learn and easy to use.

The results are seen in the apparent growth of literacy in the Syrian-Palestinian area, where the uses of writing expanded from the political and economic to the religious and the historical-literary: of this the Old Testament of the Hebrews may be considered one of the first great products. However, the real extension of literacy, certainly as far as the range of writing was concerned, took place in Greece, with its fully developed alphabet and a system of instruction that placed literacy outside the constraint of a religious system. In this new context, writing managed to place some restrictions on the development of centralized government, which it helped to promote, by providing an instrument of control in the shape of the ballot. At the same time, it saw the development of new fields of knowledge as well as encouraging new ways of knowing; the development of the visual scrutiny of text now supplemented the aural input of sound over wide areas of human understanding; linguistic information was organized by means of tangible records, which affected the way in which man's practical intelligence, his cognitive processes, could work on the world around. This potential was there with logo-syllabic systems; indeed, in China great advances in the accumulation and development of knowledge have been made using the earliest system of full writing. But the development of a democratic form of writing, one that could make the easy transcription of language a possibility for the vast majority of the community, followed the invention of the alphabet in the Near East, though it was not until the invention of mechanical reproduction of these texts by means of movable type that the alphabet came into its own.

The invention of the alphabet meant that the benefits of writing were potentially available to all: but universal literacy has in reality only resulted from long historical processes, in which controlled access to writing has served to reinforce the political and social position of élite groups. This photograph of a letter-writer in Mexico City eloquently demonstrates the dependence of those who do not have the skills of writing for themselves.

VI
PRINTING

Henri-Jean Martin

PRINTING

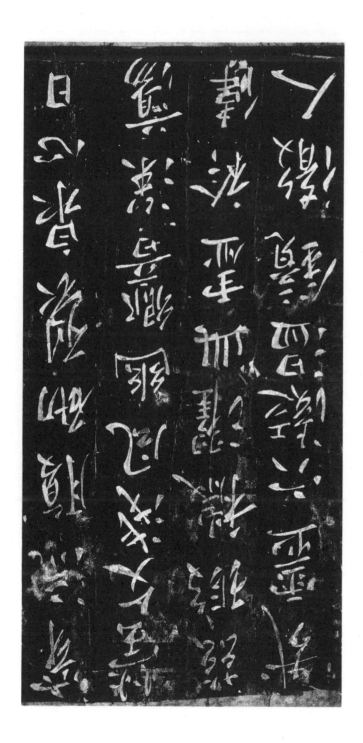

Everyone knows that it was in the Far East, in China and among some of her neighbours, that an interest in reproducing continuous texts – as opposed to the reproduction of words or brief sentences on seals or coins – first appeared. The ancient chronicles credit one of the retinue of the Emperor Ts'ai Lun with having invented paper in AD 105, a material used as a medium for writing made from the cellulose in rags or hemp. Later, in the 7th century AD, the idea arose of cutting out reliefs in wood and inking them as a means of reproducing sacred pictures and texts on paper. Later, incised stone blocks were used to impress Confucian texts on paper. Such methods were well suited to reproducing the countless characters of Chinese writing. However, the idea of making individual characters and placing them side by side to form a text had occurred by the 10th century when Pi Sheng made them in clay, baked them and attached each one with a form of glue to a wooden shank. In the 13th century the Uighurs, a Turkish people, used wooden letters for the same purpose and copper was used in Korea in the early 15th century.

These inventions made little headway in static oriental societies but, adapted or reinvented in the West and fuelled by the dynamism of the system we call capitalism, paper, movable type and the printing press became a form of liberation and the agent of far-reaching changes in social and intellectual life.

The apprenticeship of writing

The invention of printing marked the end of writing's long apprenticeship in the West. The barbarian invasions beginning in the 5th century had paralysed trade in Western Europe and brought a return to an oral culture in place of the literary culture of the Roman world. By the 10th century, or certainly by the 11th, there was a revival of commerce, towns were growing again, pilgrimage approached the proportions of seasonal migration and the Crusades were beginning. Europe was in ferment. The balance of trade with the East was once more in her favour and there was a new influx of gold. From this time the West began to acquire new resources of intellectual capital, taking from Byzantium, for instance, Justinian's great compilations of Roman law and rediscovering Aristotle from the Arabs. Universities were founded, Paris

The Chinese invention of movable type arose out of a general preoccupation with reproducing continuous texts. This example, dated AD 654 and said to be the oldest print in existence, is an impression from a stone block of a composition of the T'ang emperor T'ai-tsung in his own hand.

specializing in theology and Bologna in law; then followed others, among them Oxford and Cambridge.

In this climate writing revived. From the 11th to the 13th centuries the notarial system reappeared, allowing the use of contracts to be established and refined; trade and commercial transactions were facilitated by bills of exchange; double-entry book-keeping was invented by Italian merchants; and business correspondence developed. Everywhere writing was fixing fluid oral traditions while adapting the literary traditions of antiquity to vernacular languages.

The recurrent crises and calamities of the 14th and early 15th centuries – plague, the Hundred Years War, the Great Schism and social unrest – paradoxically favoured the written word, which by now had a foothold. In the fight against trade recession, and to mitigate the shortage of specie, business techniques were constantly improved. To reinforce their authority kings and rulers enlarged their chancelleries, their bureaucracies and their courts of justice. Often they were patrons of letters, if only in the interests of their domestic propaganda. And, struggling against all odds, there were the movements of religious self-determination, where the search for direct contact with God was aided by books.

It must be emphasized that writing was accessible only to a few restricted groups. These sometimes had their own vocabulary and language and nearly always their own handwriting, like a trade mark. This fragmentation was reflected in library collections. The important cathedral and abbey libraries guarded the heritage of pagan and Christian antiquity, but were not correspondingly endowed with the materials of the new scholasticism from the universities. On the other hand these were the staple of the libraries of the Dominican and Franciscan convents, together with doctrinal works, while books of spiritual devotion were the preserve of women's convents and of the Carthusians. In northern Europe the Brothers of the Common Life copied and distributed textbooks which they wrote for educational purposes. Vernacular literatures occupied little worlds of their own, usually centred on royal courts.

Divided into so many small communities, Europe lived at different levels. France, remaining largely rural while inheriting a magnificent university tradition, seemed content to develop, alongside its higher education, traditional elementary schools where reading was equipment for learning the Latin prayers, and which were primarily intended to provide a supply of clergy. The Italian cities, on the other hand, introduced schools of a new type from the 13th century, geared to commercial needs, which made literacy available to a considerable proportion of the population. Later on a style of education in some respects anticipating what we know today thrived, mostly thanks to the work of the Brothers of the Common Life, in the Rhine valley and the Low Countries and the ports of Germany. At the same time, however, in a Europe whose élites were more and more acceding to the world of writing, the need was felt for a language of greater clarity, more universal and more suited to the elaboration of argument. Hence the recourse to the

The growth of secular administration assisted the slow spread of writing in Europe after the setback caused by the barbarian invasions. An illustration from a work celebrating the conquest of Sicily by the Holy Roman Emperor Henry VI in 1194 shows Greek, Arab and Latin scribes in Henry's court at Palermo.

models of classical antiquity by the humanists, in particular to Ciceronian Latin. Starting in the chancelleries of Florence and the Papacy, the new humanism rapidly spread out across Europe, primarily thanks to the relationships that developed among the men who drew up diplomatic correspondence and state documents. Typically, they turned to the handwriting of antiquity, as they thought they saw it in Carolingian minuscule, in preference to the Gothic scripts in all their variety.

Like an individual person learning to read and write, Western Europe acquired the arts of literacy only by a slow and painful process. For a long time the medieval man of letters, like his Roman forbear, knew no alternative to reading the text aloud, or at least murmuring it under his breath. Memorizing sacred texts was quite a muscular discipline for the monks who meditated upon them. Confronted with a manuscript of the time, badly punctuated, or at any rate punctuated not so much to indicate the logical division of the text as to serve as a guide for reading aloud, the reader might be able without much difficulty to understand an official document drafted according to a stereotyped formula, or a text

conveying concrete facts, but he could not at first reading grasp the finer points or the subtler overtones of a literary work. For a long time writing was seen merely as a means of fixing the spoken word, especially in the universities, where the noble art of disputation had pride of place, and whose primary purpose was to train preachers and orators. So the rigid structure of scholasticism with its emphasis on logic and dialectic stood in the way of any original ideas. Likewise vernacular literature only very gradually ceased to be primarily intended to fix oral traditions, taking on a more independent existence as syntax evolved. Advance in all these fields was increasingly rapid between the 13th and 15th centuries. It was again typical of the way progress was achieved that the efforts of the humanists in the direction of evolving a logical system of punctuation were inspired by their attempts to get to grips with classical Latin, which they so admired but which was to them like a foreign language. Thus were initiated ways of reading more rapidly which printing, with its tendency towards standardization and its effect on the appearance of texts, was to promote so much further.

For a long time writing remained secondary to the spoken word. Punctuation would be according to the rhythms of speech. An anonymous drawing of c. 1400 shows St John Gualbert reading to monks in the North Italian monastery of Vallombrosa.

The birth of printing

Printing was at the heart of the intellectual, literary, economic, technological and political movements which anticipated the Renaissance. In the early 15th century, a period of relative peace, a new economic take-off occurred in Germany with the exploitation of her silver mines to meet the shortage of specie in Europe – what amounts to the birth of modern industrial metallurgy. A vigorous urban culture grew up here, in contact with both Italy and northern Europe. The German bourgeoisie was keen to overcome the disadvantages of political fragmentation and catch up with its neighbours – who, because of their relatively earlier cultural advance, were now wedded to out-of-date ideas.

Already at the end of the 12th century technology had come to the aid of culture. Paper had been introduced into Europe by the Arabs via Spain and Italy just at the moment when the upsurge of written culture was coming up against the limits of the available supply of parchment (related to the numbers of hides available from slaughtered animals). From Italy, where the imported techniques had been more or less perfected, paper-making had travelled to France and by the end of the 14th century had reached the western fringes of Germany. Thereafter, the idea occurred quite naturally of using the new material not just for legal documents, accounts and manuscripts, but also for reproducing images by a technique widely used for decorating fabrics – relief engraving on wood. Thus appeared, probably at the end of the 14th century, the first woodcuts. Subsequently the process of intaglio engraving in copper was perfected by the goldsmiths. Soon brief texts were added to the woodblock or plate to accompany the picture. Exceedingly rare today, these printed pictures were distributed in millions. Common subjects were scenes from the life of Christ, portraits of favourite saints, even a series giving instruction in the art of dying – in fact all the traditional objects of piety, migrating here from the altars and decorated vaults of the churches to permit prayer and meditation in solitary privacy. It was at just this time, and for similar reasons, that painting on canvas made its first appearance.

So the reproduction of images had been achieved. Not long after came the reproduction of text. Here recourse was made to the skills of the metalworkers – the goldsmiths and the coin-makers. The problem was to reproduce exactly by mechanical means the comparatively small number of signs that make up the Latin alphabet. The solution that emerged is familiar to us as the one used up until modern times. Each letter or sign is cut on the end of a shank of hard metal – the letter-punch – which is then struck into a softer metal, usually copper, making the matrix. The matrix is placed in a mould into which a heated liquid mixture of lead, tin and antimony is poured. By this means quantities of exactly identical characters are cast. Metalworkers had been familiar with the various processes involved for some time. The printing press, equally, had a precedent in the wine press, and there were no serious problems involved in perfecting an ink of the thick consistency required. So, in fact, printing came into being, not as the result of an autonomous invention, but when the need for it was recognized.

However, the different elements still had to be brought together, and their application to printing had to be perfected. There may have been attempts to do this in Holland, at Harlem; some were certainly made at Avignon, where a Prague goldsmith called Procopius Waldfogel was engaged in teaching the city's Jews an *ars scribendi artificialiter*. But at the centre of the experiments from which the technique of printing with movable type emerged – and perhaps behind them all – stands the powerful personality of Johann Gänsefleisch, better known by the name Gutenberg, from a house he owned called *Zu guten Bergen*, 'at the sign of the fair mountain'.

Printing before movable type: text accompanies printed image in a 15th-century German devotional metal cut (produced by a technique of relief engraving in metal akin to woodcut).

The events of his life are too well known to need repeating at length. Born about 1399, the son of a goldsmith who was mint-master to the Archbishop-Elector of Mainz, Gutenberg had to leave Mainz after a revolt by the guilds of the city, and took up residence in Strasbourg. There between 1435 and 1444 he devoted himself to developing various inventions, in which he instructed three townsmen, one of whom was a paper-maker. Already he was applying himself to the achievement of a process of printing. We hear nothing of him for a few years until 1448, when he reappears in his native city. There he went into partnership with a banker named Fust to pursue his experiments with type. Their partnership came to an end in 1455, so that it was with his son-in-law, Peter Schoeffer, that Fust opened the first printing establishment of which we have definite knowledge and in 1457 published the first printed book bearing a printer's imprint, the famous Mainz Psalter. In fact numerous earlier examples of printing have come down to us, but none of them is positively identified as to origin. The point to be made here is that many of them are unpretentious items – indulgences, almanacs, little grammars – whose numbers testify to the mundanely practical preoccupations of the first printers, as much concerned to provide multiple copies of documents as to produce books. But others are major undertakings that rank as masterpieces of typographical perfection, like the 42-line Bible, attributed to the partnership of Gutenberg and Fust, or the 36-line Bible. So we can see that from the beginning printing was destined to play a part in speeding up communication at several cultural levels.

The new technique spread rapidly across Europe. In 1458 Jean Mentelin, a notary and illuminator of manuscripts, opened a printing shop in Strasbourg. Gradually, from 1460, apprentices who had worked for Gutenberg, Fust and Schoeffer spread out through Germany, reaching Italy in 1464. They in turn taught others, and printing reached France (Paris, 1470; Lyons, 1473), the Low Countries (Utrecht and Aalst, near Liège, 1473), Poland (Kraców, 1474) and England (Westminster, 1476). In 1470 there were twelve places which had printing establishments. By 1489 there were 110, and by 1500 more than 200. One cannot fail to be struck by the speed with which all this happened. Almost at a stroke Europe was covered by a network of a quite new kind; and the first modern 'medium' established itself just as quickly as television and data networks have done in our own age of generally much more rapid communications.

A printer's shop at the end of the 15th century. The print referred to in the text, an illustration in a work entitled the *Danse macabre*.

The printing press only slightly advanced 300 years later: the illustration from Diderot's Encyclopaedia referred to in the text. After the type has been inked, the tympan with paper in place is closed and folded down on top of it, and the complete carriage slides under the press on rails.

The craft period of printing

The structure of the trade thus established and the methods it used remained the same for the next four hundred years. Contemporary woodcuts show what the inside of a printer's shop looked like in the early days. A print from Lyons of 1499 or 1500 shows the printer's 'case', the pigeon-holes varying in size according to the frequency with which the different letters are used. The way the compositor places the letters in the 'stick' he holds in his left hand is exactly as it remained up until the present day, likewise the stand holding his 'copy' positioned above the case.

The heavy printing press was made entirely of wood except for a few iron fittings. Two uprights on a solid base supported a massive cross-beam, through which the wooden screw passed. The screw was turned with a bar to lower the heavy platen, pressing the blank sheet of paper on to the 'forme' containing the inked type. In addition to this vertical movement, a horizontal action enabled the carriage holding the forme to be moved forward beneath the platen or

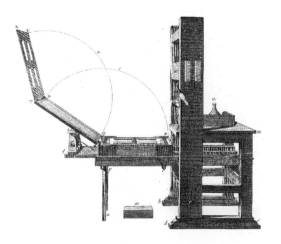

withdrawn. So as to prevent it shifting each time the screw was tightened, the press was restrained by timber beams fastened to the ceiling joists.

We learn more from another illustration of a press some three hundred years later, in Diderot's Encyclopaedia. It shows the paper held between the two frames called the 'frisket' and 'tympan' to keep it clean, and the carriage running to and fro on rails. It appears that some increase in pressure had been achieved by the substitution of brass for wood in the screw and through a more refined control of the mechanism. But the pressure was still not sufficient to allow the whole forme to be printed with less than two pulls; and it was only by slow degrees, starting at the end of the 18th century, that this basic technology was to be improved upon.

Still, it must be said that this simple and sturdy machine, handled by men who were prepared to work twelve or fourteen hours a day, achieved an impressive output. For instance, about 1650 the printers of France were supposed to produce 2500–3000 impressions (i.e. 1250–1500 sheets printed on both sides) per working day. This implies, at least in theory, 1250–1500 copies of 16 octavo pages per day, or the same number of copies of a 300-page book in twenty days. It also produced at a tremendous rate the posters and broadsheets which always constituted a major part of the printer's business.

The evolution of the book

Primitive as this technology may seem to us, it entailed a rationalization of work which in itself gave the cue to other forms of standardized production which were to effect a complete revolution in the intellectual outlook of the West.

Our evidence for such a conclusion comes from a study of the varying output of the presses between the 15th and 19th centuries. The first books aimed to reproduce the appearance of manuscripts. Initial letters were illuminated by hand and there were elaborate coloured borders, and a printer would not hesitate to cut a new type-face in imitation of the manuscript that was to be copied. But such practices were immensely labour-intensive. Gradually elements of standardization began to emerge as certain categories of books came to be printed in particular type-faces. Woodcuts began to be used in place of hand-drawn initials. At the same time, a more fundamental change was occurring. Taking a lead from the humanists, with whom they were in the closest contact, the printers quite naturally found themselves regularizing spelling, adopting and standardizing more logical systems of punctuation and making clearer the division of the text into paragraphs on the page. So we find an early Paris printer,

Guillaume Fichet, congratulating his colleague Heynlin on his technique of typesetting, which made his edition of Cicero's *De Officiis* 'so clear, so easy to read, even for children'.

Meanwhile the printed book was attaining what Lucien Febvre called its *état civil* – its defined place in the social order. The *Incipit* (literally 'Here begins') at the top of the first page of a manuscript developed into the title page, setting out, as well as the definitive title and the name of the author, the printer's device and his address. Practical considerations led to the appearance first of signature numbers or letters, then of folios or page numbers, and clear contents pages referring to page numbers rather than to the divisions of the text. All these innovations were more or less established by about 1530 and, with the triumph of humanism, Roman letter-forms, like the trade mark of the new spirit, spread from Italy and France to most of Europe, displacing the less legible gothic letter-forms which were dying out outside Germany.

Thus the modern book was born. The title page, proclaiming what the book is about, making a name of the author and informing the buyer of the publisher's address, can be seen as the earliest piece of modern publicity. The efforts that were made to make the text more accessible, breaking it up into units which made it easy to return to any passage, lightened the labour of reading. It must be obvious that all this made possible new ways of reading, faster and more individual, and new ways of using books, so that the door was opened to new realms of intellectual enrichment – which would at the same time widen the gulf between the cultivated élite and the oral or semi-oral culture of the majority.

But it would be wrong to present an image of the book in the craft period of printing as a uniform object. It was even more multifarious than the book in the industrial age, speaking many languages to those who knew how to address it and fulfilling a host of different uses.

Let us enter in imagination some ancient library in order to better our understanding of these old books and to hear what they have to tell us. The library at Wolfenbüthel, belonging to the Dukes of Brunswick, was a palatial building with a great dome and at one time had the German dramatist Lessing as its librarian (the present library replaces this earlier building). On the shelves, carefully arranged in categories, are medieval manuscripts taken from old abbeys after the Reformation, large 15th- and 16th-century folios in pigskin bindings, with blind stamping on the heavy wooden board covers, then vellum-bound books of more recent date with their titles written on the spine by a secretary, or even by the bibliophile Duke himself. What does this represent? The fruits of a collector's passion, for one thing; a symbol of prestige, also,

A page from Gutenberg and Fust's 42-line Bible, a typographical masterpiece with rich hand-decoration, closely resembling a contemporary manuscript.

Recognizable book typography: a page from a book of lives of the saints printed in Florence in 1495 by Lorenzo Morgiani and Johann Petri, with folio and indented paragraphs.

and obviously a storehouse of information. But most importantly it represents a collective memory, a temple raised in honour of a high traditional culture, and the tangible affirmation of that culture. The grandiose baroque library of the abbey of St Gall – to take an example of a different kind – proclaims in its architecture the sacred or quasi-sacred nature of the books and manuscripts it contains – the Word itself, the interpretation of the Word by the early fathers and the Church, and some of the wisdom of the Ancients – while at the same time it glories in the triumph of the Counter-Reformation and resoundingly asserts its permanence.

So books affirm their owners' participation in the culture of their day, and the character of a library can tell us something about the intellectual milieu it represents. Hence the

characteristic enthusiasm for folio volumes bound in red morocco or immaculate vellum with the family crest on the covers. Hence, too, the tendency for élite groups in strongly hierarchical societies to imitate the styles of their social superiors in their tastes for books.

Did the owners of these collections assiduously read all the books they possessed, then – as Montaigne certainly did? What we know of the way they lived – and this is particularly true of the lawyers, for whom the venerable classical inheritance was something to set against the ancient lineage of the landed nobility – indicates that they led a quiet, cloistered, absorbed existence, and suggests that many of them were great readers. But with the 18th century rest-lessness and distraction overtake this studious tranquillity,

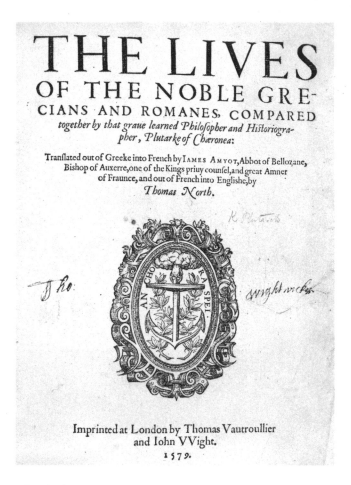

The book acquires its social identity: the printer of
an edition of Thomas Aquinas's *Summa theologica*
printed in Mainz in 1471 is identified only by a
colophon at the end of the work.

A hundred years later an English edition of
Plutarch's *Lives* has a proper title page which
includes a clear statement of the printer's name
and city and the date of publication.

and at the same time we see the appearance of the bibliophile collector of the modern kind, with his heightened
discrimination but also in some ways his perversions. This new
kind of connoisseur would relish an edition of La Fontaine
illustrated by Oudry, or a Molière comedy with plates after
Boucher, not for their well-known texts but for the
contemporary artist's interpretation of them. In just the same
way today a Virgil with illustrations by Dunoyer or Segonzac
might be owned by a rich banker or a second-rate work like
Dorat's *Baisers* might be prized in some lavish inlaid binding.
Who can suppose that the collector flipping through his little
typographic masterpiece, with its delicate illustrations
attempting to elevate a banal text, is doing any more than
savour it as an object?

But books of other kinds appear alongside these,
suggesting other ways of reading and other attitudes. In the
mid-17th century there were the aristocratic romances of
Aphra Behn in England and Mlle de Scudéry in France,
surprising to modern readers in view of their sparse
typography and bulky extent. Reading them must have
involved constant turning of the page. The inference is
inescapable that the young women for whom they were
written, newly emerged from the convent, were slow readers.
The progress made in reading ability a century later is equally
obvious from the cramped pages of the books, edifying or
amusing, that their grand-daughters read in the 18th century.
Then there was a wide variety of more modest publications,
from ballads and 'street literature' sold by packmen and

pedlars to utilitarian books like almanacs, alphabets and books of recipes. The very cheapest literature – traditional medieval tales accompanied by crude woodcuts – was wretchedly printed in type that seems scarcely legible to our eyes. How else can the humble artisans for whom these books were intended have made use of them than by slowly making out the words under their breath, constantly re-reading them, and no doubt pausing at every sentence to lose themselves in the scenes that the words conjured up?

The conclusion is inevitable that access to books has contributed to the structuring of a hierarchical social order in modern times. The culture of the book that printing has produced could only be fully possessed in the course of a long apprenticeship in which the mental equipment for reading was slowly acquired – the ability to make connections and associations, familiarity with idiom, facility of expression, skill in following an argument, an understanding of fine distinctions and, in the end, greater confidence and an increased aptitude for acquiring new knowledge. To the man who could profit from such an accomplishment the effort yielded returns which could be reinvested to further advantage. Then the long-established prestige of classical learning seemed to offer access to a charmed circle. Possessed of this skill, the educated man could aspire to political power. Hence the desire to proclaim his education with his library, his correct spelling and his accent. But at the same time, a middle-class culture developed among less experienced readers who used writing in their work and in everyday life but who inherited a more oral cultural tradition. In this connection mention must be made of other books, generally of more modest pretensions, which were published alongside all those that were accessible only to the educated. Foremost among them was the Bible, a passage from the crowded pages of which the father would read aloud to the household every night. It can occasion no surprise that a profound belief in the powers of the written word and the privileges it carried should arise among people who were half educated, half deprived culturally. In France they sought revolution: in England they looked to self-improvement and the Mechanics' Institutes.

The book trade

With the appearance of printing the book, always an equivocal object, became a piece of merchandise, and capitalist profit became a driving force of culture. We must then look briefly at some economic aspects of producing and distributing ideas in print.

Leisured reading, already the inheritance of several generations for this young French woman *à la mode* in 1778.

Reading is likely to have been a much more painful, hesitant exercise for the customers of this itinerant seller of news sheets, almanacs and popular literature, in a print of c. 1630.

First, the relationship between the unit cost and the print run. Everyone knows that a mass-produced article costs less and less as the production run increases. But there are thresholds. After a certain number of copies the proportion of the non-recurring costs (buying the text, type-setting, origination of illustrations and machine make-ready) attributed to each copy becomes insignificant in relation to the recurring costs (paper, machining and binding). Calculations suggest that in the craft period the number of copies at which this position was reached was 1000. (By contrast today the figure for a typical colour-illustrated children's book printed by web offset (where admittedly the initial investment is unusually high) would be 50,000 to 80,000 copies.) This being so, a publisher would have no interest in tying up capital in editions of thousands of copies of, say, an almanac or a schoolbook, if he was not sure of selling out in a short time. He would simply print a new edition when it was needed. Though these figures seem modest by today's standards, they were not so in a Europe whose population was much smaller than today, with a relatively small literate élite. The publisher-bookseller had to have a wide and effective commercial network at his disposal. Since the banking system was not well organized, he usually had recourse to a system of barter with his correspondents, settling accounts by means of bills of exchange. Thus he had to wait a long time for the return on his investment, and had to lay out relatively large amounts of capital.

From these circumstances an organized book trade gradually emerged. From being isolated individuals the publisher-booksellers came to form a coherent group in each centre of the trade. These centres had to be commercial as well as intellectual capitals, where credit was available and communications were good – often they were maritime or river ports. Everything also pointed towards booksellers' working in close collaboration with their printers – often small artisans – so as to be able to respond with maximum speed to new market demands.

Great risks were taken by the first publishers, at the mercy of uncertain transport and very slow communications. Failure to pay was commonplace, and there was no protection under international law. In an effort to overcome such handicaps periodic fairs were organized (the most famous of which was held at Frankfurt in the years 1500–1630) where the members of the trade settled accounts, exchanged information and books, heard all the gossip and made new contacts. Still, bad payers remained a problem, and the earliest systems of copyright and exclusive privileges in certain titles were inadequate safeguard against piracies. Finally, the most profitable titles would frequently be banned by the authorities, though this resulted in the development of underground networks parallel to and interlocking with the official ones – especially so in the so-called Enlightened Despotisms of 18th-century France, Austria, Prussia and Russia.

Yet the output of this little world of the book was immense. At least 45,000 titles survive that were published prior to 1 January 1501, and if we conservatively assume an average edition of 500 this amounts to more than 20 million books, not including all the titles that have been lost. Given that there were only a few hundred thousand readers in each generation, we can see how great was the intellectual revolution begun in 1455. For the 16th century the statistics are even more impressive: more than 200,000 titles are recorded, implying 200 million books if we assume an average edition of 1000 (of this Luther's Bible accounted for several millions by itself). In the first half of the 17th century production doubled or tripled. Then recession gathered,

A prosperous publisher-bookseller in France at the end of the 18th century disappoints a hopeful author.

lasting in France as late as 1720; thereafter revival set in with the first stirrings of the Industrial Revolution.

So the fortunes of culture were closely bound up with wider economic fortunes. But the production of books was also tied to economic and social geography. From the beginning, significantly enough, printing flourished in commercial centres with credit available and good communication links. Germany soon lost out to Italy here. Venice, poised between the two, became the first printing capital of Europe. Paris, now established as the political and intellectual metropolis of the Kingdom of France and an important commercial and transport centre, quickly followed. But then also Lyons, without any great cultural tradition but the site of an important fair, a banking city and a bridge to Italy and the Holy Roman Empire, flourished as a centre of the book trade in the period 1530–60. Then, as Germany emerged from the wars of religion on which France now embarked, the Frankfurt Fair tilted the balance again in favour of the north and, at the same time as Venice surrendered its supremacy in the cloth trade to the Flemings, its position in the book trade gave way to Antwerp under Plantin and his successors. Later the Protestant strongholds of Leiden and Amsterdam took the lead under publishers like the Elseviers.

The circuits of the book

It must be emphasized that in this period the circuits of the book were various and discrete, rather than forming a single, integrated network.

For a long period books in Latin were the vehicle for the transmission of the major currents of ideas – mysticism in the 15th century; humanism in the 16th century with the publications of Aldus in Venice, Froben in Basle, Estienne in Paris and Gryphius in Lyons. Then Latin was the medium of the hierarchical literature of the Counter-Reformation in Antwerp, Venice, Cologne, Paris and Madrid.

In time market forces prompted the production of smaller, cheaper books for a wider public in vernacular languages. This kind of publishing came of age with the rise of national literatures. With the fading of the Counter-Reformation and the economic recession of the mid-17th century it became a factor in the break-up of Europe and the forging of nation-states. Law and ideology reinforced the divisions of language. From now on the authorities – governments in particular – sought to control the printed word by licensing, the granting of exclusive privileges in certain works, and censorship. While England succeeded in casting off such controls in the 18th century, they survived in some measure throughout the rest of Europe. In their wake came underground publishing and bookselling networks and the multiplication of pirated and contraband editions. Presses producing such material naturally sprang up beyond the reach of government officials, their products reaching the market in the hands of undercover street-vendors. For France these presses were located in such places as Antwerp, Strasbourg and Geneva during the Reformation, and in the time of Louis XIV in Amsterdam, Liège, Neufchâtel and Geneva.

The periodical press and the newspaper

But it would be quite wrong to think that up until the appearance of the newspaper the press was primarily devoted to the production of books. From the very beginning it had been a medium for information of all kinds. Pamphlets with descriptions of military victories, festivals, royal progresses and funerals appeared from the 15th century onwards. Gradually printing began to be used for official decrees, proclamations and notices. Soon also popular accounts of monstrous apparitions and other apocryphal happenings became common. Religious and political controversy gave rise to a particularly large output, ranging from crude propaganda to learned treatises. And then the printing press was increasingly used for all kinds of publicity. For example, recent research has pointed to a host of small printers up and down England in the 18th century turning out tickets, posters, electoral addresses and candidates' replies to their opponents – so that we see here the beginning of 'public opinion'.

Some of the products of the press naturally tended to be periodical publications – things like almanacs and calendars. These became more and more numerous in the 17th century, and especially in the 18th. In 1770, the Stationers' Company in London printed 207,000 copies of fourteen different almanacs, one of which alone, called *Vox Stellarum*, accounted for 124,000 copies. Gradually these publications added news of political events to astrological predictions, while specialist annuals also proliferated.

At the same time the demand for up-to-date financial and political news on the part of a substantial public led to the emergence of real periodicals. In 1597 Samuel Dilbaum started a monthly news sheet in Augsburg, the home of the banking house of Fugger, and around 1605 a fortnightly commercial bulletin was started in Antwerp, the great trade entrepôt of Europe. The honour of inaugurating a regular news service belongs to the Netherlands and Germany, where several weekly and fortnightly news pamphlets were issued in the early 17th century. In London weekly gazettes started

A 17th-century ballad sheet: part of the very varied output of the press from which the newspaper emerged.

A similarly humble product of much later date – a popular Catalan woodcut in favour of a federal republic, printed in 1873.

circulating in 1620 and Thomas Archer launched his *Weekly News from Italy, Germany, Hungaria, Bohemia, the Palatine, France and the Low Countries* in 1622. In January 1631 two small Protestant booksellers in Paris, Martin and Vendôme, started the *Nouvelles extraordinaires de divers endroits*, also modelled on the Dutch gazettes. But four months later Cardinal Richelieu, all too aware of the potential of the new press, granted an exclusive privilege for its publication to Théophraste Renaudot. In 1632 a supplement of announcements called *La Feuille du bureau d'adresses* was added to it.

In fact the attitude of governments was crucial in determining the character of the emergent periodical press in different countries. Germany's subdivision into many small

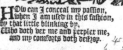

principalities and the existence of multiple forms of censorship and exclusive licensing made periodical publishing the province of governments, but at the same time encouraged the appearance of hand-written news sheets and the formation of copying 'factories' which played an important part in the dissemination of subversive ideas at the beginning of the 18th century. Holland, where toleration flourished and which had taken in a substantial proportion of the French Protestant intelligentsia after the Revocation of the Edict of Nantes in 1685, was the seat of a press opposed to the absolutism of Louis XIV. In Britain, on the other hand, press freedom experienced changing fortunes with the changing currents of political life. Eight years after the Revolution of 1688 James II's Licensing Act was repealed, but the rapid growth of the periodical press which resulted and its political independence frightened Parliament into imposing a Stamp Duty in 1712, putting up the price of journals and thus limiting circulations.

It is impossible to give here even an outline impression of the diversity of the periodicals produced by the presses of Europe at the turn of the 17th century. The *Journal des savants* (1665) in Paris was the model for the *Transactions* of the Royal Society in London (1665) and other learned journals like the *Nouvelles de la république des lettres* published by Pierre Bayle in Amsterdam from 1684 and Leibniz's *Acta Eruditorum*, published in Leipzig from 1682. In and around France a vigorous literary press emerged in the period of the Enlightenment; and censorship in France did not succeed in stifling the growth of specialized periodicals or of the advertising sheets for which the *Affiches de Lyon*, first published in 1748, provided the model.

But it was in Britain that the really spectacular developments occurred. The most brilliant organs were often the most ephemeral, but they were edited by satirical wits like Defoe, Addison and Steele whose leading articles in the *Tatler* (1709) and the *Spectator* (1711) gave them a powerful hold over the public mood. London produced the first daily newspaper in the world, the *Daily Courant*, in 1702, and gave birth to the *Gentleman's Magazine*, first published by Edward Cave in 1731. With this fertile output, print-runs increased eightfold, Stamp Duty between 1712 and 1757 notwithstanding. Such was the impetus of this development that Parliament felt obliged to agree to the publication of its proceedings in 1771, and in 1787 Edmund Burke could talk for the first time about the 'fourth estate'. Total circulation reached nearly $9\frac{1}{2}$ million copies in 1780, nearly $24\frac{1}{2}$ million in 1811, and nearly 30 million in 1820. The era of the Sunday paper began with the *Sunday Monitor* in 1779 and the *Observer* in 1791. In 1785 *The Times*, the greatest of all British

newspapers, was started by John Walter, to reach a circulation of 10,000 by 1820, 40,000 by 1850 and more than 60,000 after the Crimean War.

At the same time in France the Revolution freed the press from the shackles of the privilege system. Article XIX of the *Rights of Man* declared 'Free communication of thought and opinion is one of the most precious rights of man. Every citizen can therefore speak, write or print freely except in such cases as are provided for under the law.' Political pamphlets proliferated and in fact many of the Revolutionary leaders, like Mirabeau, Camille Desmoulins, Marat and Hébert, were journalists. Up until 1792 freedom of expression was secured by a rough balance of power between opposing factions, but it did not survive thereafter (though a clandestine royalist press went on publishing in the vicinity of the Palais Royal). As Jules Janin has put it, the free press extinguished itself by its own excesses. The Convention and the Directory were no different from the Committee of Public Safety in this respect, and Napoleon in his rise to power was assiduous in muzzling the press in practice while paying lip service to the principle of press freedom.

But these political ups and downs should not make us forget the profound general changes then taking place in Europe. The rise of the newspaper, first making itself apparent in Britain, coincided with the inauguration of the Industrial Revolution, reminding us that this was essentially a revolution in communication. The newspaper emerged as an indispensable source of fast and regular news just when the railway, the steamship, the screw propeller, the metal hull, the optical and then the electric telegraph were making their appearance, in a process which virtually amounted to the speeding up of history. In the same period, manufacturing became more and more important and agricultural workers poured into the towns; and the newspaper on the one hand served to orchestrate the aspirations of the rising bourgeoisie, and on the other played a vital role as an organized voice for the rootless and abject urban proletariat, so many of whose hopes lay in the direction of the rise of education, scientific progress and – at any rate in France – the ballot-box.

Revolutionary pamphleteers take to the streets of Paris. We recognize in the background the printing press from the Encyclopaedia, illustrated on page 132 above.

The newspaper as the mouthpiece of the dispossessed urban proletariat: a Parisian cobbler, from a German popular illustrated periodical, 1845.

Serialized literature by prestigious authors for the popular press. Grandville's cartoon has an author slicing up the production of a hack ghost writer while in the background inspiration is distilled into 'macaroni-style' literature.

Hence the fear of the press on the part of the authorities, and the long struggle for freedom of the press. In France passions ran high as governments veered between tolerance and repression, and the Revolution of 1830 can be attributed to this cause. For a long time the press made slow, if definite, progress: by 1830 the *Constitutionnel* had 20,000 subscribers, the extreme royalist *Quotidienne* 6,500 and the *Journal des débats* 12,000. In Britain the establishment fought to suppress the growth of the radical press (which it referred to as the Pauper Press) by severe sentences on editors and by taxation (the 'taxes on knowledge'), which so burdened newspapers that the seventeen London dailies in 1830 had only 40,000 subscribers between them compared with 60,000 in Paris.

A new development was inaugurated in 1835 when Émile de Girardin, an illegitimate child of good family, launched the *Presse* at a subscription half that of its rivals and below cost, relying on advertising revenue. He argued that, since advertising success depends on the number of subscribers, the price must be kept as low as possible in order to gain the highest possible subscription figure. With this philosophy he quickly achieved a circulation of 20,000 and a rival paper, the *Siècle*, which copied his methods and had the advantage of coming second into the field, rapidly made 40,000. By 1846 the twenty-five dailies in Paris had 180,000 subscribers.

To attract and hold readerships of this size Girardin and his imitators copied the editorial techniques of English popular newspapers. They established the use of the serialized novel, which had made its first appearance in England in 1719 with *Robinson Crusoe*. They employed the most prestigious names in French literature to write novels and regular columns – such as Chateaubriand, Victor Hugo, Lamartine, Balzac, Dumas, George Sand and Eugène Sue – and gradually got them to tailor their writing to the demands of the public and turn out 'best sellers' instead of addressing themselves to the literary *salons*. Then new techniques of reproduction – first wood-engraving and later the half-tone process – brought back the printed image (see Chapter 8). Following the use of wood-engravings by the *Observer* from 1791 and (though in a characteristically restrained manner) by *The Times*, heavily

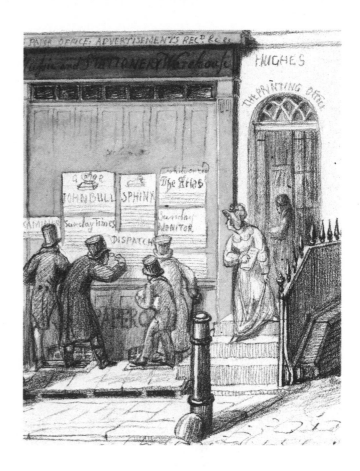

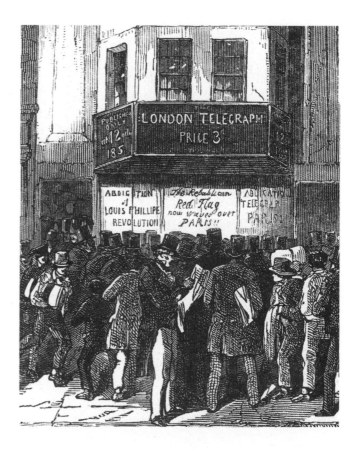

'News paper office: advertisements received': an engagingly candid drawing of a newspaper office in Bloomsbury in London alludes to the at first modest and subsequently more and more important role of advertising in the financing of newspapers.

'Rush for the daily newspapers': the growth of popular newspapers reflected in a wood-engraving from an illustrated periodical. The news of the hour is the Revolution of 1848 in France.

The idea of popular education is satirized in a mock page 1 of the first issue of the *Penny Magazine.*

The technology of mass production: paper, printing, type-setting

All this would not have been possible if the Industrial Revolution had not supplied the essential technology at each stage.

Innovation in paper-making had begun early. In the 17th century the appearance of the 'Dutch cylinder' ended France's near-monopoly in paper-making. About 1750 the English paper-maker James Whatman began to supply the printer John Baskerville in Birmingham with a high-quality wove paper of even texture, suitable for good book-production, known as vellum. The first successful attempts at a continuous roll process were made by an employee of the paper-mills at Essonnes in France, Louis-Nicolas Robert, before the end of the century. Shortly afterwards the proprietor of Essones, Didot Saint-Léger, took the process to England and perfected it there with his brother-in-law John Gamble, two other paper-makers, Henry and Seely Fourdrinier, and an engineer named Bryan Donkin. Production soared and as steam replaced water-power the industry was able to supply the vast requirements of the printing presses. By the mid-19th century there were more than 300 steam-powered paper-making machines in Britain, 200 in France and about the same number in Germany. Production in Britain increased tenfold between 1810 and 1860, by which time only 4 per cent of paper was being made by hand.

This vastly accelerated production required new sources of raw materials to replace the rags which it had always been hard to come by. In 1718 Réaumur had shown that cellulose fibre could be obtained from wasps' nests, but much more research was needed and in fact it was not until the middle of the 19th century that a process of producing mechanical pulp by grinding up the soft white wood of the spruce was achieved in Germany. The chemical pulps followed in the second half of the century, and the way was open for today's giant mills consuming vast forests of timber every year.

Meanwhile there were further improvements in printing techniques. One problem was to find a means of duplicating the formes to enable reprints to be made without keeping type standing. In 1739 William Ged of Edinburgh published an edition of Sallust from primitive moulds. The French government's need to print the paper money known as *assignats* between 1789 and 1797 in a way which would prevent counterfeiting by the English stimulated further progress, and it became common practice in France to produce stereotypes from plaster of Paris moulds. Between 1830 and 1840 Louis Hachette went so far as to correct an

illustrated periodicals began to appear in the 1830s and 1840s like the *Penny Magazine* (1830), the *Pfennig Magazin* (1833), the *Caricature* and the *Charivari* (1832), *Punch* (1841), the *Illustrated London News* (1842) and *Illustration* (1843). With the continuing growth of literacy throughout Europe, the circulations of newspapers were to go on increasing impressively – nowhere more so than in Britain, which, thanks to the abolition of the 'taxes on knowledge', was to outstrip other countries in the Victorian era. The traditional press was defenceless in the face of the penny newspaper so that the circulation of *The Times*, faithful to its traditional readership, stagnated while the *Daily Telegraph*, founded in June 1855, achieved 144,000 copies by 1861 and 191,000 in 1871. The provincial press flourished at the same time, and before long everyone would have access to a newspaper.

edition of Alexander's Greek dictionary on the stereotypes so as not to tie up the type.

Of greater importance was the need to increase the output of the presses. Numerous efforts in this direction were made in the years 1770–80, notably in France. Then, about 1800, the Earl of Stanhope, aided by the mechanical engineer Robert Walker, invented an iron press to replace the traditional wooden one. The famous Stanhope press had many descendants, the Columbian and the Albion among them. But other solutions were desperately needed to supply the demand for newspapers and periodicals. The German Friedrich König worked on the idea of a steam-driven mechanical press between 1777 and 1803. It occurred to him to replace the flat platen by a cylinder as used in copperplate engraving or like that used by Valentin Hauy to make relief impressions for blind readers; he also adopted the ink roller invented by William Nicholson, an 18th-century London doctor, to replace the old hand ink dubbers. On 29 November 1814 *The Times* was printed for the first time on König's steam press, and in the following year he found a way of coupling two presses so that the recto and verso of each sheet could be printed at once: the 'perfecting' or 'backing' press had arrived. Later, Edward Cowper and John Applegath improved on this and secured further increases in output.

Still the reciprocating movement of the type-bed limited output to a few thousand sheets per hour. A faster rate of output could only be achieved by adopting a cylindrical printing surface on the model of the engraved cylinders used for printing cotton in the 18th century. In 1790 Nicholson took out a patent for this idea, but the first effective machines were produced by Applegath and the American Robert Hoe. The type was locked up in chases, the columns and pages divided by rules and secured to the impression cylinder. This enabled them to build monster machines with large-diameter vertical cylinders, with teams of men feeding the sheets of paper individually at the rate of 12,000 per hour. It is difficult to imagine how these machines, using a fragile printing surface that was not perfectly cylindrical, could have worked. The arrival of a flexible stereotype provided a better solution. The Frenchman Jean-Baptiste Genoux suggested replacing the plaster of Paris type-mould with a 'flong' made of a kind of flexible, non-inflammable papier-mâché, in 1829 and Worms

An engraving of 1831 shows a Stanhope press at work. Again the similarity to the press illustrated in the Encyclopaedia is striking; but the Stanhope press was made of iron.

A giant cylindrical newspaper press, Robert Hoe's eight-feeder vertical dated 1862.

The Walter press, introduced by *The Times* in 1866, used stereotypes to print both sides of a continuous roll simultaneously, giving an output of 10,500 complete newspapers per hour.

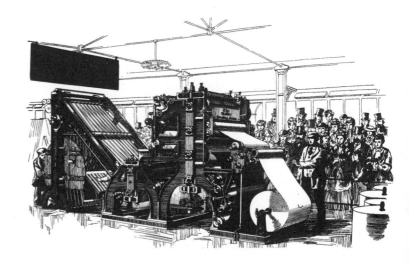

and Phillips had the idea of applying this to making cylindrical stereotypes in 1845. The technology was perfected and brought into use between 1857 and 1860. This made it possible to print newspapers from continuous paper rolls, and so the gigantic paper-making machines were matched by huge rotary presses capable of printing, folding and trimming tens of thousands of complete newspapers every hour.

It would have been no use being able to print newspapers at an ever-accelerating rate if type-setting had been tied to the old, slow, manual methods. This problem proved more difficult to resolve than any other. The first attempts to reduce the tedium of letter-by-letter composing were made by *The Times* at the end of the 18th century, when they introduced cases containing the most frequently occurring words and combinations of letters cast in single slugs. Machines were then devised which enabled the letters to be called up by means of a keyboard. Although some use was made of these in the absence of a better alternative after 1840, they did not deal with line justification and page make-up and the magazines of these 'pianotype' machines, as they were called, could only hold a relatively small number of characters. In 1845 Gérard de Nerval glimpsed the real solution when he set out to make a type-casting machine which could type-set from its own matrices to a specified text measure. However, it was only in the decade 1880–90 that the first linotype machine, producing automatically justified lines cast in one piece, was perfected by a recent immigrant to America from Germany named Ottmar Mergenthaler; and only at the beginning of the 20th century did the monotype machine make its appearance, producing justified lines made up of individual characters under the instructions of a previously prepared punched paper tape.

NEW YORK, DECEMBER 26, 1846.

MESSRS. CLAY & ROSENBORG'S PATENT TYPE SETTING MACHINE.

An early attempt at mechanical composition resembling a piano in more than name.

The popular press and the image explosion

Thus bit by bit the technology that was needed to make possible the era of so-called mass journalism was assembled. The penny press gave way to the halfpenny press with Lord Northcliffe's launching of the *Daily Mail* in 1896, and by 1914 the circulations of a number of British dailies were approaching the million mark. In France, where a law of 1881 finally secured the freedom of the press, print-runs continued to rise and on the eve of World War I there were four morning papers with more than a million readers each.

Nowhere could match the explosive growth of the press in the United States, however. Here an aggressive style of popular journalism emerged, with arresting headlines and plentiful illustration, making much use of comic strips like the famous 'Yellow Kid' (started in 1894), skilfully addressing itself to the very basic culture of the millions of new immigrants. This was the era of the great press barons, like Pulitzer (1847–1931), a Hungarian Jew who arrived in America at the age of 17, and William Randolph Hearst (1863–1951), son of a Californian millionaire.

By 1910 there were twenty-two daily papers in New York and in the USA at large some 2430 papers were printing 24 million copies every day. Geography prevented the appearance of national dailies on the British pattern, and individual circulations were never as much as 1 million copies. Instead the USA saw the formation of chains of newspapers about the turn of the century and the growth of the syndicated column carrying the words of nationally-known journalists across the nation. Between 1920 and 1940 the combined circulations of all American dailies rose from 27,800,000 to 41,100,000; in the same period that of the Sunday papers (often 250 pages in length) almost doubled from 17,000,000 copies to 32,400,000. Finally, new techniques of telecommunication made it possible for chains of local papers to be centrally coordinated even to the extent of remote type-setting input or the transmission of complete pages for common sections of, say, national or financial news or syndicated features.

While the newspaper was in its heyday in the first thirty years of this century, the weekly and the illustrated magazine were in process of development. This coincided with developments in two new processes for reproducing text and pictures – offset lithography and photogravure (see Chapter 8) – to the point where they seriously challenged traditional letterpress methods. Although the innovations concerned were mostly made prior to World War I, it was only afterwards that they began to have an impact. Devised to meet the requirements of glossy magazines and the hugely increased output of publicity material, brochures and advertisements, they enshrined the image at the centre of printing; and by treating type, set and proofed by traditional hot-metal methods, as material for the camera in the same way as illustrations, they made possible a much greater degree of flexibility in page-layout than was possible with letterpress methods employing type on the one hand and blocks on the other.

Since the 1950s, however, electronic technology has begun to make these processes obsolete in turn, or to impose radical changes on them. Type-setting was the first area to be affected. Everyone knows that it is now possible to set tens of thousands of words in hardly any time at all from a punched tape, with automatic line justification and simple page make-up using a computer with a relatively straightforward programme. The computer can control a mechanical type-setting machine, but it is particularly suited for use with modern photo-setting techniques, of which the earliest was the Lumitype process invented in France in 1954 by Higounet and Moyrand and manufactured commercially in America. The newest film-setters generate their own letter-forms from a matrix of light impulses and are capable of setting a whole book in a few minutes. This technology in turn marries particularly well with offest printing processes, since it is by photographic means that the image on a lithographic plate is produced. So it seems that today's constellation of graphic processes is favouring planographic techniques and relegating type to the dustbin.

Traditional journalism: a poster advertising the *New York Times* in 1895.

The front page of *El Liberal*, a Spanish middle-class newspaper, for 5 October 1902, carrying an illustration by Picasso.

The new popular journalism: the front page of an issue of Joseph Pulitzer's *World*. Note the emphasis on circulation figures and advertising success in the mast-head.

A revolution in books

Whatever the objective merits of these new processes, there is no ignoring that they are specifically tailored to the needs of the so-called mass culture, involving very high origination costs and thus demanding huge print-runs. Created as they were to meet the requirements of press and advertising, they have continually shifted the ground on which the book stands and over the last century and a half have constantly changed the terms in which we must consider the problem of the relation of creative writing to contemporary economic processes. Hence Marshall McLuhan's somewhat premature pronouncement that 'the book is dead' just when, according to some book-trade experts and as statistics confirm, it is experiencing a new access of vitality. Perhaps we should look at the question with the benefit of the distancing that a historical approach can offer.

To begin with we must point out the existence of a basic difference between the two halves of Europe. Recent historians have drawn a line from Saint-Malo through Geneva dividing northern France and Europe, more extensively literate and at an earlier stage, from the generally less book-oriented south. This tendency, already established in the 16th century, clearly assisted the rise of Protestantism, so much a religion of the book. Undoubtedly the hallowed Protestant practice of a daily reading from the Bible before the assembled household placed a premium on education in the Protestant countries. In the 18th century the comfortable bourgeois family in Britain and Germany turned from the Bible

Protestantism, the religion of the book:
Rembrandt's painting of his mother conveys an intimate familiarity with the Bible reflecting habitual reading.

to improving novels like Richardson's *Pamela*, and now we see the growth of circulating libraries serving the small circles of leading citizens in northern European cities from Bremen to Edinburgh.

Meanwhile France, nominally Catholic throughout, saw a comparable advance of literacy, even if children were often first taught to read their prayers in Latin. By the middle of the 18th century it was common to find devotional books, 'histoires' (novels) and radical literature in the homes of the more prosperous artisans; but, in general, resentment of the obstacles to cultural advancement – as of the obstacles to advancement in so many other spheres – was the dominant motif among the craftsmen, shopkeepers and petty clerks that were the backbone of the French bourgeoisie on the eve of the Revolution. This explains the efforts in the Revolution to establish public libraries out of the collections seized from religious houses and from *émigrés*. Alas these somewhat unsuitable book stocks were rarely topped up with new accessions, so that the libraries became primarily prestigious repositories of the past. The new leaders among the victorious bourgeoisie contented themselves with lining the libraries in the châteaux they had seized from the aristocracy with the kind of books that gave sanction to what they had done, i.e. principally the works of the philosophers of the Enlightenment. Bringing out editions of these on a subscription system was the mainstay of bookselling in the Bourbon restoration. Otherwise for the middle and lesser bourgeoisie it was the circulating library, which now began to proliferate in France on the same scale as elsewhere.

One can thus see why the sizes of editions remained exceedingly small, especially for new literary works, even if the number of titles published annually increased impressively (in France the figures are estimated to have been about 2000 in 1750, 4000 in 1780 and 6000–8000 in 1830). In England (where the growth in the annual output of titles probably exceeded that in France) the first edition of a new novel would be 750 copies if it was expected to sell mainly to individuals, or 250 if reliance was being placed on sales to libraries. Here Walter Scott, whose poems could achieve 10,000 copies and his novels 20,000 copies in several reprints, was a prominent exception. In France, Lamartine's *Méditations poétiques*, the inspiration of the Romantic movement, ran to eight printings, but in general new works of literature continued to be published in small editions at high prices. Thus in 1835 Girardin, the creator of the *Presse*, could put Victor Hugo and Paul de Koch at the head of a list of French authors ranked according to the size of the first printings they enjoyed, with 2500 copies. Balzac and Eugène Sue followed with 1500 copies, Musset with 600–900, and Théophile Gautier with less than 600. It comes as no surprise to hear Gladstone, in a speech in the House of Commons in 1853, reckon that 90 to 95 per cent of new books still sold less than 500 copies each.

With the economic downturn in Europe about 1830 publisher-booksellers looked for every available means of encouraging sales. Thus they put out books with illustrations in instalments so as to facilitate payment, or started up illustrated weekly periodicals. Chapman and Hall launched *Pickwick Papers* in monthly parts from 1836, with enormous success.

So traditional publishing methods began to be abandoned. During the century a number of entrepreneurs in the classic Protestant mould arose, who vied with each other in highly profitable crusades to bring good books to a huge public. They increased print-runs in order to bring down prices, just as the new newspaper publishers were doing. Space does not allow us to conjure up the often colourful personalities of these men. Some like Colburn and Bentley concentrated on cheap editions of novels, reducing the price to six shillings and eventually to one shilling (60 cents and 10 cents in terms of today's exchange rates). Others produced original publications of a practical kind, like Henry Brougham, whose Society for the Diffusion of Useful Knowledge founded in 1826 was to produce tens of thousands of pamphlets on popular science for the clientele of the Mechanics' Institutes; or later like John Cassell, the self-taught carpenter turned tea and coffee merchant, who began by printing his own price tickets and in 1852 launched *Cassell's Popular Educator* at a penny a copy in 1852. His *Illustrated Family Bible* sold 350,000 copies in six years.

This lowering of prices and increase in print-runs went hand-in-hand with increasing use of industrial production methods: first, particularly after 1830, stereotypes and the steam press; shortly afterwards mechanized binding; and later on the rotary press which, for instance, Macmillan's used for novels aimed at the popular market, like those of Charles Kingsley, whose total sales exceeded one million copies.

Thus popular books seemed to have the won the day in Britain by the end of the 19th century, and were shortly to do so in the United States also. It was not so unequivocal in continental Europe, however. In France Louis Hachette dominated the trade. He had been expelled from the University of Paris during the Bourbon restoration because of his too liberal opinions, which he then channelled into publishing. With the advice and help of teachers and sympathetic professors he began publication of textbooks, students' manuals and periodicals based on new educational principles, marketing scores of thousands of them throughout France, and like W. H. Smith in England he organized a chain of railway bookstalls which he supplied with reading matter; some of this, in blue paper covers, later blossomed into the famous *Guides bleus*, and a series of romances called the Bibliothèque Rose included improving tales by the Comtesse de Segur. After his death the Messageries Hachette had the virtual monopoly of newspaper and periodical distribution in France.

Alongside the power of the Hachette empire other French publishing houses remained small family enterprises, though of course they too sought wider publics. Gervais Charpentier and Calmann-Lévy set about bringing down the prices of their novels. Larousse and Flammarion embarked on a programme of popular education. Arthème Fayard II launched his Modern Bibliothèque at the beginning of this century, offering good authors at 95 centimes per copy (about 10p or 20 cents at today's exchange rates). His Bibliothèque Populaire included titles like *Chaste et Flétrie* and *Aimée de son concierge* which sold more than 100,000 copies each, or cloak and dagger mysteries by Paul Feval or Michel Zevaco, many of which first appeared in instalments in the *Petit Journal*. Then there were the popular information books like the *Manuels Roret*. But it is significant to note that the only rotary presses employed were newspaper presses, and it was actually not until 1929 that the first rotary press specifically intended for book-work was brought into use by Hachette.

So the revolution in books seemed not to have been completely accomplished in France by 1914. It is interesting that by this date both Britain and the United States had established public library systems, whereas in France efforts in this direction in the 1870s and 1880s had come to nothing, and it was only in recent times that the situation was changed. If one remembers that the Scandinavian countries, Germany to some extent, and since more recently the communist countries all had efficient lending library systems, while Italy and all the countries of the Spanish- and Portuguese-speaking world had none, one can see how long-established cultural patterns have continued to prevail. Again the same pattern can be seen in the fact that the paperback, initiated by Penguin Books in 1935 and introduced in America by Pocket Books in 1939, did not become commonplace

The travelling library of the Warrington Mechanics' Institute in one of the industrial areas of the north-west of England.

outside the English-speaking world until after World War II, in many cases until quite some time after.

These changes were associated with an increasing division of labour in the world of books. The functions of publisher and bookseller began to be distinguished as the old system of bartering stocks was abandoned in the late 18th century. By the early 19th century publishers had stopped retailing books, while second-hand books became a distinct area of the trade, concentrated in the hands of the great antiquarian booksellers. With many more booksellers to be persuaded to buy their books, publishers began to place expensive advertisements and announcements of lists in both literary periodicals and the general press. The practice of reviewing assumed more importance, developing from the mere 'puffery' of the early Victorian period into the sustained and substantial review articles which appeared in the responsible literary journals. Catalogues and leaflets proliferated.

Thus now the effects of longer print-runs in reducing prices were being offset by increased costs. Lending libraries and bookselling chains were increasingly insistent on having special discounts. The London publishers who, a century earlier, had held banquets to sweeten their correspondent booksellers were forced to make ever-larger concessions to these demands, and the first Net Book Agreement in 1899 was an attempt to control the situation by collective action. At the same time booksellers were getting tired of dealing with innumerable publishers on an individual basis and whole-saling activities like those of W. H. Smith and Simpkin, Marshall became a new element in the commercial structure of the trade.

But it was in Germany that a really rational book trade organization was worked out. For some time the Leipzig Fair (successor to the older Frankfurt Fair) had served to resist the anarchic potentialities of the situation of the German book trade, operating across the frontiers of a multitude of small states. In 1773 a copyright agreement was put into effect. The booksellers began to meet annually at the end of each fair to hand out their orders and settle accounts. Soon they acquired an office and then they built their own headquarters, known as the German Book House. Most important, they set up a highly-organized orders clearing centre, based on the warehouse maintained by the Leipzig commission agents on whom the publishers relied to maintain stocks of their books (numbering fifty-seven in 1936).

So the book trade's distribution arrangements were developed and elaborated. But there are still problems to be resolved. One is the question of whether the publisher or the bookseller should be responsible for unsold books. Selling firm on the British pattern prevents the bookseller from ordering

with confidence, and various means have been devised to remedy this. In the difficult times of the 1830s Didot and Hachette started the system of 'correspondent booksellers' to whom they consigned their publications on a sale or return basis, while Werdet set up a central book agency placing stocks of books with provincial booksellers. Gradually in France and Germany a system evolved whereby supplies of new titles were automatically sent to correspondent booksellers for them to return any unsold copies within a reasonable period of time. But the weight of centuries of tradition can still be discerned in the variety of practices, the overlapping sales networks of publishers and wholesalers and the bewildering multiplicity of discount-rates that apply to different types of sales.

The same diversity of practice explains the slow advance in international copyright protection. For a long time publishers were free to publish any title from abroad in their own country without making any recompense to the original publisher. In the 19th century Belgian publishers made fortunes at the expense of their French colleagues, English publishers were exploited without reward in Paris and Leipzig and, most notoriously, American publishers pirated editions of English authors for sale in colonial markets (though the British retaliated by pirating American titles). In the Italian states prior to unification in 1870, complete anarchy prevailed. Gradually the situation was remedied, initially in innumerable bilateral agreements, leading on to the various international agreements (the Berne Conventions of 1886 and 1908, the Brussels Convention of 1948 and the International Copyright Convention of 1952, in which the United States was a signatory for the first time). But it is well known that there are still gaps giving rise to significant abuses.

The German book trade has led the world. A cartoon in the periodical *Simplicissimus* celebrates 100 years of the German Book House in 1925.

The author in society

The book was inexorably turning into a mass-produced commodity. How did this affect its role in society? Let us think about this in terms of the 'circuits' in which book culture travelled. By making the book a commercial commodity printing gave the publisher-bookseller a new role at the heart of the networks of communication, that of choosing what texts to multiply in print. To start with, it was a question of choosing from among the manuscripts in circulation, perhaps making selections and then even adapting them for printing. Later publishers competed for books in manuscript appearing in the world of letters, and more and more they commissioned books on subjects that they judged would appeal to wide audiences. Hence the characteristic ambiguity of the author's dealings with his publisher, and the complications of the author's standing in relation to society at different periods of history.

For a long time after the invention of printing the professional author served a patron, typically an aristocrat or prince. He would often act as a kind of cultural major domo in the patron's household or court and would look after his public relations by writing verses, philosophical pamphlets or historical accounts of an appropriate slant. In return, the patron would provide board and lodging for his protégé, respond to dedications with generous presents, grant him annuities, and on a wider front proclaim his genius to the world and assist him to a diplomatic or clerical career.

This oversimplified statement must be modified to the extent of saying that many authors of books were not professional writers strictly speaking. But even then – say if they were clerics, lawyers, doctors or courtiers – they invariably anticipated advantages to their careers or reputations from the publication of their books, and frequently they gained financially as well. At the same time, they put themselves in touch with other sections of society frequently superior to their own. The writer might find himself acting in the role of broker between the differing social groups whom he addressed through his writing. He was rarely an isolated figure. He could expect to meet other men of talent at court or in the circles surrounding his patrons and would benefit from these contacts. Gradually we see the emergence of literary *salons*, providing a meeting-place for writers and making and breaking literary reputations. From the beginning of the 17th century various groups took institutional shape as academies or societies which enabled aristocrats and other men of power to meet writers and artists on terms of apparent equality, but they in turn were expected to have at least a few good words for the status quo in their writings and to

reconcile new ideas to it. Of course writers have always bridled at these sorts of compromises, as they still do today. Then as now they often dreamed of making direct contact with the vast public that they so longed for, bypassing the approval of men of influence or the sanctions of the literary circles where they had failed to gain recognition.

Meanwhile it was becoming increasingly common for writers to be commissioned by publisher-booksellers. This practice had honourable precedents in the Renaissance, when humanist printers, themselves well versed in the new ideas, gathered around them other humanist men of letters to edit, translate or supply commentaries on the major writings of antiquity. In the following centuries, in what we have called the craft period of printing, the literary élites were little more than enlarged special-interest groups in the hierarchical societies of their day, and the publisher-bookseller only occasionally intervened in the literary world. Gradually, however, he began to pay the author in relation to the success that his books enjoyed and to commission work, and this had become quite a significant feature of publishing activity by the 18th century, especially in Britain. In France writers who were hostile to the establishment, or even rejected the form of society in which they had to live, saw new hope in these commercial initiatives of a release from the bonds of patronage. Then from the 19th century to our own day there has been an ever-growing preference for dictating subjects and commissioning specific titles on the part of publishers out to maximize their sales. It may be that things today are not so different as we sometimes think. It is true that the majority of books – especially popular information books – are written by writers (one hesitates to call them authors), often working for a fee. But it appears that this kind of book has always been produced in this way, and since the 19th century London has had its Grub Street, Paris its Rue Saint-Jacques, peopled with hopeful hacks in search of employment. And if libraries today seem to the cultural élite to be full of nothing but category fiction in series – hospital romances, science fiction, crime novels and so forth – this kind of writing has antecedents of quite respectable antiquity in the enterprises of men like Barbin in 17th-century France or John Dunton and Edmund Curll in 17th- and 18th-century London.

But what about the position of creative writing, literary and scholarly? It is easy to think of literary masterpieces that were destined to be best sellers from the start – some early examples are *Don Quixote, The Pilgrim's Progress, Robinson Crusoe* and Richardson's *Pamela*. But usually the serious writer has to make his reputation among the literary minority, just as a professional historian or scientist first has to secure the respect of his peers before he is interviewed as a pundit on television or achieves wide sales for his books. Hence the perennial smallness of first printings, the always precarious foothold of any kind of originality and the chance or partly chance nature of major successes, which depend not just on the author's talent, but also on the way the publisher promotes the book and on the capricious and perhaps not specially well-informed decisions of magazine editors and television producers.

Print in the electronic age

How much have the new media – cinema and radio between the wars, television today – changed things? They appeared on the scene at a time of accelerating change and speedier communications and like popular journalism were a response to increased demand for information and entertainment. Historians know that new systems and structures never completely drive out older ones but are superimposed on them. So the new technologies of information storage and retrieval have required the print media in this field to regroup and find new niches, often of a more specialized kind. From another point of view, the audiovisual revolution has been attended by a deluge of printed promotional material, sometimes in danger of strangling the mails and choking our letter-boxes. And then international statistics reveal that books are constantly reaching new publics; and as recently as 1971 the United Nations thought it worthwhile to proclaim the right to read as one of the fundamental rights of man. That is not to say that there have not been changes affecting the book too. For instance, conventional type-setting is now so expensive that much larger print-runs are required to justify it. But then again a variety of easier and cheaper methods of reproduction have become available, such as photocopying and cheap litho printing from typed copy, for circulating literary writing and research papers on a limited scale.

All this is not to say that fundamental changes are not in store. In the instant society with its information overload we are less amenable to the ordered thinking of which the well-turned book represents a model. Writing habits are changing in significant ways: decent authors think nothing of putting their thoughts straight on to tape, and most make practically no alterations to the first typescript draft. Certainly no publisher today puts up with the kind of second thoughts and changes that an author like Balzac went in for. Television is responsible for spreading habits of speech that a linguistic purist would regard as corrupt, while correct spelling is losing its age-old stature as the hallmark of a proper education. So, in some ways, the traditional book with its sacred aura and its implications of perfectionism, is indeed under threat as McLuhan has said. Looking ahead, we ought now to reflect on the new forms of print and printout produced by the contemporary retrieval techniques. But that is another story.

Passport to Print

The invention of writing was a momentous step in the history of mankind. It enabled us to break loose not only from the limitations of time and place in the transmission of messages, but also from the limitations of what one man could think and remember in the acquisition and accumulation of knowledge.

The final step in the representation of speech in graphic form was the alphabet. With a minimal number of signs, every possible variant of language could be expressed without any further innovation. All alphabets have a common parent in the one invented by Canaanite merchants in the area of present-day Palestine-Syria around 1500 BC. The two systems which inspired it, Babylonian cuneiform written in wedge-shaped strokes with the end of a stylus impressed into wet clay, and the highly pictorial Egyptian hieroglyphic writing, survived into the Christian era and the non-alphabetic writing of China survives today. But otherwise it can be said that the whole stream of human cultural development in this respect passed through one narrow sluice-gate.

It was not until three thousand years later that the invention of printing with movable type in turn opened the way to the fulfilment of the potential inherent in the invention of the alphabet.

86 'The very stones shall cry out': sacred Buddhist inscriptions lining the road leading up to a place of pilgrimage in the Himalayan province of Ladakh aptly suggest the transformation of the world of man through writing, even to the remotest corners of the earth.

GRAFFITI

We can be reasonably sure that the first written words were graffiti, and this may therefore be claimed – no doubt to the surprise of its present-day practitioners – as the most venerable of literary forms. In fact graffiti should not be lightly dismissed. Typically, they are statements of protest, or unlicensed assertion, reminding us of the controls which societies effectively place on all forms of communication, and of the role communications in turn have played in the structuring of societies.

87 Lovers' initials united in hearts on a tree trunk.

88 'Death to the Shah': the Shah's name appears upside down to accentuate the message on the wall of a mosque in Teheran University in January 1980.

89 'Ulster not for sale': Protestant slogans in strife-torn Northern Ireland.

90 'Munich 1938 – Bratislava 1968': Czech patriots compare the invading Russians to the Nazis, in words and potent symbolism.

WRITING
IN PICTURES
OR
STRIP CARTOON?

There is more than one way of using a picture to embody specific meanings. Formally these two specimens of communication employing graphic signs, both from north-east Africa, have much in common: they are both sequences of representational drawings. But looked at in terms of their connections with spoken language they are poles apart.

91–4 The ancient Egyptian hieroglyphs, here produced in a decorative art context, are true writing with a determinate relationship to spoken language, each picture or picture group denoting, through fixed conventions, a precise word.

95 This modern rendering of the traditional myth of the origins of the Ethiopian nation is a 'story in pictures', the equivalent of a strip cartoon, and could serve as a prompt to numerous alternative oral renderings of the same general story. It is emphatically not 'writing'.

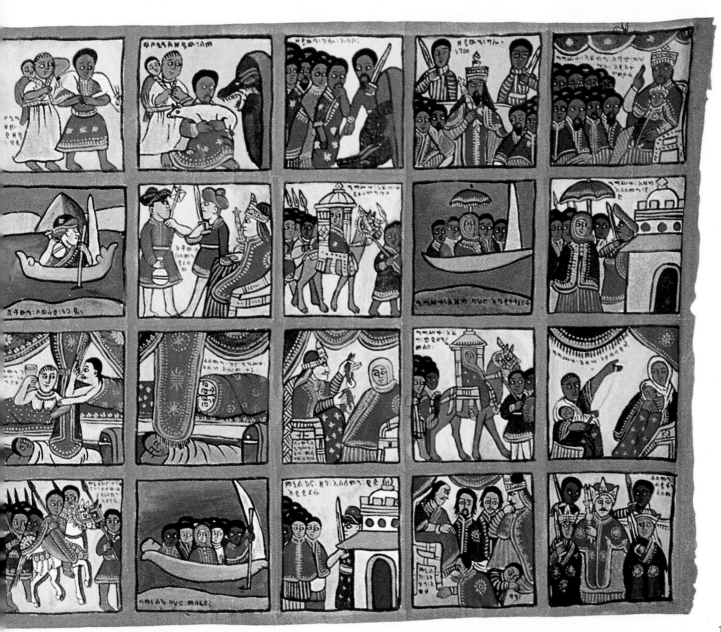

WRITING AND READING: PRESTIGE AND POWER

Prestige reflects power. From the earliest times, access to the written word, upon which most human knowledge and any advanced civilization depend, has been wielded as a valuable form of power.

Throughout medieval and Renaissance Europe it secured membership of priestly or scholarly élites. In the West today, near-universal literacy and new forms of communication which offer universal access, at least for consumption, have taken away the prestige of the word; but in directed societies, as in theocracies in earlier centuries, the word is still power.

96 An angel records the good and bad deeds of men in a late-13th-century Islamic manuscript.

97 A Dominican friar transcribes a manuscript in a fresco at Treviso by the 14th-century Lombard master Tommaso da Modena.

98 A philosopher, who is also a saint in the clandestine symbolism of early Christian art, reads a scroll on a 3rd-century sarcophagus in Rome.

99 The Virgin reads in rapt attention: from a painting by the 15th-century Flemish master Rogier van der Weyden.

100 Three *electi*, the equivalents of monks in the Manichean religion, are shown writing in an 8th- or 9th-century manuscript.

101 In Mao Tse-tung's China reading the Little Red Book was a demonstrative and ceremonial political act.

PICTURE-WRITING
AND PICTURE LETTERS

If the Ethiopian creation myth was a strip cartoon, this example of picture-writing does represent a definite sequence of words. But it is a formulaic sequence likely already to have been learnt by oral repetition, and it could be 'read' in any Indian language. So it is still not 'writing', a precise and sufficient representation of linguistic forms by fixed graphic signs.

102, 3   The Ten Commandments: four pages from an early-19th-century version of the so-called Testerian picture-writing (after the name of the Spanish friar with whom it is associated), a catechism owned by Princeton University. It was used by Catholic missionaries to instruct native Indians in the faith after the conquest of Mexico. Translation is far from straightforward. The rows of circles represent numbers, marking off the end of each Commandment. 'Thou shalt observe the Sabbath day and keep it holy' (fourth) and 'Honour thy father and thy mother' (fifth) are two of the more easily made out Commandments.

Making letters into pictures seems to have a strong general appeal. It tells us nothing about the development of writing, however, except by alluding to the origins of some letters in pictorial symbols. The best-known example of this is the Hebrew letter beth (the first letter in the second line opposite, reading from right to left), which is said to have come to stand for the initial letter of the word it represented and whose meaning it originally depicted: bayit, a house. The same principle is applied in children's ABCs: A is for apple, though the child must not get into the habit of drawing an apple to stand for A.

104   Hebrew letters colourfully animated into human and animal forms in a 13th-century Spanish manuscript of the liturgy for the Jewish religious service held at home on Passover eve, known as Haggadah. The horse with its rider in contemporary dress is an allusion to the Exodus.

כַּמָה שְׁנֵא וַיִּרָא אֱלֹהִים אֶת
בְּנֵי יִשְׂרָאֵל וַיִּרַע אֱלֹהִים·
עָמַלֵינוּ אֵלּוּ
הַבָּנִים כְּמָה
שֶׁנֶּאֱמַר

כָּל הַבֵּן הַיִּלּוֹד הַיְאֹרָה תַּשְׁלִיכֻהוּ·
וְכָל הַבַּת תְּחַיּוּן· וְאֶת לַחֲצֵנוּ
זֶה הַדְּחַק כְּמָה שֶׁנֶּאֱמַר וְגַם רָאִיתִי
אֶת הַלַּחַץ אֲשֶׁר מִצְרַיִם לוֹחֲצִים
אוֹתָם·

PAYING THE PIPER

The printed book was born into a world of patronage, ecclesiastical or courtly. Changing winds of fortune or political interference made the nascent European book trade a fragile growth: paying the author in relation to his success was a novelty when it occurred. It was the 19th century that saw the beginning of the book trade as a powerful commercial force, most often calling the tune in its relationships with authors.

105 Rabanus Maurus, abbot of Fulda in northern Germany, **presents his verse book** De laudibus Sanctae Crucis **to Pope Gregory IV, about 831–40: from a miniature painting on vellum preserved in the monastery.**

106 Philip the Good of Burgundy receives the Chroniques de Hainault **from the hands of his client-author Simon Nockart; 15th-century patronage recorded in a contemporary miniature.**

107 Le colporteur, **an anonymous painting of a street vendor of books in Paris in 1623.**

108 The book trade starts to find its feet as the ideas of the Enlightenment prevail. Léonard Defrance de Liège's painting shows a late-18th-century printer-bookseller advertising the works of Rousseau, Helvétius and the Encyclopédistes.

109 The title of the magazine which this 19th-century American lady puts into her handbag as she prepares to return home by train from a holiday by the sea aptly captures the sententious moral tone that animated many of the pioneer publishers to the new 'mass' market.

110 Universal literacy, advances in printing and cheap paper all led to a boom in light reading as the 19th century neared its end. And new skills, whose art lay in appealing to the greatest number in the shortest time, were born – journalism and publishing as we know them, modern publicity, mass production and 'mass' marketing. This turn-of-the-century advertisement alludes to the railway bookstall empire which was the foundation of the commercial might of the British bookseller W. H. Smith.

HOT NEWS

The newspaper no longer literally provides the news, now that
television and radio have overtaken it in speed. But it still has the
power to engross us, with its diversity of coverage and, perhaps
more particularly, its production and reinforcement of outlooks on
the world.

111, 112　The primary urgency of a mid-19th-century newsboy
rushing to get the Pawtucket Record out on to the streets harks back
to older traditions of itinerant street-selling, as with the Parisian
colporteur on the previous spread or this 18th-century Japanese
bookseller.

113 The 'devourer of news-papers' in a French cartoon of 1815 is a politician scouring the newspapers in a coffee house or club for news of current events.

114 A poster by Savignac hu-morously suggests the role of a newspaper in the 1970s in form-ing and reinforcing opinions.

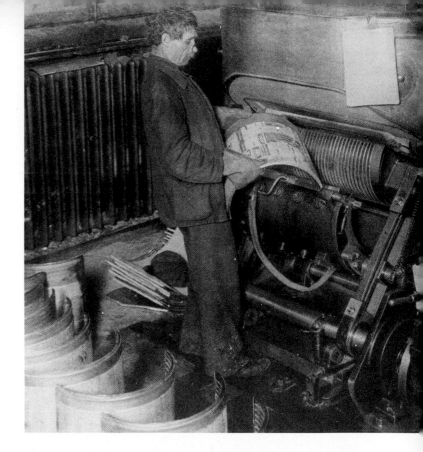

PRINTING THE NEWS

During the last fifty years electronic techniques have widely replaced mechanical in the printing industry. These changes are eloquently summarized in photographs comparing the production of Pravda in Moscow in 1931 with aspects of newspaper production today.

115 Linotype machines in the Pravda composing room.

116 Casting curved stereotype plates for the rotary presses from the flexible papier-mâché mould known as a 'flong'.

117 Electronic technology enables a compositor to read and correct the stream of electronic pulses recorded on magnetic tape that will drive a high-speed filmsetter producing, in some instances, completely corrected, justified and made-up pages ready for printing down on to litho plates.

118 Facsimile transmission makes it possible to supply complete made-up pages of a newspaper for printing at distant plants. This technology is widely used in America to supply centrally-owned chains of local newspapers with common pages of national news.

119 Complete folded and trimmed copies roll off a Pravda press at a rate of tens of thousands per hour.

VII
EXTENDED SPEECH
AND SOUNDS

Ithiel de Sola Pool

The latest printing machinery employs huge capital resources and the most sophisticated electronic technology to make material printed for 'mass' distribution dramatically cheaper. While this enlarges the possibilities for certain types of communication, it may also operate to impoverish the range and richness of communication by pricing out of the market printed matter of less than universal appeal.

One of the largest gravure printing plants in the world is operated by Purnell and Sons at Paulton in Somerset.

120 An oblique view of one of the presses in operation, showing separately the four colour impressions on one side of the sheet.

121 This control panel electronically regulates the flow of ink to every part of each printing cylinder to achieve fine adjustments in colour balance and printing quality.

EXTENDED SPEECH
AND SOUNDS

The robot talks

In the fifth century after the birth of print a strange thing happened. A new technology made it possible to do with voice, that most primitive form of human communication, what before could be done only with print – to store it, repeat it, and move it over great distances.

Three inventions that transformed the use of human voice, the telephone, the radio, and the recording machine, were all first conceived as improvements in telegraphy. Thomas A. Edison devised the phonograph because he thought Bell's telephone somewhat less practical than the telegraph that had preceded it. Since few people could then afford a phone in their home, it would be better, Edison thought, if the voice message could be sent to a local office (like the local telegraph office) and the recipient then called to hear the message in its stored form. He did not anticipate the use of the phonograph as an entertainment device.

Alexander Graham Bell had been financed to develop a multiple telegraph, i.e. one that could send several messages at once down the same wire by separating their frequencies. But Bell, a teacher of the deaf, had a different goal and produced a device that could reproduce the interpretable range of the human voice. Bell came to his interest in speech naturally. His father was the professor whom George Bernard Shaw (himself in the 1880s a telephone company right-of-way agent) parodied as Henry Higgins in *Pygmalion*. The elder Bell (like his fictional counterpart) had invented a system for phonetic transcription, which he called Visible Speech. The young Bell too was an expert in voice and hearing, and not in electricity. The latter he had to teach himself. That he did, and invented a device that could carry not just monotonic dots and dashes over a wire to a distance, but one that could reproduce the modulation of sound.

Radio broadcasting, too, came out of wireless telegraphy. Marconi first sought to interest the Royal Navy and other shipping interests in his new device. Something that could send messages long distances without wires or cables was of obvious value to ships at sea. If it became reliable enough and free enough of interference, it also promised to save enormous sums invested in copper for wires on land. (Before 1900 copper was a quarter of the total telephone investment in the United States.) But with the model of the telephone already in front of them, many inventors saw a logical progression from the easier task of transmitting Morse code by wireless to that of transmitting voice. As early as Christmas Eve of 1906, only five years after Marconi's first transmission of code across the Atlantic, R. A. Fessenden successfully sent a spoken greeting to ships at sea.

But if phonograph, telephone and radio were all originally conceived as refinements on telegraphy, telephone and radio were half-brothers at most. In their social significance they were in many ways polar opposites. What emerged as radio broadcasting was a 'mass' medium, even more so than the penny newspapers that had emerged in the 19th century. It was a one-way medium that gave a few producers in the capitals a means to address the whole nation. It was an instrument listened to in the home alone or with one's family. It was the companion of the lonely hour, the addiction of those without other friends.

The telephone was the opposite. It was originally an élite instrument for busy people. When it became more general, it was still the instrument for two-way interaction. Its social importance in that respect cannot be underestimated. It came at a time of the evolution of 'mass' society. Early in the century sociologists described how an expanding urban civilization was replacing the rural primary communities in which most people had lived for millennia. Big cities, big factories, geographic mobility, bureaucracy and the mass media were creating (they said) a society marked by anomie, impersonality and undifferentiated products. Broadcasting, as it displaced the corner pub, or church gathering, or local band or concert hall, fits that description. The telephone was its antithesis. It was one invention that went against the easy generalization about what was happening. It enabled those who had moved away from old neighbourhoods and relatives to stay in touch. It allowed friends and lovers to talk. Perhaps, in being the counterpoint to what was happening in all the other media, it preserved society from becoming as much of a 'mass' system as it might have become. Suppose the telephone had proved technically impossible and all electronic messages could be delivered only in a broadcast stream to the population *en masse*; how much more collectively standardized and regimented (we may ask ourselves) would our social organization have been?

Long-distance sound and human settlement

The telephone and radio have each had profound but different effects on the ecology of human activity. Most profound, perhaps, was the impact of the telephone on the structure of the city. From the ancient world until the turn of the last century, urban structure everywhere was a patchwork of small occupational neighbourhoods. Clothiers, furniture-makers, jewellers, bankers, butchers, each had their own small districts, and so did dozens of other trades. The city as a whole was a walking city; one had to be able to go from any part to any other part on foot. For trade to be carried on efficiently, the suppliers or customers that one wanted to see needed to be gathered within a few blocks. To locate in the heart of his trade's neighbourhood was so important to any businessman that property values and rents there were very high.

In industrial cities of the 19th century the pattern changed a bit. Large factories were at the heart of manufacturing towns. The workers had to be able to walk to their place of work. The capitalist, too, had to be where he could keep track of whatever was going on, so typically the company's head office was right in the building with the plant.

All that changed with trams and streetcars and the telephone. For the first time it became possible for workers to commute, for traders to travel longer distances across town, and for people to deal with each other without having to walk down the street to the other man's shop. Company presidents moved their offices away from the plant, for they could give orders to the superintendent by telephone; they moved nearer to the people with whom they had more difficult negotiations: their bankers and their customers. So the heart of the city became a collection of office blocks, where executives from all sorts of companies congregated far from their plants. At the same time the small single-trade neighbourhoods broke up. A business could move close to its customers instead of being next door to its competitors. Equally important, it could pay less rent if it moved its premises out from the centre or up off the street into one of the new high-rise buildings, and yet it could still stay in touch.

Indeed skyscrapers would not have been possible without the telephone. In 1902 someone calculated that if offices had had to continue relying on messenger boys, as they had in the past, the traffic up and down the elevators of a tall building would have been about double what it was. With an elevator well of the size needed to take that traffic, a high-rise building would have been uneconomic. So the use of skyscrapers stemmed from the invention of the steel frame and the elevator, of course, but also from the telephone.

Not only did business move; so did homes. The new suburbs became more attractive when one could talk with those who stayed in town.

These processes of urban change, which began around the turn of the century, were flowering in the 1920s when broadcasting began. The first full-fledged commercial broadcasting station, KDKA in Pittsburgh, opened in 1920. The BBC was organized in 1922. Two stations were transmitting from the Eiffel Tower in Paris by 1923. The coincidence of broadcasting and rapid urbanization was a matter of chance, but it meant that radio became the home entertainment medium for the first generation in which a third to a half of the population were not lifelong inhabitants of a community to which they belonged by heredity. They were rather migrants thrown together in the anonymity of the new cities, often not knowing their immediate neighbours, often not belonging to any organized group with its own cultural tradition. The radio for such people had to provide much of what for their parents or grandparents had been provided by the fête, or county fair, by weekly church gatherings, or by sociability or casual entertainment in the market square.

Radio was an excellent substitute, indeed in some ways an improvement. The soap operas or variety shows, bad as they were, were several notches better than the average of what one might pick up in the local 'opera' or burlesque house, or travelling troupe; the radio networks had the national talent pool to pick from. Yet, better or worse, radio was different. It was in the home; it was ideal for the isolated farmstead or for the equally isolated urban dweller to whom his neighbour and his neighbourhood were alien. It was an individual or family activity, not one shared with his community or his church. And if it contributed to 'mass' society by taking people away from community groups, it also did so by exposing them to 'mass' preachments from the centre. In the United States where radio was commercial it provided a new and important channel for Madison Avenue in its growing efforts to market brand-name products. In countries like Great Britain, where radio from the start was non-commercial but national in origination, it was a channel by which an approved culture was disseminated to all regardless of the subculture to which they belonged.

How the twig was bent

It would be easy to interpret what we have said so far as a kind of technological determinism, and with some justification. Our lives are changed by the tools we use. But there is also interaction between the tools and men's ideas about how to use them. A steel knife may have a sharper edge than what came before it, but one society may use it for a sword in war and another to save work in cutting crops. So too with the electronic reproduction of sound either with wires or with radio waves. The device did not foreordain the things for which it was used. That came out of an interaction between what the technology worked well for and what people wanted and were ready to think about. The determinants were not only the technology, but also a stock of ideas with which innovators approached the new device.

The telephone was invented often in fantasy before Bell produced his working model. The word is found in a number of sources in the 19th century, such as Charles Bourseul's article on 'Electric Telephony' in *Illustration de Paris* in 1854. What such futurists had in mind was something very much like the telegraph, but able to reach from end user to end user, for it would not require the intermediation of a Morse key operator. *Punch* repeatedly played on this theme in science-fiction notes like an 1858 one on 'The House Telegraph'. The satirist concedes that it 'would be pleasant to be within five minutes of such a message as "Dine at the Club with me at seven"'. But against that, 'When I leave my suburban retreat at Brompton, at nine a.m. for the City, I am insured against Mrs P's anxieties, and tribulations, and consultings, on the subject of our little family, or our little bills ... at least till my return to dinner. But with a House-Telegraph, it would be a perpetual tête-a-tête.' So when Bell showed how to make the technology work, at least the germs of the system were already in mind.

Nonetheless, when the telephone became a reality, there were rival conceptions as to its use. One notion was that of person-to-person applications which correspond to the phone as we know it today; the other was of uses that correspond to what we now call broadcasting.

To earn money from his new invention, Bell in 1876 and 1877 went on the lecture circuit. At his talks he would have someone declaim a dramatic speech or sing on the phone from outside the hall. The idea of what Asa Briggs calls the 'pleasure telephone' which would carry entertainment over wires to people's homes antedates the existence of the telephone. *Punch* magazine in 1848 ran a piece on 'Music by Electric Telegraph'. It reported (wrongly) that 'pieces of music are now sent from Boston to New York.... Our American brethren have among them such remarkable musical instruments, and in fact such astonishing lyres, that nothing coming from the other side of the Atlantic can take us by surprise.' In the illustration a lady reclines at ease facing three boxes that look much like radios of the 1930s, with dials and aerials, one box labelled Exeter Hall, one Philharmonic, and one Hanover Square.

In Paris, London, Newark (New Jersey), Budapest and elsewhere, entrepreneurs set up services for transmitting entertainment to subscribers by telephone. The one that lasted longest was the Telephon Hirmondo in Budapest, whose formula of music, news, public announcements, market reports and weather was that of many radio stations twenty years later. While the telephone business in the form that we now know it thrived, these broadcast applications all failed, and most of them quickly. The economics were wrong. The fidelity of early telephones was inadequate for pleasurable listening to music or drama, but that probably did not matter much. After all, early radios or phonographs were not much better. The magic of listening via an electric device to Nellie Melba or Enrico Caruso overcame aesthetic quibbles. But there were very few people who could afford a telephone, with the miles of wire, operators, repeaters and other equipment that it entailed. The average American telephone bill at the turn of the century was not very different from today's: advances in technology have more or less cancelled out inflation. But that same bill, which now might be 2 or 3 per cent of an average worker's salary, would then have been about 50 per cent. There was no general market for that.

If some entrepreneurs made the mistake of thinking that they could make a go of broadcasting by telephone, Bell and his associates did not. They quickly recognized that the early market for telephones consisted of business firms and very rich individuals who had activities in more than one site. Bell himself was an idealist and a reformer. So was his father-in-law and financial backer, Hubbard, who had recently engaged in a Ralph Nader type of crusade against the giant Western Union Company. These telephone pioneers, and the man who came in as the first President of the American Bell Telephone Company, Vail, all anticipated the day when the telephone would be in every man's home at a price even the poor could afford; they talked about that. But their market entry strategy was to offer the device to those who could pay.

The initial marketing decision against the pleasure telephone has left its stamp on the system today. It has been engineered with switches, directories, and low bandwidth, and it has been optimized and tariffed for short conversations, so that it works well for people who need to talk briefly to each other. The possibility of a later shift to use in broadcast mode was pre-empted by the coming of wireless.

The idea of avoiding the cost of wires and cables by sending electric signals through the air antedated Heinrich Hertz's discovery of radio waves in 1887. Electrical induction, by which a current flowing through a wire had an effect through the air on objects not attached to it, was already known. Experimenters ultimately succeeded in sending induction signals for a few miles through the air or through the earth.

The discovery of Hertzian waves, which we now call radio waves, stimulated such research. One of the people whose imagination was caught was young Marconi. His important idea was not a scientific theory, but an intuitive conviction which turned out to be right, that these waves for some reason would travel very long distances. His great experiment, in 1901, was transmitting a signal from Poldu, in Wales, to Newfoundland. Before that, writings on the uses of wireless telegraphy talked about such applications as communicating to lighthouses from the shore. Now it became clear that the new technology might compete with wires and cables for telegraphy or for long-distance telephony.

That prospect caused a certain amount of panic in the cable, telegraph and telephone companies. In 1903 Sir Ambrose Fleming, Marconi's principle scientific adviser, gave a lecture at the Royal Institution in London on the marvels of radio. It was to end with a transmission from somewhere thirty miles outside London into the hall. In the middle of the speech the receiver began to chatter, and the engineer who had set up the demonstration, Arthur Blok, listened to the dots and dashes with horror. There, interrupting the speech, but fortunately not understood by those who knew no Morse, was a limerick which began:

> There was a young fellow from Italy
> Who diddled the public quite prettily.

Then happily it fell silent till the demonstration at the end. As Mr Blok looked around him his eye fell on a man involved in a cable company, Nevil Maskelyne, appearing as though he had just swallowed a canary.

After the talk Sir Ambrose penned an angry letter to the London *Times* about 'scientific hooliganism'. Lo and behold, Maskelyne replied saying he clearly had no evil in mind for he let the lecture proceed. He only sought to show that this new technology of radio had no future, for there was no way to protect privacy.

In the United States, Vail at AT & T (the American Telephone and Telegraph Company, which by now had taken over the Bell Telephone Company), was worried too. In 1907 he wrote to a London banker assuring him that the difficulties of wireless telephony were such that it was unlikely to displace the wired phone system. That turned out to be right, but Vail was in fact not quite sure, as his exchanges with his chief engineer make clear. They reprimanded themselves that they had let this technology develop out of their hands, for if it should work it might supplant their whole system. They thought the problems of radio interference would prove too great for that, but they were not certain. The lesson they drew was that they should expand their research programme, so as

to be the principal developers not just of telephony, but of the technologies on its shoulders too. Out of this effort grew Bell Labs, and its extraordinary contributions over a wide range of technologies such as the invention of the transistor and of sound movies, giving AT & T for a while in the 1930s a dominant position in cinema.

What radio was obviously good for was long-distance transmission of messages to places to which the telegraph or cable circuits did not go. Besides ships at sea, it became a means of reaching aeroplanes in flight, and high-frequency radio soon became a message system for remote stations and for defence. It also became a favourite plaything of hobbyists. But 'plaything' is an unfair word for, even if amateurs, they were in fact scientific experimenters. There was much to be learned about where and under what conditions signals would reach and when they would fade. Different kinds of equipment needed to be tested, and also the characteristics of different frequencies. The amateurs were therefore given licences, and they were instructed that the only uses for which they were allowed this privilege was to exchange information about reception with other amateurs. That remains today the limit on what amateurs are supposed to communicate. They ask the world 'Can you hear me?', and they exchange cards reporting what callers they have heard.

But why these restrictions? At first it was because of the interference with what the navigators and governments considered to be the serious uses of radio. The amateurs, like American CBers today (see page 254), enjoyed the thrill of talking to each other at a distance, and of proving the quality of their transmitters by playing music on them. Various amateurs started broadcasting, that is to say they started periodically entertaining their radio friends. In the United States the Navy objected that amateurs were interfering with their communications, and so Congress in 1912 passed a law requiring that all transmitters be licensed. (Since receivers caused no interference Congress could see no justification for requiring licences for them, under the assumption of freedom of speech; and so it has always been in the USA.) In Great Britain licences were required for both transmitters and receivers and until 1922 special permission had to be asked of the Post Office if a radio transmitter wished to send music or other material not directly related to transmission and reception. Indeed, permission had to be asked for each individual broadcast. The issue came to a head in 1920 when the Marconi Company's Chelmsford transmitter was (with permission) transmitting Lauritz Melchior, the opera singer, and it interfered with communication with an aeroplane lost in fog over the channel. The official view was that this was a 'frivolous' use of a 'national service'; it was a 'stunt', 'more propaganda than scientific', 'a toy to amuse children'. Licences for the Chelmsford broadcasts were suspended.

If that view had prevailed, radio would not have become broadcasting. It would have remained a technical means of transmission for high-value messages. But the pressure of demand for general entertainment overwhelmed those objections. In January 1922 the Postmaster General withdrew his veto in response to a petition from 3000 members of wireless societies. The same impetus that led people to try to develop the 'pleasure telephone' was at work in radio, and this time the economics were right.

If one could make a receiver cheaply enough, radio transmission (requiring no investment in wires and switches) was an ideal means for bringing news and entertainment to the home. The radio receiver itself turned out to be, in its simple forms, a relatively cheap device. There were, however, two problems. The first was the electricity required for higher-fidelity receiving sets. The second was how to charge someone for the costs of doing the broadcasting. The first of these problems was resolved when improvements in valves (vacuum tubes) made it possible to run a radio off the wall current instead of from large expensive batteries. The second was solved in different ways in different countries. The solutions tell us more about the social and political philosophies of the time than about the technology.

Radio, ideology and society

An old cliché contrasts democratic broadcasting which 'gives people what they want' with authoritarian broadcasting which 'gives people what is good for them'. In fact there are really three philosophies: that which gives people what they want, that which gives people what the broadcaster wants to produce, and that which gives people what the authorities think is good for them. Each of these three emerged in an almost prototypical form in different countries in the first two decades of broadcasting. In the USA commercial broadcasting sought to gain for the advertiser the largest possible audience by giving the audience whatever it wanted. In the UK, the Reithian BBC brought together a remarkable group of talented men and allowed them an almost unprecedented freedom to be creative according to their lights, unpressured either by politicians or by the audience. In the totalitarian systems in the USSR and Germany, broadcasting was used as an instrument of indoctrination to mobilize the public for what the authorities thought was good.

These three formulas were not adopted in each case in full awareness of what the alternatives were and what the result would be, but rather in an instinctive way that expressed the mood and spirit of each society.

Democratic commercial radio: the US model

No one thought at the start of broadcasting around 1920 that advertising could support the broadcasting system. The pioneers puzzled about how to arrange that producers of entertainment for the public should get paid: otherwise the system could not develop. Two main ideas are found among the early entrepreneurs, though what emerged was different from either. One idea was put forward first and most clearly by David Sarnoff in 1916 in a memo to his superiors at the Marconi Company, which they disregarded at the time. Sarnoff saw that radios could be used as a kind of music box as well as for transmission of messages. If these 'music boxes' were sold to the public there would be a large market for radio set manufacturers, but of course the public would not buy sets unless someone put on some programming. Sarnoff's idea was that the manufacturers would do this so as to sell sets. In 1926 RCA set up a broadcasting network subsidiary, NBC, to help supply the entertainment that the public would want. By that time, however, it was clear that advertising would pay much of the cost, though as late as 1922 Herbert Hoover's Washington Radio Conference 'agreed that it was against public interest to broadcast pure advertising matter.'

The alternative conception of how to market radio to the public was held by the American Telephone and Telegraph Company. AT & T saw radio as simply one more part of their business of electrical communication. As with the telephone system, they had no desire to get involved with programming; they saw themselves as a common carrier providing radio transmission to anyone with a message that he wanted to broadcast. AT & T proposed in January 1922 that the telephone company build a broadcasting station in each city and lease time on it to all comers. As an experiment in that concept, AT & T opened up station WEAF in New York; but no one came to buy time. With only a small number of sets in the hands of the public, and with no way of billing the customers in the audience, there was little incentive for independent producers to offer programmes. So to keep their station going WEAF had to start producing programmes themselves, just as RCA'S or Westinghouse's stations had.

Then one summer day in 1922 a real estate developer came to WEAF and asked to put on the air a plug for some vacant apartments that he had built. That was not quite the kind of use that AT & T wanted out front. They were already being attacked for having 'mercenary advertising purposes'. They wanted dramatic producers, musical companies, public affairs groups and similar users to rent air time. So they suggested to the realtor that he do what today we call a 'soft sell'. He would be allowed to give a speech on housing in which he could work in a plug for his development. In that back door way commercialism came to American broadcasting.

But even so, AT & T's conception of an entertainment common carrier was not going to work. The market was not ripe for it. So AT & T threw in the sponge. In 1926 AT & T and RCA signed a pact. AT & T would stay out of radio broadcasting; RCA would leave radio telephony to the telephone company and would use AT & T lines for networking.

The commercial system worked even better than the set manufacturers had anticipated. Driven by the dynamism of promotion and salesmanship in a competitive market, the number of sets in the USA grew extraordinarily. In 1917 there were about 125,000. By 1925 there were $5\frac{1}{2}$ million, nearly half the world's total. By 1950 there were about 72 million, or substantially more than one for every household. And as the audience grew the advertisers became increasingly interested. Broadcasting, supported by advertising, became not merely a loss leader to help sell sets, but a profitable operation in its own right. When that happened, money began to pour into programming. Instead of one or two people in the studio playing phonograph records and reading news and announcements, radio dramas began to be written and serialized. Whole orchestras were created by the newly formed networks, and the revenue became adequate to bid for personal appearances by movie stars or famous musicians.

What was broadcast in this system was loved by millions, but a horror in the eyes of élite intellectuals. True, every Saturday afternoon one could listen to the concerts of the Metropolitan Opera live and every Sunday afternoon one could listen to the Symphony. For America's intellectuals, these became almost religious rituals. But most of the music was tin pan alley. Radio drama was the soap opera. And of course the ads themselves offended sophisticates; but they did not offend the general public. As was later equally true of television, the ads were produced with a care and a level of dramatic quality that far exceeded what was in the programmes. The advertising agencies discovered the power of the singing commercial. The tunes were lively, the words were catchy. A couple of generations of Americans grew up whistling and humming these ditties to themselves, and enjoying them.

The best study of the reaction of the American public to the advertisements that interrupt their programmes is Raymond A. Bauer and Stephen A. Greyser's *Advertising in America: the consumer view*. It deals with television, but its well-researched findings were apparently true of radio too. The study finds that the public as a whole do not dislike the

ads. They find them informative and practically useful. They are aware that they make possible free delivery of entertainment that they want, and are grateful for it. Ads, however, like any other material, are seen as of varying quality. Some are identified as offensive. Most of all, however, the public are annoyed by what the industry calls clutter, i.e. a lot of ads packed into the programme time. The positive reaction of the public to ads is not just an American phenomenon. In Italy television ads have been put all together in a single half hour of solid advertising. That had the highest audience rating of any programme.

One byproduct of the dependence of American radio programming on advertisers was the development of social

science audience research as we know it today. The advertiser had to be persuaded that there was someone out there listening. There was no physical evidence of circulation, as with a magazine. Survey research, ratings, sampling theory, all got strong support from the audience studies sponsored by the broadcasters and advertisers. Much of what we know about communications in modern society came out of a burst of remarkable studies of radio in the 1930s.

Guided by the ratings, the broadcasters zeroed in on making the kinds of programmes that the public chose to listen to. But, just as with television today, it was not an economist's ideal market. To use the economist's jargon, the most serious departures from optimality arose from restrictions on entry. The shortage of frequencies and the problem of interference between broadcasters had made broadcasting from the beginning a regulated market. With a limited number of stations in any given community, they each tended to strive for the widest audience, and so to concentrate on the most popular material: popular music, soap operas, variety shows, and sport. Specialized stations existed in the United States, but not with the plenitude that makes the free market in print media such a prolific and diverse thing. There were religious stations, foreign language stations for immigrants, good music stations – particularly after the development of FM broadcasting opened up the airwaves to a large number of additional and static-free stations. There was even a station belonging to the American Federation of Labor in Chicago. But the mere mention of this as an oddity suggests how much less diverse the airwaves were than the printed media.

American broadcasting was regulated first under an Act of 1912, requiring all broadcasters to obtain a licence. Until 1927, however, the issuing of licences was a purely administrative act of the government intended to ensure that each broadcaster was on a different frequency; there was no basis for restriction on who should be broadcasting or the type of material they could broadcast.

In 1926 the 1912 law was ruled unconstitutional by the US Supreme Court because Congress had given the Secretary of Commerce no criteria for issuing or denying licences. The result of the decision was considerable chaos on the airwaves as broadcasters tried to get the best frequencies for themselves. Radio science in those days did not permit very fine separation of stations or good control of drift. The industry itself asked for regulation and Congress passed the Radio Act of 1927 which, in a 1934 rewrite as the Communications Act, remains American law today. That law did set a number of criteria for licensing broadcasters. One of the principles adopted was localism. The Federal Communi-

Franklin Roosevelt delivering a 'fireside chat'.

cations Commission has not issued licences for powerful stations that could reach the whole country; it has issued licences in an elaborate pattern that allows each city to have a number of stations. Cities soon came to be linked in national networks, but to earn licences in a competitive situation in which many more entrepreneurs were seeking licences than could receive them, the stations had to promise to do a certain amount of local programming. The FCC also tended to give licences to stations that would promise to do a rounded package of kinds of programmes including news, religion and public affairs, as well as just the enormously popular jazz and soap operas.

American radio, for all its commercialism, became in the 1930s a powerful political factor and source of information. KDKA started its broadcasting in 1920 in a great rush so as to be on the air in time to carry the national election returns of that year. By the 1932 presidential campaign radio had become an important factor, and Franklin Roosevelt's mellifluous voice and skill in the use of the medium was a major source of his political success. Unlike many of his contemporary politicians, he understood the difference between delivering a speech to a crowd of devoted partisans in an auditorium and talking to the general public in their living rooms. His 'fireside chats' gave him direct leverage on the moulding of public opinion. Other politicians, like the mayor of New York, Fiorello La Guardia, took the cue and developed a new, highly personal style; La Guardia during a newspaper strike read the comics that they would have missed to the children.

With World War II, and with the development of short-wave transmission technology in the 1930s, radio became one of the main sources of international information for the American public. Direct short-wave listening was never important in the USA, but the radio networks began delivering reports from their correspondents abroad live, and sometimes the sounds of the events themselves, like the ranting of a Hitler speech.

So by the time that television came to pre-empt the franchise on the airwaves around 1950 radio broadcasting was a large, mature, and diverse system with 2829 stations scattered across the country. A few main genres of popular entertainment filled the great bulk of the air time, but radio was also a major transmitter of culture and news.

Elevated radio: the British model

In discussing American broadcasting we did not even mention the option of public ownership, for it was an idea with very little constituency. At the end of World War I the US Navy proposed that, but Congress rejected it out of hand. There were some publicly owned broadcasting stations such as New York City's WNYC or a number of stations owned by state universities. These were no more inconsistent with the free enterprise system than was the Government's having printing plants. They were simply one minor element in the pluralism that the system was supposed to foster. In Europe the situation was totally different. Two converging though contradictory forces made it seem natural for broadcasting to be a Government function. These two forces were, on the one hand, the bureaucratic conservatism of the post offices and, on the other, the rise of social democracy.

The principle of the postal monopoly goes back to when the King issued letters patent to the operators of horse posts to handle official messages. To make the business more profitable and so to enable Government to have its letters carried free or at a low price he extended the monopoly to private mails too. Libertarian writers at the time demanded freedom to carry messages, just as they protested against government licensing of the press. One John Hill published a pamphlet in 1659 entitled 'A Penny Post: Or, a Vindication of the Liberty and Birthright of Every Englishman, in Carrying Merchants & other men's Letters, against any restraint of Farmers of such Employment'. But John Hill did not win; the patentees kept their monopoly. Indeed, two-and-a-half centuries later Marconi ran into the same kind of problem with the cable monopolists. When he proudly announced transmission of a radio signal from Cornwall to Newfoundland, a sharp letter arrived from the solicitors of the Anglo-American Telegraph Company, noting that they had a monopoly of telecommunications in Newfoundland; legal action, they warned, would follow further infringement.

Alexander Graham Bell (whose invention ironically is, in most places, now a postal monopoly) was infuriated at this action and offered Marconi the use of some land that he owned at Cape Breton, Nova Scotia. While early postal monopolies were conveyed to entrepreneurs by patents, the growth of State bureaucracies in the 19th and 20th centuries led to the Post Offices' becoming Government departments. By the 1920s in Europe they had absorbed the telephone and telegraph along with the mails. In Great Britain the telegraph was nationalized in 1869 and the telephone in 1912.

Post Office resistance to the idea of anyone else transmitting messages was bolstered by the idealistic notions of the socialists. Ironic as it may seem today, in the early years of the century socialists often used the Post Office as evidence that a public monopoly could be as efficient as a private enterprise or more so.

It so happened that the date when radio broadcasting arrived on the world scene more or less coincided with a high point of socialist advocacy of nationalization. With the end of the War the Labour Party in Britain had displaced the Liberals as a major party. In Germany the Social Democrats were the leading party. The Russian Revolution had flanked them with Communists on the Left and seemed to prove that private enterprise could be abolished and a socialized economy

The first *Radio Times*, published by the BBC's commercial predecessor, the British Broadcasting Company, in September 1923.

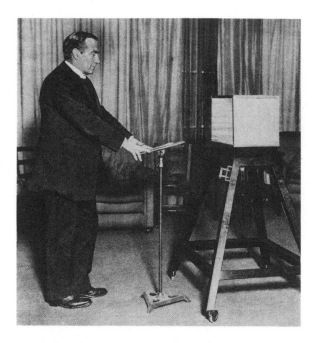

'Elevated' radio: an election address from Conservative leader Stanley Baldwin, 1924, and a song recital, 1922, from the studios of the British Broadcasting Company.

could work. In the centre of the political spectrum moderates too were caught up in the ideology of mixed economy and planning. The success of large corporate organizations both provided a model of how central planning could displace market forces and at the same time was a target for regulatory action. And socialism too, which in its early-19th-century versions tended to idealize co-operative communities, had been caught up in the *étatisme* and gigantism of the 20th century. In every political debate people were calling for the nationalization of one industry or another, as too important to be left to the supposedly anarchic operations of private enterprise. In the New York Public Library, under the subject heading 'telephone', there are more pamphlets and tracts for and against nationalization than about any other subtopic, and these are virtually all from before World War II.

In that atmosphere, the idea of turning over valuable resources of radio spectrum and the broadcasting system itself to private enterprise impressed many as socially irresponsible. Society was considering reversing a century or two of private operation of major industries; to allow a new and culturally significant industry to fall under that questioned sway would have aroused enormous opposition.

But the ideological atmosphere of the day was at most a supporting factor. In Europe the influence of the postal and telegraph monopolies was probably decisive. The legal authority of the British Post Office derived from the Telegraph Act of 1869 (which gave it the monopoly in telegraphy) and the Wireless Telegraphy Act of 1904 (which extended its control to radio). The philosophy of its high civil servants attached little significance to recreational use of limited frequencies, and certainly saw little benefit coming from a *laissez-faire* process of pluralistic private decisions about use.

It was the rapid growth of broadcasting in America that forced the Post Office's hand. It might not have decided to use radio for entertainment broadcasting at all. With the American experience in front of the public, the Post Office could no longer refuse what was so clearly attractive. But the disorder, the competition, the lack of planning, the commercialism and the radio interference in the American system filled the orderly minds of civil servants with horror. So, while the American example was of decisive influence, it was also a cause of alarm. It was frequently cited as a lesson of what to avoid.

The Postmaster General, then, concluding that 'it would be impossible to have a large number of firms broadcasting,' compelled the various radio manufacturing companies which sought to broadcast to join together in 1922 to form a single broadcasting organization, the British Broadcasting Company. That was not the BBC as we know it today. It was a privately owned commercial company. Out of that, in 1927, the BBC was formed as an independent public corporation. It would be easy to exaggerate that change. In both incarnations the BBC was headed by J. C. W. Reith, and inside the organization the transition was hardly perceptible.

The change, however, highlights some ideological issues about the BBC. In Parliament and among the public there had been concern about the monopoly position of the private company. That and other issues led the Postmaster General to appoint the first of many investigatory commissions, the Sykes Committee, in 1923. It started a process that led three years later to the forming of a public corporation. Broadcasting, it concluded, was too powerful a force to remain in private hands. 'The control of such a potential power over public opinion and the life of the nation ought to remain with the State.' But the Sykes Committee worried about full subordination of broadcasting to the Post Office, and recommended an independent board. Among the witnesses, only Herbert Morrison, speaking on behalf of the London Labour Party, spoke for full State ownership and control. From his Labour point of view, an independent body, whether profit-making or otherwise, was an élitist institution, shielded from democratic political control.

For those like Reith and his associates who sought the status of an independent institution, the critical question was how to finance it. There was general agreement that no advertising should be allowed. The solution was to give broadcasting a share of the licence fee; that source of revenue is now used in many countries as a protection, not only against commercialism, but also against dependence on the whims of the Treasury or other funding authorities. In periods of inflation a fixed licence fee has proved to be a poor support for broadcasters, but in the early years of British broadcasting it was an adequate basis for growth that was healthy, though less rapid than in the USA. The UK started with 400 licensed receivers in 1921. By 1926 there were a million and a half.

The quality of the BBC won world recognition. Its staff were an élite from the universities. To become a broadcaster was something an intellectual aspired to, not a matter for apology as in the USA. The BBC was their organization, not merely an employer. The programming reflected this. The élite, class-conscious BBC accent became a cultural norm as well as a condition for employment. Probably no other broadcasting system in the world had as much good drama, as much good music, and as much good serious talk as the BBC, at least from the time of the Third Programme.

Oddly, though, the weakest part of the BBC programming was news. The newspapers sought to prevent radio from becoming a competitor. Until an internal revolution, about 1938, the radio news was nothing but a reading of bulletins that had already appeared in the papers. In the 1920s the rule that the wire services and the press imposed was that there should be no more than a 1200- to 2400-word bulletin, written by the wire services, and not to be read before 7.00 p.m., by which time the papers had taken full advantage of the day's events. The BBC was not allowed to do any of its own news collection. Newspaper pressure was the primary restraint, but one may also wonder whether a monopoly élite medium would ever have become an aggressive investigatory medium.

The very detachment that was a disadvantage for journalistic enterprise was, however, the key to the success of the BBC as a news medium in another arena, namely international broadcasting. In credibility, among world broadcasters the BBC has no peer. During the darkest days of World War II it told the story as it was, and millions of people on both sides of the lines came to depend on it. There was a curious replay of this pattern during the war in Vietnam. Americans interrogating captured Vietcong officers found that their preferred news source was the BBC. They would not trust the Voice of America, and they knew they could not trust their own broadcasts. The BBC could be believed.

So some audiences were served very well by the BBC: those who wanted unvarnished news bulletins, those who liked good music and good drama, those who wanted to hear informed talks and discussions. But there were other tastes that were less well served. And also not served were advertisers with products to sell. Since radio waves are no respecters of frontiers, those who were dissatisfied with the BBC turned to foreign broadcasts, particularly Radio Luxembourg, and in the postwar years to some pirate stations at sea. In the early 1930s the BBC, the Foreign Office, and the International Telecommunication Union all brought pressure on Luxembourg to cease commercial broadcasting to foreign countries in their own languages. With righteous indignation they protested at the 'forcing of advertising programmes into Great Britain'. But, of course, the advertisers who made the programmes possible were British firms, and the reason they did it was that the British public listened. A survey in 1935 showed that half the British audience tuned to Radio Luxembourg on Sundays when the BBC as a matter of policy ran a very restricted programme. On weekdays the Luxembourg rating was 11 per cent.

Eventually the pirate stations on the high seas were put out of business by force, but international commercial broadcasting remains, and so does its audience. And today, indeed, domestic pirate radios are springing up in many countries. In

Italy they are there by the hundreds, and are now legal. In France they are beginning to show up too. The technology of radio broadcasting makes it possible to sustain a vastly increased number of stations on the air and so makes it harder to justify denying to the public programming of kinds that it likes, whether the broadcasting authorities approve or not. Indeed, the British model from 'the golden age of radio', when channels were few and nationalized, gave way in the 1970s. Local commercial stations were allowed and came to play an increasing role, though national broadcasting is still exclusively the BBC's domain.

Propaganda radio: the totalitarian model

'Genuine sincere radio,' said the 1939–40 *Handbook of German Radio*, 'is simply propaganda. . . . It means fighting on the battlefields of the mind ... to destroy, to weed out and annihilate, to build and to abolish.' Radio played a key role in Nazi propaganda doctrine. In that day, like satellite communication or computers today, radio had the mystique of the newest technology. Just as, today, worried people fear these new devices as having some mind-controlling impact far greater than the old fashioned media, so people then thought of radio as a key to the control of society. That image of power and dominance was, of course, just what the Nazis wanted.

Secondly, the Nazis saw in radio a means of addressing the whole nation at once and of forming a unified national will. 'Well prepared political broadcasts can produce such a strong mental current that a community, a people and even groups of peoples may be induced to common action.' A medium through which every citizen could be made to listen to the same demonstration on the same afternoon was for them an ideal means of national mobilization.

Third, and most important, radio permitted a personal link to the charismatic leader. People listened to the voice of the Führer himself instead of reading a journalist's report. It permitted 'direct talk by the Leader to every single member of the Nation.' Hitler would address a screaming mob of thousands, while the whole nation listened in by radio. Both personal leadership and the spoken word were thought, in the Nazi theory of propaganda, to be far more effective for reaching the masses than cool written tracts.

In radio as in so many other areas, the Nazis copied in caricature their arch rivals, the communists. They believed they were turning the Devil's tools against the Devil. The Soviet Union had launched a massive programme of international broadcasting, and the communists in Germany had organized an extensive and powerful network of listening groups for it. The fact that the communists believed in the power of international radio propaganda helped persuade the Nazis that it was vital.

From its inception the USSR gave high priority to broadcasting. In 1918 they established a radio laboratory. Lenin wrote to the laboratory director 'The newspaper without paper and "without boundaries" you are devising will be a brilliant achievement.' By 1922 they had begun regular broadcasting.

But in the years immediately after the Revolution, Russia was a very poor country indeed. Radios were expensive items in that pre-transistor era. So the Soviets devised means for extending the reach of listening cheaply. One way was collective listening. Radios were placed in clubs, and played at work in factories. Another means was wired radio. Many loudspeakers could be attached to a single receiver. That way a residence need only have one simple piece of equipment, the loudspeaker, not the tuner, amplifier, batteries and tubes which receivers required. Today we are familiar with this system as used in China: their scheme was borrowed initially from the Soviet Union. In the USSR the number of actual radio sets came to exceed the number of wired loudspeakers only in 1964, at which time the total of both together was approaching 70 million sets, or about one per household.

Wired loudspeakers had another advantage besides cheapness. There could be complete control of what was heard. Stalin's Russia had a paranoid concern that people should not be exposed to any deviation from the correct line. Linotypers for the printed press were sent to Siberia for minor printer's errors, since a politically meaningful 'typo' might be passed off as a mistake. On the radio, no news was broadcast until after *Pravda* had carried it, to make sure that broadcasters followed the correct line. In the case of major events that broke at the wrong time of day, there might be a 36-hour delay in mentioning them. And, of course, what was said was highly stereotyped. So while radio was treated as a matter of great importance, it was in fact dull.

On Stalin's death a measure of change ensued. A channel of light music and news was added to the standard two channels with their heavy mix of serious material, music, news and propaganda. In 1960 the broadcasters were instructed no longer to wait for *Pravda* before giving spot news. They still, of course, had to be guided by the Party in analysis, but radio was given the task of carrying an immediate flash on current events.

These changes were in part a competitive response to the growing impact of short-wave broadcasting from abroad. It is hard for people who live in societies where information flows freely to realize how important short-wave listening can be in a society where the domestic media provide no alternative views. No one knows, of course, with any exactness how large the audience for short-wave broadcasts is. (Listening is not illegal, but is discouraged, and repetition of malicious reports is illegal.) But the best evidence, based on years of careful research by various international broadcasters, is that the majority of Soviet households have short-wave sets and the audience on a given evening may be as much as one-sixth of the adult population. Today only a few foreign stations are jammed, most notably Radio Liberty and Radio Peking. The rest are jammed only when they become politically aggressive, which they rarely do.

The reader may wonder why there are so many short-wave sets in the USSR. Partly it reflects the preference of the population; people are reluctant to buy sets without the short-wave band. Partly, however, it is because of the vast distances within the Soviet Union. For Moscow broadcasts to reach Siberia, the Soviet regime has used fairly high frequencies, and so sets are built with that capacity. In the days when most of the population was listening to wired loudspeakers, the Government did not have to worry much about the reception capability of the radio itself. Those days are past, however.

Increasingly Soviet broadcasting has to compete with other voices; to do so it must concern itself with audience appeal. It is ironical that a broadcasting system that in its origin was seen as an instrument of mobilization became, because of its protected monopoly, rather dull and ineffectual; but as it once more faces competition, it becomes more of a normal entertaining radio system, while striving to recapture its propaganda effectiveness.

The social effects of radio

From the days of Socrates on, people have worried that the media of information were bringing change and corruption. In the rich countries today no one asks what effect radio is having; television bears the burden of the attack. But in the 1930s the effects of radio were a matter of much concern. There was, for example, a complex revolution going on in the public's appreciation of music. The number of people who enjoyed classical music grew rapidly as radios and phonograph gave millions a chance for daily listening to what before they could hear only on rare occasions. But if the taste for classical music was growing, that for popular music was exploding. Jazz, crooning, rock, in their myriad forms came, went and changed with unprecedented speed. Songs hit the hit parade for a moment and then disappeared. Styles passed almost as fast, but left residues in a whole new art form.

While that is perhaps the most obvious outcome of records (and now tapes) and radio, some more subtle effects were also explored by social scientists, who, as we noted before, got a

'Propaganda' radio: assembling loudspeakers in a Moscow factory in 1931 (*top*) and *Design for a loudspeaker for Lenin* (1917) by the Russian Constructivist Gustav Klutsis.

major boost from the broadcasters' need for audience research. For example, in 1940 Paul Lazarsfeld, the Director of the Office of Radio Research (later the Bureau of Applied Social Science Research) at Columbia University, published a book, *Radio and the Printed Page*. A question that bedevilled newspapers at the time was whether radio would destroy them. Publishers worried, as we have seen that they did in England, that if people heard the news on the air they would not buy newspapers. In many places publishers at first refused to print radio schedules, though finally they found they gained by doing so. Even regarding news itself, one could argue that broadcasts stimulated interests that led people to buy newspapers more. Which way was it?

That, in essence, was the question that Lazarsfeld set out to answer. It applied not just to newspapers. Librarians, too, worried about what radio would do to reading habits. Would serious material on radio create a taste, as it did for serious music and sports, or would it satisfy a taste, thus reducing the audience for books?

The answer from the research was both disturbing and reassuring. Radio, it seemed, had far less direct effect than either the panic-mongers or the educators believed. People used radio according to their own cultural level. The ones who listened to serious programmes were the ones already interested in that content. Radio was not a school for the uneducated. For those who were already predisposed, it could serve to draw their attention to the matters it covered. So the publishers could be reassured. Those listeners who were satisfied with just the short radio bulletins were the ones who did not read news in newspapers anyhow. Those already interested in news would listen to the news programmes and then also read the newspaper for further explanation. The survey, in short, found an 'interaction'. There were those who were already news addicts and radio might draw them to the printed page more. There were those who did not care and read little anyhow; radio might make them read less.

Indeed, as we look back over forty years, what Lazarsfeld told the publishers seems obvious. We now know that radio did not kill the newspaper. It changed it somewhat. The extras that newsboys used to hawk shouting the latest breaking news have long since been forgotten. No print medium can outpace what comes over the airwaves. So papers have turned to more interpretation, but they have not declined. Radio and the printed page have each found a niche – as the existence of this book testifies. But in the 1930s the publishers were not sure of the future; they looked at broadcasting with alarm.

The point is not that radio had· little impact. On the contrary it had much. Some obvious effects are easy to catalogue. Radio brought entertainment from the theatre to the home. It promoted a youth culture and a star system. It made political campaigns more personal. It reduced dialects and brought a standardization of national languages. Some interesting questions concern less obvious matters like the effect on print, or what people took away from the programmes that they listened to.

Among the most interesting findings of radio research is that on the appeal of soap opera. This is a universal phenomenon. In almost all countries the serial family dramas are among the most popular programmes, now on television, but once on radio. Propaganda-oriented broadcasters, such as those of Eastern Europe, have used such programmes (often the most popular in their country) to inject low keyed instruction. They are not a good medium for blatant ideology, but they teach easily about such ordinary rules of life as 'do not hoard' or 'line up in queues'. Indeed, that kind of preachment is found not just in preceptorial broadcasting systems. In the USA a constant theme in soap operas has been against racial prejudice.

So radio serial drama has had an improving purpose. The puzzling question is why the audience put up with that. One might have assumed that viewers of such banal, cliché-ridden material sought only light entertainment; but that is not so. In a 1944 study on daytime serial listeners Herta Herzog found that a 'commonly unsuspected form of gratification concerns the advice obtained from listening to daytime serials.' 'The stories are liked because they "explain things" to the inarticulate listener.' Women who listened felt they were learning how to handle their husbands or boyfriends or bring up their children.

Here is what some said:

I am fighting old age, and having a terrible time. Sometimes I am tempted to go out and fix my hair. These stories give me courage and help me realize I have to accept it.

Husbands do not really understand what a wife goes through. These stories have helped me to understand that husbands are like that.

Most mothers slap their children. She deprives them of something. That is better. I use what she does with my children.

I learn a lot from these stories. I often figure if anything like that happened to me what would I do. Who knows if I met a crippled man, would I marry him? If he had money I would. In this story he was a lawyer so it was really quite nice. These stories teach you how things come out all right.

VIII
EXTENDED IMAGES

Garth S. Jowett

EXTENDED IMAGES

One of the earliest deliberate uses of symbolic imagery was to denote personal property. Long before the development of writing, the Sumerians had developed a system of indicating formal ownership of various items by marks pressed into clay with personal seals. These were usually small, soft stone cylinders carved with scenes of religious practices, or other symbolic representations of particular significance to the owner. The need for a permanent form of personal identification, for both trade and ownership purposes, was accentuated by the growth of population centres in the period after 4000 BC. Once the previously nomadic tribes began to congregate into communities and cities took shape, the complex social interactions which resulted required a means of dealing with conflicting claims and recording agreements. No longer was the human memory totally acceptable, and so a more permanent method was developed, at first with simple seals, and eventually with the development of the earliest forms of writing.

With the development of alphabetic writing, and the demise of cuneiform and other types of early writing which required making marks on wet clay, the cylinder seal gave way to the stamp seal which was better suited to the harder surfaces of the papyrus and leather manuscripts. The stamp signature seal as a mark of personal identification and authentication almost died out after the decline of the Roman Empire in the West, but was revived by the Carolingians under Pippin. Eventually, all monarchs, important officials, bishops and other dignitaries, as well as private individuals of some significance, required their own identification seals.

The seal as the visible embodiment of the governing power gradually gained importance and was adopted throughout the civilized world. Each nation has developed its own seal as a symbol of its authority and sometimes, as in the case of the United States, its founding philosophy. The Seal of the United States, after considerable discussion between 1776

and 1782, was eventually adopted by Congress with a design showing 'the American eagle displayed proper, holding in his dexter talon an olive branch, and in his sinister a bundle of thirteen arrows, all proper, and in his beak a scroll, inscribed with the motto "E Pluribus Unum".' This symbol has subsequently become a major icon of American culture, and no doubt has significant but different meanings for those around the world who recognize it.

In 44 BC Julius Caesar was granted the right to have his portrait on Roman coins, an unprecedented step for it was the first occasion that this privilege had been granted to a living Roman. It indicates a conscious decision to symbolize the might of Roman imperialism to the furthest reaches of a structure that was already becoming unwieldy.

In origin coins were much more mundane. There had always been some form of barter in trade negotiations, and cattle, axes, cauldrons and precious objects had been used as items of exchange long before the development of coinage in the ancient Orient, Greece and Rome. The use of metal bars (valued according to their weight) was common in the ancient world, while gold and other precious metals were often used as currency in the form of rings. Once gold and silver were accepted as more convenient equivalents to base metals, the first stage of true coinage was reached.

The first coins which we would recognize as such were developed soon after 650 BC in Lydia, in Asia Minor, whose King Gyges issued regular, bean-shaped pieces of metal, stamped with a lion design, which guaranteed their weight and therefore their intrinsic value. They were made of electrum, an alloy of gold and silver which was found in a natural state in Lydia. The practice of using coinage very quickly spread to the Ionian cities, and then to the other states of Corinth, Athens and Megara. Attributable in origin mainly to commercial convenience, coinage quickly became a means to satisfy civic and political pride. It was also the first

Reproduced images from the dawn of history: a Mesopotamian cylinder seal from the mid-3rd millennium BC and an impression from it.

form of the reproduced image to receive wide circulation and recognition.

The images on Greek coins were usually simple, and often taken from the animal world, like the owl of Athens, the eagle of Zeus, or the bee of Ephesus. Sometimes the staple product of a city was proclaimed, such as silphium at Cyrene; often the coin depicted cults associated with the region, like the Minotaur of Knossos. Human or anthropomorphic figures were comparatively rare on early Greek coins, the idealized heads of deities being much more common. The famous tetradrachms of Athens had the head of Athena on one side and the owl on the other.

With the economic expansion of Athens in the 4th and 5th centuries BC, the Athenian coinage became the dominant form of currency in the Greek world. The symbolic importance attached to it can be seen from the edicts prohibiting the striking of silver coins by Athenian allies, and providing that previously minted currencies should be handed in for exchange for the currency of Athens.

It was with Alexander the Great that coinage became a symbol of regal power. But only after his death did his deified portrait appear on coins in the widespread empire he had established, and it was not until 306 BC that Ptolemy I of Egypt became the first king to put his own portrait on coins.

The use of coins as an integral part of imperial Roman policy was marked by Julius Caesar's use of his own portrait; following this precedent the imperial portrait was an essential element of every gold, silver and bronze coin of the official mints, and nearly all provincial coinage. The image of the stylized portrait of the emperor (or sometimes his wife or sons) emphasized his personality, and was an important symbol of power in Roman life, as these images were distributed widely throughout the Empire. After the decline of Roman power in the West, the gold currency of Christian Byzantium took the lead in European coinage for almost 1000 years.

With the Renaissance naturalism was introduced into coin portraiture, together with a greater use of ornamentation. This new artistic expression was greatly aided by more mechanized means of coin production, and religious symbolism gave way to civic or feudal emblems. The practice of placing a portrait (or other symbol) on the obverse, with a national badge or coat of arms on the reverse, became generally established from the 16th century onwards.

The printed illustration

With the appearance of the first printed books in the West in the middle of the 15th century, the illustration gained new importance as a means of conveying information and as a vehicle for powerful archetypal images. In the period before the development of printing with movable type, hand-written manuscripts were often elaborately illustrated, but this was a costly and time-consuming process. Illustrated manuscripts were usually confined to a few privileged members of society, though a few hand-copied manuscripts without elaborate illustrations were available at low prices (Plato says that in his time a copy of Anaxogoras could be bought for a drachma – about twelve pence or twenty-five cents).

The Greeks and the Romans were impeded in the development of their scientific thought by being unable to reproduce illustrations of their discoveries so as to permit further discourse. Greek botanists, for example, realized that visual statements were needed to make their verbal statements intelligible, and they tried to develop pictures for this purpose. But distortion at the hands of successive copyists meant that the pictures actually obscured the meaning of the verbal statements, and the legacy of Greek botany was little more than lists of plant names.

The earliest technique for reproducing illustrations was the woodcut, a relief process in which the white areas were cut away leaving the image to be inked and printed. Woodcuts and paper were being used for 'printing' in the Orient in the 6th century AD. In Europe the woodblock was first used for stamping designs on textiles at about the same time. Its use for printing illustrations had to await the manufacture of paper in France and Germany at the end of the 14th century (though paper had been introduced into Spain from the Orient in the 12th century). The earliest credible date found on a woodcut is 1423, on the Buxheim St Christopher, now in the John Rylands Library in Manchester. This simple cut, though lacking shading or perspective, has the same strength and directness as the figures in medieval stained glass.

The new process made possible the production of enormous quantities of the iconography of religious faith, hitherto available only in churches, for individual purchase. These vivid depictions of religious scenes, usually the lives of the saints, were portable and widely circulated. The early woodcut prints were also very popular as talismans for pilgrims wishing to carry a symbol of their faith about them. Woodcuts were also used for 'sheet dice' – playing cards.

Eventually some text was added to this increasing number of pictures, in the woodblock printing of posters, commercial prospectuses and calendars, where the text became more important than the illustrations. The first books, known as block books, were made by sewing together woodblock-printed sheets combining pictures and some text. These too were primarily devotional in character.

The development and use of printing with movable type eventually caused the demise of the block book, but not of the technique of printing woodcuts. Many of the earliest illustrations in printed books had known previous lives as separate prints. The earliest book printed from type to contain woodcuts is the *Edelstein* of Ulrich Boner, printed at Bamberg in 1461. It is quite clear that most of these first book-illustrations were intended to provide only the emotional enjoyment or feeling of piety which comes from a visual representation of an object of veneration. The idea of illustrations specifically to convey information, or as a direct explication of the text, was a later development, picking up from the point where the Greek botanists had left off.

In 1467, two German printers in Rome, Sweynheym and Pannartz, published an illustrated version of Cardinal Torquemada's *Meditations on the Passion of Our Lord*, which contained pictures representing decorations used by the Cardinal in his titular church of Santa Maria sopra Minerva. This was an important step, in that these woodcut illustrations purportedly represented real objects, and not mere decorative abstractions. Five years later an edition of Valturius's *Art of War* was published in Verona, containing many detailed illustrations of the machines of war and their uses. 'This was not edification at all, and neither was it mere decoration. It was the deliberate communication of information and ideas.' (William Ivins, *Prints and Visual Communication*.)

The use of printed illustrations specifically for informational purposes gradually increased as authors became aware of the possibilities of the visual mode. The author of an important German herbal, *Gart der Gesundheit*, published in 1485 complete with superb and accurate illustrations, went to some pains to point out to his readers that he had taken a painter with him to seek out at first hand those plants he was writing about. This is the first illustrated account of a scientific expedition. In the late 15th century several important illustrated books appeared, such as Sacrobosco's *Sphaera Mundi*, with its illustrations of astronomical phenomena, in 1485; Breydenbach's *Peregrinationes* in 1486, the first illustrated book of travel to come from a press; and the famous *Nuremberg Chronicle* in 1493, which contained more than 1800 illustrations. If many of these early illustrations seem crude to our eyes, we should consider them in their historical context, the products of an age before the discovery of perspective. It was only in 1504 that Pelerin published his book *Perspective*, the first printed book on that subject.

By the 16th century the woodcut had received recognition as an independent art form, most notably in the work of Albrecht Dürer. But the woodcut was also quickly recognized as a means of reaching a wider audience than ever before for messages of a political or religious nature. By 1500 there were an estimated nine million books in Europe, compared to about one hundred thousand hand-written manuscripts some fifty years before. No invention had ever done more to revolutionize intellectual life and society, and the consequences in the great schism of Europe do not need to be emphasized.

From the last half of the 16th century engraving on metal became the principal means of providing printed illustrations. Engraving is an intaglio process, where engraved lines hold the ink and the surface of the plate is wiped clean. The impression is made on dampened paper under pressure.

While the woodcut had been responsible for a major increase in the quantity and quality of pictorial information, it had limitations as a technique. The nature of the inking process, which involved pounding the blocks and type with large leather balls charged with ink, made quality work very slow and expensive; and with the paper available finely detailed work was not possible. The technique of engraving allowed the reproduction of very fine line work on relatively rough paper. While engraved plates were more expensive to produce and use than woodblocks, the increase in the quality of the reproductions obtained was sufficient to offset the added cost. What is important about engraving is that once it was established as an art, a series of special techniques emerged which eventually became rigid visual codes. Different schools of engravers in Germany, Italy and France perfected their own methods of conveying the texture or shading of an object, and generations of disciples followed their conventionalized swirls, cross-hatchings and fine lines.

The virtuosity of the engraver's art: Claude Mellan's engraving of the face of Christ in a continuous spiral line, dated 1649.

Essentially, therefore, engravers were making their own visual statements about the object to be reproduced, rather than attempting a faithful reproduction. To quote William Ivins again, 'The most particular personal characteristics of the original works of art, their brush strokes and chisel marks, were thus omitted, and what was transmitted in the print was little more than an indication of iconography combined with generalized shapes and masses.' The concern for the correct engraving technique became as important as the desire for accuracy in the reproduction. Nowhere is this better illustrated than in the famous engraving of the image of Christ (1649) by the French artist-engraver Claude Mellan, which was created by a single spiralling line that thickens and diminishes to form the image.

The technique of etching was also widely used as a means of reproduction from the 16th century onwards. Here, the lines that hold the ink are etched with acid through scratches in a protective wax coating. Etchings bear the mark of the artist in a way that engravings do not. It was in the Netherlands, particularly in the 17th century, that artists such as Van Dyck and Rembrandt brought the technique of etching to its greatest period of creative expression. At the end of the 18th century and again at the end of the 19th century Goya and Whistler brought the art to new heights.

In the 19th century the printed picture, in its myriad forms, established itself as a major feature of the emerging industrial society. Given enormous impetus by the development of photography and the new high-speed printing techniques, the reproduced image became a commonplace item in the lives of all members of that society. No longer was the visual stimulus of pictures reserved for those who specifically purchased them; imagery now proliferated in cheap daily newspapers, in the increasing amount of advertising aimed at the middle and working classes, and in books and periodicals, many of which were specifically designed to make maximum use of these new techniques.

Up until the advent of the half-tone process for reproducing photographs in the 1880s, the wood-engraving was the pre-eminent form of image dissemination in the 19th century. This was an innovation in the ancient art of the woodcut. At the end of the 18th century the English engraver Thomas Bewick perfected a new technique of engraving across the grain of a woodblock, using an engraver's burin instead of a knife, which left in the printing a white line against a black background. This technique, which enabled images to be reproduced in great quantities, soon became the most popular medium for book and magazine illustration.

This new, fairly inexpensive method was the favoured medium in large-circulation periodicals, and nowhere was the wood-engraving used to better effect than in the United States. From about 20 professional wood-engravers in the United States in 1838, their numbers increased to over 400 by the 1870s, and illustrated magazines such as *Frank Leslie's Illustrated Newspaper*, *Harper's Weekly* and *The Family Magazine*, and a great variety of illustrated books, soon became the backbone of American popular culture. In Britain and France a similar move toward illustrated periodical material for popular consumption took place.

Lithography was invented by Aloys Senefelder of Munich in 1798. After several years of looking for an inexpensive method of printing plays and sheet music, Senefelder discovered a process which made use of the fact that grease and water do not mix. Many gradual refinements made lithography one of the most important modern printing processes. The object to be printed was drawn directly on a specially prepared stone in a greasy ink, and after fixing and etching treatments the stone was wetted and inked for printing with a grease-based printing ink. Because there is little interference between what the artist draws and the final printed image, lithography was widely used for the reproduction of visual material, and spawned the development of an entire industry devoted to the reproduction and sale of popular prints to the general public. In the United States the best known of these are the productions of the firm of Currier and Ives, founded in 1857, whose hand-tinted prints of city and pastoral scenes soon became important popular icons for the American middle class.

The wood-engraving as the medium of popular illustration in the early industrial age: mastheads of two of the publications which took advantage of this technology, the American *Frank Leslie's Illustrated Newspaper* and the *Illustrirte Zeitung*, published in Leipzig.

Coupled with the increase in the speed of printing brought about by the introduction of the steam press in the early 19th century, the new techniques of reproduction effected a revolution in the production and dissemination of pictorial information. Charles Knight's *Penny Magazine*, launched in Britain in April 1832, exemplifies the new importance of the illustration as a means of enticing the illiterate to learn to read. Its copious wood-engravings helped attract a public unaccustomed to reading. At one point in the first three years of its publication, the *Penny Magazine* had a circulation in excess of 200,000. Publications such as this, and others like *Chambers's Journal* (1832), created an entirely new reading public, and provided a quality of reading material not previously available to the artisan and shopkeeper class.

In time the increasing use of illustrations, from the crudest depictions of violent crime to the most detailed rendition of mechanical drawings, taught the reading public (and even those who could not read) to expect illustrative accompaniment to their reading material. The illustration was becoming an essential part of the written narrative, particularly in newspapers and magazines, and, in turn, the standardized visual codes used by the illustrators began to create a form of visual cultural stereotyping. Thus society was able to see itself through the eyes of the illustrators. Did the image reflect or mould society? We may not be able to answer this question definitively, but undoubtedly the proliferation of standardized images did much to shape the culture in which we live today, for it was in this manner that most of our concepts about how the world 'looks' were created.

Photography and the printed photograph

Photography and the various photo-mechanical printing processes associated with it must be considered among the greatest achievements of the 19th century, and they rank with the introduction of the movable-type printing press in the history of human communication. As with so many other major innovations, photography was not the discovery of one man, but the end result of hundreds of years of attempts to capture the image by using a combination of optical, mechanical and chemical means. The realization that silver salts were blackened by light was first made in 1727 by the German physicist Johann Heinrich Schulze. 'By the end of the 17th century the camera was absolutely ready and waiting for photography', according to Helmut and Alison Gernsheim in their monumental *History of Photography*. By this time the *camera obscura*, first described in the 10th century and in its simplest form a contrivance for projecting an image of the scene outside onto a screen within a darkened chamber

through a hole in one of its walls, had undergone all the refinements in terms of portability and the incorporation of mirrors and lenses as optical devices that were to be applied to it before the advent of photography. In the 18th century it enjoyed wide popularity as an aid to artists, amateur and professional, and as an amusement.

The three major pioneers of photography all invoked the hope of using light-sensitive chemicals and the sun's rays to spare them the effort of drawing. The French amateur inventor Joseph-Nicéphore Niépce, experimenting with the newfangled art of lithography, devised a variety of light-sensitive varnishes to enable him to transfer the images of engravings onto the lithographic stone or plate without having to copy them by hand. Niépce's countryman Louis Daguerre was the founder in 1822 of the Diorama, an auditorium in Paris where spectacular painted scenery and special lighting effects created extraordinary illusions. He employed the *camera obscura* in the creation of his scenery, and his interest turned to the idea of arresting the evanescent image on the screen. In England William Henry Fox Talbot, a scientist, mathematician and linguist, was initially inspired to study the problems of photography by his lack of success in drawing landscapes on travels abroad. After 'various fruitless attempts' Talbot remembered the *camera obscura*, and his vision of photography came to him. In his book *The Pencil of Nature* (1844) he recalled that moment: 'It was during these thoughts that the idea occurred to me – how charming it would be if it were possible to cause these natural images to imprint themselves durably, and remain fixed upon the paper.'

Niépce produced the first photograph ever taken in 1826, using a type of light-sensitive asphalt solution requiring exposures of several hours. Niépce's pioneering efforts caught the attention of Daguerre, who was then also beginning to work along similar lines. In 1829 a partnership was effected between the two men which lasted until Niépce's death in 1833. The daguerrotype process which resulted from this joint experimentation consisted of burnishing and buffing a silvered copper plate to a high polish, and then sensitizing it with iodine vapour before exposure in a camera. The exposed plate was developed by placing it over a container of heated mercury, and the image was then permanently 'fixed' by washing it with a solution of sodium thiosulphate.

The daguerrotype process flourished in the period between 1840 and 1851, but it had several severe limitations. The apparatus was bulky, a lengthy exposure time was required, and the resulting prints were extremely fragile and had to be kept under glass. The pictures could be difficult to look at because of the metallic glare, and the cost was quite high for quality prints. But the major disadvantage was that the pictures could not be duplicated. Of course many engravings and lithographs were made from daguerrotype prints, but this was a painstaking and expensive process, and the result was similar to other engraving processes.

It was the work of Fox Talbot which led more directly to the development of photography as we know it today. By 1835 he had worked out a method of sensitizing paper with silver chloride; however, he put his experiments aside to concentrate on work in a wide variety of other scientific areas such as optics, mathematics and botany. Early in 1839, when Daguerre's process was being made known in Paris, Talbot frantically revived his work to establish a claim of priority, and on 31 January he read a paper to the Royal Society in London entitled 'Some Account of the Art of Photogenic Drawing; or The Process by which Natural Objects may be made to delineate themselves without the aid of the Artist's Pencil'. He originally used sodium chloride (common salt) to fix the image, but later turned to sodium thiosulphate at the suggestion of the astronomer Sir John Herschel, who also coined the word 'photography' to describe the new process of taking pictures from life. Talbot's process involved the creation of an original reversed picture, with the shadows light and the light areas dark: when the negative originals were subjected to the same printing procedure, positive pictures resulted. Thus Talbot's process was the direct ancestor of all modern photographic techniques.

By 1840 Talbot had perfected a significant improvement on his original process whereby, instead of exposing the paper in the camera until the image appeared, he used a solution of silver nitrate and gallic acid to develop the latent image produced by a much shorter exposure. He named the improved technique 'calotype', from the Greek *calos* (beautiful) and *typos* (impression). In 1844 he published the first book to be illustrated with actual photographs, *The Pencil of Nature*, which contained mounted calotypes of architecture, still-life arrangements, sculpture and other works of art. The process was so new to the public that Talbot placed a slip of paper into the book which read: 'Notice to the Reader ... The plates in the present work are impressed by the agency of light alone, without any aid from the artist's pencil. They are the sun pictures themselves, and not, as some persons have imagined, engravings in imitation.'

In 1851, at the Great Exhibition in London, there was an important international display of photographs and photographic equipment. This proved to be an enormous stimulus to interest in the new art, and led to the formation of photographic societies and clubs to facilitate the continued exchange of ideas. In the same year an English sculptor called

Frederick Scott Archer invented the wet collodion process, which started a new era in photography. It produced glass negatives which combined the sharpness of detail provided by daguerrotypes with the reproducibility of Fox Talbot's paper process. The manipulations were initially more difficult than those for Talbot's calotype, but the wet collodion process allowed for more sensitivity and greatly decreased exposure times. Small portraits could now be taken in 2 to 20 seconds, rather than the minutes often needed for calotypes. Collodion is a solution of guncotton in alcohol and ether which forms a tough, clear film when dry. After its discovery in 1847 its primary use had been as a protection for wounds. Because it was impervious to water when dry, the exposing, developing and fixing had to be done with a wet plate, so that the photographer had to carry a darkroom about with him. This process, with modifications, was the basis of the familiar tintypes, whose sturdiness and low cost made them so popular in the United States. Printed on a tin background, they were easily sent through the mails, a boon to a country where the majority of the population always seemed to be on the move, leaving loved ones behind.

The next major innovation came in 1871, when Dr Richard Leach Maddox, an English physician, made an emulsion of silver bromide in gelatin. After improvements, especially in the speed of the process, the rapid gelatin dry plate became the forerunner of the whole modern photographic industry, freeing the photographer from having to make his own plates by allowing mass production. In the period after 1878 the commercial manufacturing of photographic plates and other equipment became an important industry. The Eastman Company of Rochester, New York, was one of the first to introduce a nitro-cellulose roll-film in 1889, which finally set the stage for the modern photographic era. The cameras for taking these photographs also underwent significant improvements, with the introduction of faster lenses, and smaller, more compact equipment. Most serious photographers nevertheless continued to work with big plate cameras until the 1890s, when a variety of new equipment including the first reflex and roll-film cameras was introduced.

After 1880 the rapid increase in interest in photography by amateurs created a viable commercial photographic market. The Eastman Company, with its trade name of Kodak, led the way as this new invention captured the public's imagination. Skilful in its use of advertising, the Eastman Company appealed directly to the sentimentality of the prospective buyer, underscoring the significance of having such images available for the first time for the majority of the population. Anyone could now capture and recall impressions of their own lives, and the advertisements pointed out that 'A collection of these pictures may be made to furnish a pictorial history of life as it is lived by the owner, that will grow more valuable every day that passes.' The ubiquitousness of the camera, and the ease with which the public adapted to making its own pictures, can be summed up in the famous Kodak slogan – 'You press the button, we do the rest.'

In the 20th century there has been a continuous improvement and refinement of photographic equipment; cameras have become smaller, films faster and the use of photography seems to know no bounds. Colour photography, long the goal of experimenters, became easier and available to amateurs following the introduction of the first easily-used colour films in 1935, and the introduction of the Polaroid camera, invented by Edwin H. Land in 1947, created an entirely new concept in instantaneous photography, with the picture being produced in less than one minute (though it had the disadvantage of producing only one print).

While the acceptance of photography as an art form has been relatively slow, the adaptation of the medium for commercial purposes was immediate. The growth of photography in the 19th century coincided with movements of populations never before witnessed on such an enormous, organized scale. In particular, migration to North America created a clear need for some form of inexpensive process of providing mementos for those left behind, or those about to undertake the journey. In the United States the demand for cheap portraits was so great in the period 1850–60 that daguerrotypists and calotypists were hard-pressed to keep up with it (we have already referred to the popularity of tintypes). This competition led to a price war in which the operators 'offered the public daguerrotypes at 50 cents, at 25 cents, and

finally at 12½ cents – made "two at a pop" with a double lens camera.' (Beaumont Newhall, *History of Photography*.) It was estimated that three million daguerrotypes were produced in the United States in 1853 alone, while New York City had over one hundred studios. In England, the only country where the daguerrotype process was patented, the demand for portraits was just as great, threatening the livelihood of the painters of miniature portraits.

It is, however, in the application of photography to printing that its greatest significance in the proliferation of images lies. From the first, printing plates had been made from daguerrotypes, and Talbot had produced printable steel plates in 1858; but the effective development of the process to allow the printing of photographs together with type on the ordinary press-run paper had to wait until the 1880s. In the intervening years the major effect of photography on the printing industry was in the use of photographs for engraving purposes. About 1860 Thomas Bolton, an English wood-engraver, sensitized the surface of a woodblock in order to print a photograph on it for engraving purposes. Now an artist need no longer draw the picture for the engraver to follow.

The most important of all the 19th-century adaptations of the photograph for printing was the half-tone process. It had always been understood that the prime requirement was to find a means of breaking up the continuous tones of the photographs. As early as 1852 Talbot had suggested the use of a gauze netting for this purpose. Between the 1850s and the 1880s many different experiments were tried, with gradual improvements in quality. We owe the principle of the half-tone screen in use today to Frederic E. Ives of Philadelphia and its practical accomplishment to the brothers Louis F. and Max Levy, of the same city. It consists of two glass plates, each covered in etched parallel lines filled with an opaque substance, cemented face to face with the lines at right angles and sealed at the edges. Photographs could now be reproduced economically and in large quantities in books, magazines and especially newspapers.

While periodicals such as the *Illustrated London News* used photographs as the basis for their wood-engravings, the end product was still the result of several intermediary processes and lacked the immediacy we are used to today. In fact, the use of wood-engravings for the reporting of news events was comparatively rare, and usually required about 48 hours' preparation time. With the introduction of the half-tone process, photographers could specialize in taking photographs especially for reporting purposes. The New York *Daily Graphic* for 4 March 1880 appears to be the first newspaper to have used this process, in an article demonstrating the half-tone as one of several ways of reproducing pictures.

The camera in the hands of the amateur: from a Kodak advertisement around the time of World War I.

Despite the demonstrated success of the half-tone process, the use of woodblocks and other processes such as zinc-engravings (a technique of etching zinc plates in relief by chemical means developed early in the 19th century) persisted until well after the turn of the century. It has been estimated that in 1891 there were nearly one thousand artists at work in the United States supplying illustrations for over 5000 newspapers and magazines. In 1897 Stephen H. Horgan, an editor who had long championed the use of half-tone photographs, after several rebuffs by doubting pressmen, finally succeeded in perfecting a method for running half-tones on a rotary press, at the New York Tribune; this innovation was quickly adopted by other newspapers. The artists suddenly found the photographers taking over their role, and news syndicates now included news and feature photographs as part of their offerings. By 1907 a method had been devised for transmitting pictures by wire which depended upon the property of a material known as selenium to vary its electrical conductivity according to the light falling on it. The introduction of the valve (vacuum tube) greatly enhanced this process of 'photo-telegraphy', and in 1925 the American Telephone and Telegraph Company opened a commercial service between New York, Chicago and San Francisco. Thousands of photographs are now routinely sent all over the globe every day.

The growing importance of photography as a means of reporting news resulted in the development of popular periodicals specifically dedicated to photo-reportage, making photography a communications medium in its own right. Beginning in Germany in the late 1920s, the photomagazine spread to England with the founding of the Weekly Illustrated

in 1934 and Picture Post in 1938 by the experienced German emigré, Stefan Lorant. In November 1936 Henry Luce started Life magazine in the United States, soon to be followed by a host of competitors, including Look in 1937. It was however the British magazine Picture Post, with its use of 'candid' photography, in available light, that did most to enhance the concept of photographic reporting.

In the 1960s the photomagazines were seriously challenged by a new communications medium, television. It was not that they were becoming obsolete: but in the growing dependence upon advertising support the electronic medium could deliver to the advertiser a far greater audience much more cheaply. One by one the magazines succumbed to this financial plight. Despite a circulation in excess of six million, Life magazine was discontinued as a regular weekly publication in 1972.

Meanwhile, however, as already hinted in the previous chapter, the printed image was exploding into colour, with major consequences in our contemporary environment of super-rich, super-real colour images of poster and magazine advertisements. Following the marketing of convenient colour films for the first time in 1935 the half-tone engraving process began to be extended to colour work on a significant scale, employing the three primary colours of cyan (turquoise blue), magenta (mauve-red) and yellow first used by a German printer in France named Le Blon early in the 18th century. It has only been in the postwar period that the technologies of offset litho and colour gravure, the two colour printing processes suitable for high-speed work and permitting the flexible integration of text and pictures, have been perfected and developed in large-scale use.

The first half-tone newspaper picture: from the New York Daily Graphic for 4 March 1880.

The electronic image: a radio photograph of Queen Marie of Rumania on a visit to New York in October 1926.

The motion picture

In 1921 a British journalist, Arthur Weigall, noted with some alarm that the American motion picture had become a dangerous worldwide influence. He wrote: 'To the remotest towns of England, as to those of America and other countries, these films penetrate, carrying with them this mild but ultimately dangerous poison; and gradually the world, from end to end, is being trained to see life as it is seen by a certain group of kinema producers and writers congregated in a corner of the United States. The world is being Americanized by the photoplay ...' André Maurois expressed similar sentiments during a visit to New York in 1927: 'This is the day of universal culture. The people of the world dress alike more or less, and it is from motion pictures that they get their idea of being alike.' In the short period of thirty years after its first crude beginnings, the motion picture had become a pervasive and sophisticated contributor to the gradual shift toward a global 'mass' culture. No more effective and popular method for disseminating images had ever been seen before.

The 'magic lanterns' which resulted from the first experiments of Athanasius Kircher in 1646 were popular for over two hundred years, many being ingenious devices which allowed the simulation of movement. For example, the Englishman E. G. Robertson's version of the lantern show, the *Phantasmagoria*, used a rear-projection method together with a complex series of mirrors and lenses to heighten the effects of his macabre tales, told to an audience often actually seated in ruined castles or deserted mansions. Again, later in the 19th century, the American Alexander Black used photographic slides of posed models to develop a highly effective narrative presentation of melodramatic stories. Historians of the motion picture have not given their due to the travelling lanternists and the importance of their presentations in preparing – and perhaps whetting the appetites of – audiences for the introduction of true projected moving pictures.

Several strands of science and mechanics united in the eventual apparatus for moving pictures. The whole mechanism depended upon the physiological phenomenon of persistence of vision, which allows the human brain to hold an image just long enough to ensure an illusion of motion when the static images on the strip of film are fed through the projector onto the screen. While this physical principle had long been noted, it was not until the early 19th century that serious attempts were made to provide a scientific explanation of how it worked. One of the early theorists, the Englishman Dr John Paris, designed a series of toys to demonstrate the principle in the 1830s. His toys, called thaumatropes, quickly became a fairly successful commercial enterprise, and a wide variety of similar objects were developed by other innovators throughout the 19th century. These devices, with exotic names such as phenakistiscope, zoetrope and praxinoscope, all used drawings to demonstrate the illusion of movement which could be obtained as the result of the persistence of vision.

From the earliest days of photography the possibilities of projecting photographic images were quickly realized, and inventors lost little time in trying to develop a method of using the static photograph to create the illusion of moving images. Experiments in the nature of animal movement by Eadweard Muybridge in the United States, using cameras fired in sequence, and the work of the French physiologist E. J. Marey with his 'photographic rifle' exposing a series of images on a revolving photographic plate, were significant contributions to the evolution of the motion picture apparatus, but the real breakthrough came with the introduction of celluloid strip film in the late 1880s. Ironically as it now seems, Thomas Edison was interested in moving pictures as an accompaniment to his phonograph, to provide an added attraction. One of the first movie cameras, called the Kinetograph, was developed in his laboratories by the Englishman William L. Dickson in 1888. But Edison was not interested in a projection apparatus at this stage and was content with Dickson's Kinetoscope viewing machine, a peepshow apparatus in which a vital ingredient of the technology of the projector, the interrupted motion of the film past the light source, was missing. Wasting both film stock and light intensity, the Kinetoscope froze the images of the continuously moving film with an aperture in a revolving mask. It was the Lumière brothers, Auguste and Louis, who arrived at the essential principle in their *cinematographe*, which gave its first public exhibition in the Grand Café de Paris on 28 December 1895. In fact they used the same machine to shoot and project the film. Following the commercial success of the Lumière brothers' shows, Edison's interests were rekindled, and he now developed an improved projector invented in his laboratory by Thomas Armat. The Vitascope had its first public showing on 23 April 1896 at Koster and Bial's Music Hall in New York.

It is important to note that the tremendous speed with which the transition was made from peep show to projected motion picture exhibition was a direct result of the combination of entrepreneurship and invention which Edison represented, and it was undoubtedly the magic and past triumphs of the Edison name which inspired the confidence of the large number of investors anxious to obtain projection equipment. Thus, while Edison's claim to have 'invented' the motion picture apparatus has been largely refuted, the incredibly fast dissemination of this new entertainment would not have occurred without the use of his name, and its reception by a sceptical public would have been slowed.

Starting at first in converted storefront theatres, or in tents, the new entertainment appealed initially to the working class, where it proved to be the ideal form of urban amusement – it was cheap, accessible and easily understood. However, the motion picture industry itself almost immediately set its sights on achieving a degree of respectability which belied its lowly origins. This was as true for France and Britain as it was for the United States. By 1914, on the eve of World War I, the motion picture had become the largest form of commercial amusement in the history of the world, and 'going to the movies' was accepted as a normal part of 20th-century life. The audience for the motion picture was no longer that of the urban working class for, with the stabilization of the industry, the quality of films improved, the movie theatres became more comfortable and even luxurious, and the price of admission increased. Talking pictures arrived with *The Jazz Singer* (1927), which demonstrated the commercial attractions of the Vitaphone, an invention of Bell's Western Electric Company bought by Warner Brothers in 1925 after the other major studios had turned it down. Originally employing a phonograph disc, after a short time the Vitaphone changed to the modern principle of sound-on-film, in which the sound is converted into light impulses by means of an oscilloscope (invented just after World War I). Colour began to be introduced on a significant commercial scale following the introduction of the Technicolor process in 1932. The motion picture industry, by virtue of the enormous audiences it attracted worldwide, had become an important disseminator of mass images, but these images had a glamour and appeal unlike any other known before. It was as if the photographic innovations of the 19th century had all come together to create the ultimate in visual experience for the audience. It was not mere hyperbole when the motion picture theatres were called 'The House of Dreams'.

With the destruction of the European studios in World War I, the American film industry lost no time in rushing in to fill the entertainment void; and despite every type of political and economic effort, it has never lost its position. The American film studios do not have the great power they once had, but there is still a residue of financial and technical expertise in Hollywood which has helped the American film industry to maintain its international appeal. While countries such as Italy, France, Britain, Russia and Sweden may have achieved the pleasure of international critical acclaim for the output of their film studios, well over 50 per cent of screen time throughout the world is still devoted to the showing of American-produced films, or films featuring American performers. The addition of sound to films in the late 1920s was seen by many as leading to the end of the Hollywood hegemony, but new techniques which allow voices to be 'dubbed' into any language have made the sound film as internationally acceptable as the silent film.

The motion picture was the most prolific form of image dissemination available before the advent of television, and it was the first of the major mass media of communication to come under close moral and scientific scrutiny. Not long after its introduction in the 1890s, the medium was being subjected to censorship in all countries where it was available. This was no doubt a result of its enormous appeal to the entire public, especially to children. It was also to do with the inherent, but unascertainable, qualities of persuasion which this visual mode seemed to offer. In declaring that the motion picture should not be granted the same guarantees of freedom of speech as those afforded to the print media, the Supreme Court of the United States noted in 1915: 'It cannot be put out of view that the exhibition of moving pictures is a business pure and simple ... They are mere representations of events, of ideas and sentiments published or known; vivid, useful, and entertaining, no doubt but ... capable of evil, having power for it, the greater because of their attractiveness and manner of exhibition.'

These fears about the influence of the cinema were not limited to the United States: in Britain a report by the National Council of Public Morals on *The Cinema: Its Present Position and Future Possibilities* in 1916 pointed out:

> In the course of our inquiry we have been much impressed by the evidence brought before us that moving pictures are having a profound influence upon the mental and moral outlook of millions of our young people – an influence the more subtle in that it is subconsciously exercised – and we leave our labours with the deep conviction that no social problem of the day demands more earnest attention.

Similar concerns were voiced in every country where the motion picture became the major commercial entertainment form. The worldwide impact of the motion picture, although little understood, was deemed to be of such magnitude that the League of Nations established a special series of commissions to investigate and report on the problem in the period between 1928 and 1937. In countries such as Britain, France and Germany special tariffs and other economic sanctions were introduced in an ultimately futile attempt to enhance and protect the domestic film production industry. The importance of the motion picture as a purveyor of culture

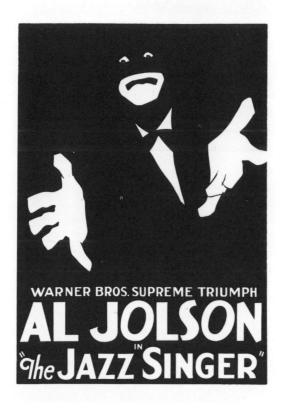

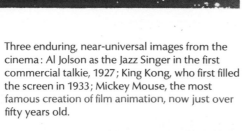

Three enduring, near-universal images from the cinema: Al Jolson as the Jazz Singer in the first commercial talkie, 1927; King Kong, who first filled the screen in 1933; Mickey Mouse, the most famous creation of film animation, now just over fifty years old.

and its influence on society as a whole were such that it was subjected to a quite unprecedented series of legislative and social controls.

Like radio and television at a later date, cinema bypassed the existing channels of social communication and authority structures in the sphere of politics, religion, education, kinship and economics, and established direct contact with the individual. Parents and teachers felt powerless to prevent the influence of these new communications forms, which seemed so readily accessible to the young. The cinema obviously had the potential for a wide range of applications in the field of education, but their integration into the curriculum has never been entirely successful. The inability of the formal education system to counter the effects of the commercial film remains an important educational issue.

The motion picture has, of course, had uses in many other areas. Like still photography, it has been extensively used in science and manufacturing; it has also been used as a means of recording personal memories, but 'home movies' have never been adopted on the same scale as the snapshot.

The motion picture emerged from its period of greatest glory as a wartime contributor to morale in the period 1940–7, only to be faced with a crisis of its own. While television had been available since the mid-1930s, the war had delayed its introduction on a national scale in the United States and Britain. Once television became generally available to the entire population, the motion picture industry went into a serious financial decline in these countries, losing almost half of its 1947 audience by 1960. Television simply took over much of the entertainment function of the motion picture, providing the same thing more cheaply and conveniently. Despite attempts to use improved technology, such as wide screens, three-dimensional projection, and such bizarre effects as 'smell-o-vision', the worldwide audience for the movies has never recovered to its previous levels, although in recent years the audience has stabilized and box office receipts, because of inflation, are higher than ever.

It will never be possible to say exactly how important the motion picture has been in the shaping of modern society, but the powerful social influence of films has become increasingly obvious. The movie image is a potent one, quite capable of transporting an audience into a new cultural experience. As the social psychologist Herbert Blumer has pointed out, 'motion pictures not only bring new objects to the attention of people but, what is probably more important, they make what has been remote and vague, immediate and clear'. But immediate and clear in very particular ways: cinematic ways. Culturally the movies are most effective in creating and reinforcing stereotypes. Where the audience's initial familiarity with a subject is least, the depiction on a screen in a definitive and familiar way often influences the way the subject is perceived. It is for this reason that so much attention is paid to movie content and influence, particularly by racial or ethnic minorities which have consistently been the victims of 'Hollywood versions'.

The motion picture is still without peer as a disseminator of memorable and durable images. The history of the commercial cinema is replete with vivid images, many of which have become important icons of the 20th century. Who is not able to identify Charlie Chaplin's 'Little Tramp' character, the comedy team of Laurel and Hardy, the animated character of Mickey Mouse, or more recently the great white shark in *Jaws*? These have become international symbols, whose meanings know no language barriers. (While television may be more ubiquitous, it has not proved to have the same qualities of endurance; it does however have its own immense power.) With the increasingly international character of film production and the stabilization of the audience, the motion picture will continue to be one of our most potent forms of communication and a shaper of universal images.

Television: the massive medium

None of the earlier visual media of communication was so clearly foreseen or so eagerly anticipated as television. From as early as 1862 experiments with electricity had confirmed the possibility of transmitting pictorial material by wire. One important breakthrough was the discovery by Willoughby Smith in 1873 that selenium was capable of producing small amounts of electricity in direct response to the amount of light falling on it. Most of the subsequent speculations assumed that each element of the image would be transmitted simultaneously over a large number of separate circuits. In 1875 George Carey of Boston demonstrated that crude pictures could be transmitted by means of electric impulses generated by a bank of selenium photo-electric cells. There were, however, obvious limitations to a system which used more than one channel of transmission.

The concept of persistence of vision, which was discussed in connection with the development of motion picture technology, was also to play an important part in the history of television technology. In 1880 Maurice Leblanc and W. E. Sawyer in the United States both proposed a system which would rapidly scan each element of the image in succession, line by line, and frame by frame, relying upon the persistence of vision to retain a complete image from the approximately 300,000 individual elements required to be transmitted. It was the understanding of this principle which indicated the possibility of using only a single wire or channel for transmitting a complex image. All subsequent technological developments concentrated upon the improvement and refinement of the single-channel scanning apparatus.

In 1884, the German scientist Paul Nipkow patented an early form of a complete television system, using a combination of the currently available technology. Nipkow's system used a rotating scanning disc which allowed the light to go through a series of tiny holes, a mechanical technique which would dominate television research until the late 1920s, when it was replaced by electronic methods. The selenium cells which Nipkow and others used in these early efforts unfortunately had a slow response to changes in light, and were therefore not entirely adequate for the task. In 1913, German scientists produced a potassium hydride coated cell with both an improved sensitivity and the ability to follow rapid changes of light, which allowed the development of the first practical mechanical scanning system. The production of the neon gas discharging lamp by the American D. M. Moore in 1917 allowed the development of modulated light, and this was subsequently adopted by the British pioneer John Logie Baird and the American C. F. Jenkins, both of whom applied it to Nipkow's mechanical principles.

In 1926 Baird was able to demonstrate the first true television system by electrically moving pictures in half-tones. Although these crude, tiny pictures were formed of only 30 lines, repeating themselves ten times every second, they demonstrated that television was a practical technology, and they were a tremendous stimulus toward further research. It was this system and subsequent refinements which formed the basis of some experimental broadcasting in England between 1929 and 1935.

The mechanical method of scanning lacked the sensitivity needed for very clear pictures, and therefore many scientists were at work trying to develop a system which would permit greater definition. As early as 1908, the Scottish electrical engineer A. A. Campbell Swinton had outlined a method that has proved to be the basis of all modern television. (The Russian Boris Rosing independently proposed a similar system at about the same time.) Swinton did not have the benefit of amplifiers, so his work was considered 'an idea only'. His idea was to use a cathode-ray tube (which had been developed earlier by the German K. F. Braun in 1897), in which the stream of electrons was magnetically deflected in both camera and receiver. The image was formed inside the camera where it fell upon a mosaic screen of photoelectric elements, which were then discharged by a cathode-ray beam tracing out the scanning sequence line-by-line. Unfortunately Swinton's ideas were much too advanced for his time, and it was almost twenty years before they found practical application.

For good-quality reproduction it was necessary to have the image broken down into at least 200,000 elements; and this required a system using about 300 lines. Mechanical systems simply could not operate at this level, and further it was necessary to amplify the weak electrical impulses produced by the photocell at the transmitter end to a level sufficient to operate the lamp at the receiver end. The development of the thermionic amplifier tube by Lee De Forest in 1907 provided the basis for such amplification, but this was still a far cry from the power required for the high-speed amplification needed for even crude television transmissions.

A major breakthrough occurred in 1923, when a Russian immigrant to the United States, Vladimir Zworykin, while working for the Radio Corporation of America (RCA), received a patent for his electronic improvements resulting in the development of the iconoscope (sending) and kinescope (receiving) tubes, which formed the basis of modern electronic transmission. This finally did away with the need for mechanical scanning, and after several years of cross-licensing agreements and further improvements, a standard form of sending and receiving equipment emerged.

In Britain, Electric and Musical Industries (EMI) created a television research unit in 1931, headed by Sir Isaac Schoenberg. This group developed a complete and practical system using a camera tube known as an Emitron, and an improved high-vacuum cathode-ray tube for the receiver. By 1935 his team had developed and demonstrated a totally workable system, including all the complex control and amplifying circuits. Schoenberg, understanding the need for a permanent type of system which would set the standard for future years, proposed the use of 405 lines at 50 frames per second, a demanding technological feat at the time. The British government authorized the British Broadcasting Corporation to adopt these standards, and using the complete EMI system (which was in competition at the time with Baird's system), the world's first public high-definition service was launched in London in 1936. (Germany had begun a low-definition 180-line service in 1935.)

All of this international activity culminated in the graphic public demonstration of a 441-line electronic television system in 1939 at the World's Fair in New York City. There for the first time Americans and thousands of overseas visitors saw the true potential of television as a form of convenient visual entertainment. The theme of this Fair was, prophetically, 'The World of Tomorrow'. But on 1 September 1939, just four months after Franklin Roosevelt opened the New York Fair, Hitler's troops invaded Poland. However, television was allowed to start in the United States when the Federal Communication Commission approved commercial television with a 525-line standard. On 1 July two commercial stations began broadcasting in New York City, being limited by regulation to about 15 hours a week. By the time the U.S. entered World War II, between 10,000 and 20,000 television sets were in use, half in New York and the rest in Philadelphia, Chicago and Los Angeles.

After the war, there was a flurry of expansion in television, but the difficulty in establishing suitable regulations to avoid the same type of free-for-all as had occurred in the early 1920s when radio was introduced prompted the FCC to suspend the granting of new station licences in late 1948. This temporary freeze lasted until April 1952, when, with a new, more carefully considered regulatory system, television was given the green light to expand all across the United States. In Britain a small London-based service was reopened in 1946, and a national television network was in operation by 1952.

There has been a continuous improvement of the technology of television since its successful introduction as an entertainment medium. The use of television in industry, education and almost every facet of modern life has been a prominent feature of the last half of the 20th century. The introduction of colour television, although a first crude colour system had been demonstrated by Baird in 1928, had to await the solution to many complex technical problems, because the transmission of colour images requires a 'multi-gun' cathode-ray tube. Once again competing systems vied for the lucrative market for colour sets which was foreseen once the market became saturated with black-and-white models. Even today the United States uses a different system (NTSC) from that generally used in Europe (either SECAM or PAL), although there is a degree of compatibility between the systems. The United States has standardized to the use of 525-line definition, while the Europeans have decided upon a finer definition of 625 lines.

Television cameras also became much more portable, and were increasingly able to operate in available light conditions. This has allowed the television camera to become much more akin to the portable microphone of radio, and given television news virtually the same degree of mobility. This has brought about a fundamental change in the way in which populations in many countries now receive their daily news, as the trend is increasingly toward a reliance upon television as the major news source, and a decline in both newspapers and radio.

The rate of growth of this new visual entertainment medium was unprecedented. Never before had there been a form of cultural activity quite like television, with its enormous worldwide audiences, its increasing absorption of available leisure hours, and its ability to create instant celebrities or to focus attention on important or unimportant

events with equal emphasis. Television, already the most prolific disseminator of images, has become the most widely shared general culture in the history of mankind. Technological developments like satellite transmission and large, life-size screens are making television even more powerful and widespread. This possibility has raised fears that total worldwide 'cultural dominance' by a few countries is already taking place. One outspoken critic of 'cultural imperialism', Herbert I. Schiller, has said, 'The free flow of information, reinforced by economic power, has led to a worldwide situation in which the cultural autonomy of many (if not most) nations is increasingly subordinated to the communications outputs and perspectives of a few powerful, market-dominated economies.'

This, and other serious questions concerning the social and cultural impact of television, have only begun to receive detailed attention in the last decade. As the power of television increases as an advertising vehicle, as entertainment, as a source of news and other information, and even as a means of formal education, the true dimensions of the

Television, the most widely shared general culture in the history of mankind: issue No 1 of *TV Times* marks the inauguration of commercial television in Britain in September 1955.

impact of this new, all-encompassing form of visual communication will become clearer.

With daily television usage in most industrialized countries now exceeding three hours per home, the participation in this form of activity has clearly become more a prescribed routine than a chance decision to 'be entertained'. Of course the television set is often switched on while no one is actually watching; but the presence of the soft, glowing light, the sound of the modulated tones of the announcer, or the obviously controlled laughter from the laughter-track – all serve to provide the sense of comfort that comes from familiarity and reliability. Thus our interaction with television is becoming increasingly a prescribed code of behaviour, at times almost a ceremonial act. Much of television's success as an entertainment medium comes from providing precisely the type of content that has familiarity, easily accessible common symbolism, and dependable frequency. Television is not only a means of bringing images into the home; it also brings a sense of comfort and belonging.

Raymond Williams observes elsewhere that broadcasting was the ideal form of entertainment-communication for a society that was increasingly mobile, but conversely developing a self-sufficient family home; a concept he calls *mobile privatization*. First radio and then television were capable of bringing news and entertainment directly into the home, where they 'served as a form of *unified* social intake, at the most general level'. Perhaps more than any other 'mass' medium of communication, television is considered 'part of the family'.

The amount of time that is spent watching television, again especially by children, has raised the question of 'media influence' to a minor social science of its own. The role of television in shaping our ideas and subsequently our values has always been acknowledged, but the behavioural and cultural mechanisms by which this is accomplished, and their relative importance in comparison with the other socializing influences in our lives (such as the school, the family, the church and peer groups), is still a matter for considerable speculation. What is known is that television can, under certain conditions, become a very important source of information and therefore contribute to the formation of our ideas; and that so-called 'entertainment' programmes have built-in 'message systems' which act as potent devices for communicating those values about which such shows are structured. These values are reinforced by constant repetition, in every episode, week after week.

The last five hundred years have witnessed an astonishing increase in the use of visual material in all sections of society, and a corresponding increase in the reliance upon the visual mode. The proliferation of images was achieved as a result of the complex set of social, cultural, economic and even political conditions which form the web of human evolution. Urbanization and industrialization resulted in new communication needs and changed the uses of communication and entertainment. A demand for the reproduction and wide distribution of all types of images was part of this. Spurred on by the obvious financial rewards, inventors and later industry responded to the challenge; the result is a world permeated by images, and a population which has come to depend on visual stimuli to an ever-increasing extent. With the new technologies currently in use, or on the horizon, there is much to suggest that the 'extended image' in its myriad forms will continue to proliferate and play an increasingly important part in our cultural evolution.

Media Messages

The power of communicating at a distance is now so much a part of our lives that we can easily forget how recent an innovation it is. Up to the 1830s every message intended for a recipient out of earshot required a messenger to carry it. The great breakthrough came with the invention of telegraphy. Immediately, the world shrank. The time-lag between the occurrence of an event and its being known in many parts of the world (which had been weeks and even months) diminished remarkably. The telephone was in this respect only a refinement of the telegraph, and radio did the same thing without needing a physical link. The results of this unprecedented ease of communication are still hard to assess, but we have only to think of such diverse fields as nagivation, air travel, administration, diplomacy, war . . . to see that most aspects of modern life could not exist without it.

By comparison, the ability to transmit visual images has had fewer directly measurable effects, though this may be less true in the future than it has been in the past. Over the last sixty years the cinema and television may have changed people's ways of thinking, of seeing each other and the world, even more radically than the invention of printing in the 15th century. The social and political consequences of these changes will be examined in the next chapter. Here we look at some of their effects on individuals – their influence on private and domestic life, and the strange mixture of the mundane and the exotic, the real and the illusory, the sordid and the beautiful, with which they have furnished the imagination.

122 An advertisement issued jointly by the British and German governments stresses the way in which the telephone holds friends and families together. The wires and handset make up two faces, while at the bottom a map of the globe is surrounded by the words 'International Direct Dialling'.

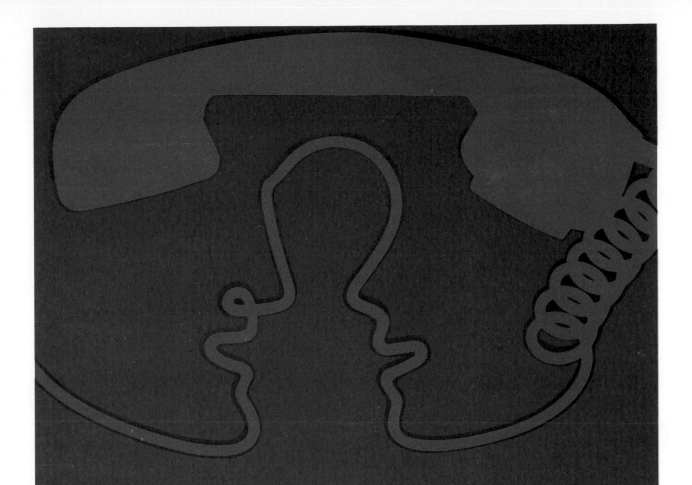

Get closer, make a call.
Ruf doch mal zu Hause an...

It makes good sense to keep in touch by 'phone. Why not give your family and friends a pleasant surprise—'phone them, it may cost less than you think.

Aus dem Urlaub grüßen und ein paar liebe Worte sagen. Es kostet nicht die Welt.

Produced jointly by the British Post Office
and the German Federal Republic Telecommunications Administrations.

THE TELEPHONE: LIFELINE OF THE 20th CENTURY

While many new technical devices tended to divide social groups and isolate the individual, the telephone has worked in the opposite direction. As towns expanded, as people began living away from their work and offices became divorced from factories, the telephone was the means of keeping them in contact

I feel so shy when she is nigh
So I'll tell Tilly on the telephone.

It can say: 'I love you'.

Your phone gets you closer to someone.

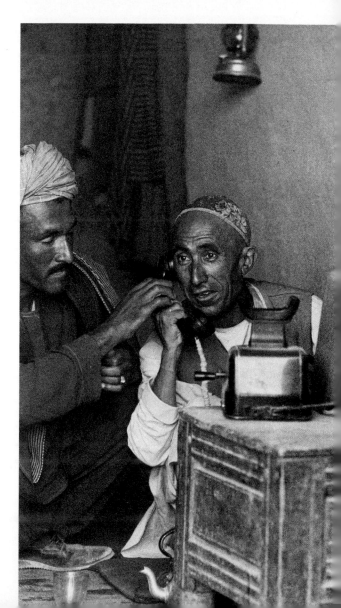

123 A Bell Telephone advertisement of 1915 neatly summarizes the telephone's role in making possible the separation of homes from workplaces, of factories from offices.

124, 125 Romance by telephone, evidently as useful at the turn of the century as it is now. What differences are there between our kind of phone call and the exchange of love-letters?

126 The telephone is now at home in every part of the world: here, a coffee-bar post office in Afghanistan in the early 1960s.

127 A sketch (on a telephone message pad) by Jean-Michel Folon alludes to the telephone's contribution to a specific urban form, the skyscraper. Without it, the liftshafts needed to accommodate hundreds of messengers would have made skyscrapers uneconomic.

128 Help in an emergency is as near as the nearest telephone: beside a desert road in New Mexico.

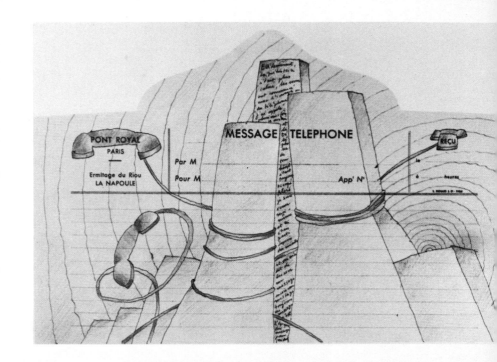

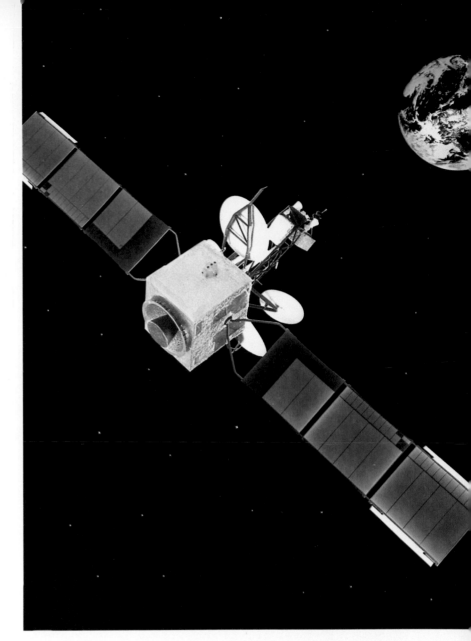

DISTANCE NO OBJECT

Telephone wires criss-cross our streets and stride across deserts; cables alive with voices lie on the ocean bed; and by the latest devices electronic messages stream into outer space and are bounced back to earth by satellite. These are the monuments of our culture, as roads and aqueducts were of the Romans'.

129 Mile after mile of wire in the Mojave Desert between Los Angeles and Las Vegas – an uncompromising symbol of communication across vast, hostile distances.

130 Intelsat V, the latest satellite of the global communications system set up in 1964, able to reflect from earth station to earth station up to 12,000 telephone calls simultaneously.

RADIO POWER

In direct or indirect forms, and over a range from selection and suggestion to straight exhortation, the use of radio for political propaganda is now in effect universal. We notice this more readily when it is in distant or foreign forms.

131 A propaganda post in a railway station during the Russian Civil War. The banner above says 'The stronger the Red Army, the more quickly the Civil War will end.'

132 'The whole of Germany listens to the Führer, with the people's wireless': a striking image of the power of Hitler's rhetoric through the voice alone.

133 The Islamic revolution uses radio to consolidate its power: Muhammad Montazavi, a leading member of Iran's Revolutionary Council, reciting traditional Friday prayers.

134 'The voice of freedom in the German night': an advertisement for the short-wave broadcasting station set up by the underground left in Nazi Germany in 1937.

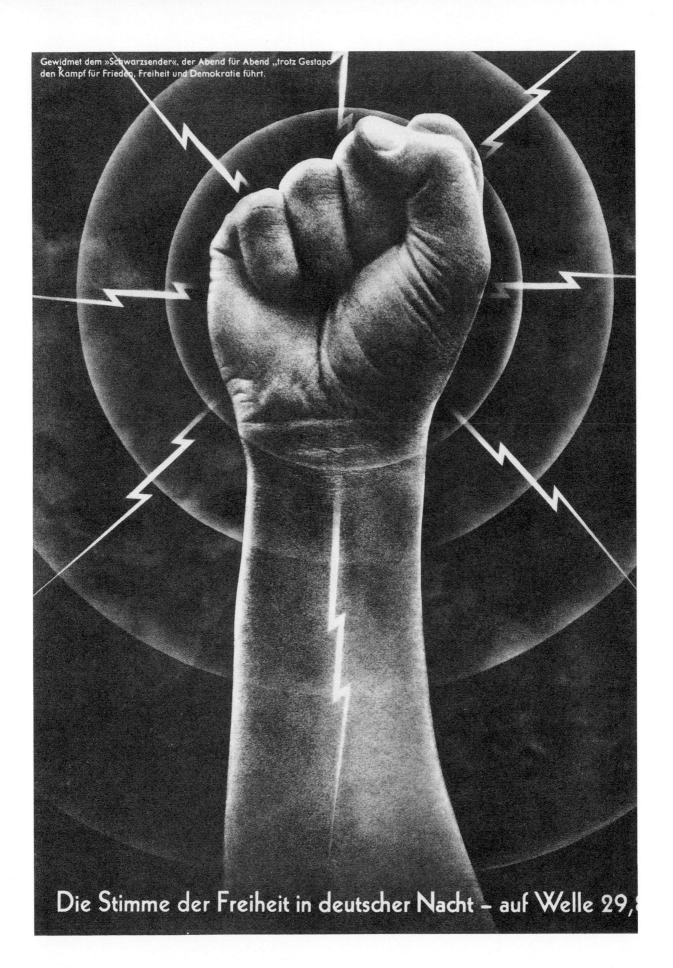

Gewidmet dem »Schwarzsender«, der Abend für Abend „trotz Gestapo
den Kampf für Frieden, Freiheit und Demokratie führt.

Die Stimme der Freiheit in deutscher Nacht – auf Welle 29,8

MUSIC, MUSIC, MUSIC

The services of the radio and gramophone to classical music are widely acknowledged. Less analysed, perhaps, but more pervasive, is the way in which they have made possible a whole new sub-culture: Pop. Truly international in appeal, undemanding, unending and hypnotic, it seems able to cross all frontiers – racial, economic, linguistic and ideological.

135 As long ago as 1925 the Italian company SITI was promising the unification of all nations in riotous entertainment through radio.

136 In love with a voice: an Austrian Art Nouveau postcard by Maria Likarz Strauss. But who in the early part of the century could have guessed the power that records would acquire over the adolescent's fantasy life?

137 Roller-skater in a world of his own. Today's portable radio/cassette player – even more so when used with earphones – makes possible total enclosure in a cocoon of rich musical sound from morning to night.

HOMO PHOTOGRAPHICUS

The first commercial photographs were portraits. In a world where groups and families tended to be on the move, photographs were a way of keeping in touch. Later, amateur photography filled this need, while professional photography moved on to fields with a much wider influence on our world.

138 A Victorian street photographer, with his barrow bearing an array of portrait photographs.

139 'Media man', a montage portrait of the German communist reporter Egon Erwin Kisch by UMBO, c. 1920.

140 The actor David Hemmings portrays the epitome of a glamorous fashion and advertising photographer in Antonioni's film Blow Up.

141 'You press the button, we do the rest'. An Eastman Company advertisement of 1889 used this picture of a boy snapping his friends against the Genesee Gorge.

142 The keen – and affluent – amateur can now match the professional in the sophistication of his equipment. Here a group of Japanese with long-focus lenses concentrates on a sporting event.

THE
IMAGE MARKET

Up to the 19th century a picture was an expensive commodity produced by and for a relatively educated élite; this was true even of etchings and engravings. Today, pictures are universal, direct reflections of popular taste. But the continuities are striking.

143 Detail of a picture dealer's stall in the Great Hall of Prague Castle in 1607.

144 Postcard stall in Palermo, 1960s: an iconography for our age. The reproductions of old masters are the most direct link with the past – 'holy pictures' even when the subject is secular; the flowers are conventional symbols of greeting and affection; the babies and the wholesome young men appeal to family values, the racing cars to those of novelty and adventure; best of all is the placing of a nude next to Pope John XXIII.

FROM PEEPSHOW TO VISTAVISION

Unlike radio and television, the cinema could be inserted into an already existing social pattern, the theatre, which it then changed. It became the first example of fully generalized entertainment.

145 Edison's first moving pictures were viewed through a peephole apparatus in 'kinetoscope parlours'.

146 The early cinema as a theatre: the Rialto was one of a chain owned by the legendary 'Roxy', S. L. Rothapfel.

147 Vitaphone brought sound to the cinema in 1927, increasing its popular appeal, though making it more difficult for films to cross linguistic barriers.

148 Film stars of the 1920s and 1930s like Greta Garbo were probably more famous than any men or women before or since. Remote yet glamorous, accessible in a way that flesh and blood could neve be, they aroused a devotion that had something akin to belief in the supernatural.

149 An early attempt to combine pictures with sound was the Biophonographe, in which a gramophone (the horn in the centre) kept pace with the pictures on the screen to tell the story of Molière's *Médecin malgré lui.*

150 Drive-in cinemas arose in response to the automobile culture of the USA. While increasing the viewer's rapt involvement in the private world of the film, they forfeited the shared experience of a large audience.

THE BUSINESS OF SHOWBUSINESS

The dominant influence of the cinema persisted until at least the 1940s, but what was its nature? For most of its career, the prevailing image was one of luxury, and cinemas almost became what their promoters called them, 'picture palaces'.

151 'Cathedrals of Broadway' by Florine Stettheimer, 1929. All the plush surroundings are there: the arrival by taxi, the lobby with fountain, the obsequious commissionaire, the magically lit auditorium.

152 The Indian cinema today still enjoys the same enormous popularity as that of Europe and America before television; this scene is at Jaipur in Rajasthan, 1972.

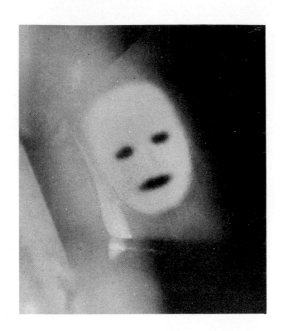

TELEVISION:
THE ALL-SCANNING EYE

Television's rate of growth outstripped that of even the cinema and radio. Since it emerged as a picture version of radio it went straight into people's homes. There was never any question – as there might well have been given different circumstances – of its becoming a 'theatre' entertainment, though this may be happening in Asia and Africa.

153   The first television used a mechanical form of scanning invented by the British pioneer John Logie Baird. This face is the first image ever successfully transmitted by television, in 1925.

154   Baird's apparatus consisted of a rotating disc, which allowed light to go through a series of tiny holes onto a sensitive surface, where each change in the strength of the light was transformed into an electrical impulse. This whole system, however, led nowhere, and during the 1930s it was replaced by an electronic system which involved scanning the picture in a grid of parallel lines.

155   Syncom III television pictures from the 1964 Tokyo Olympics – the first Olympic Games to be shown via satellite.

156   We now expect to see every important event on earth – and sometimes on the moon – immediately visible on our screens. This Hughes mobile ground station was erected to transmit pictures of President Nixon's visit to China.

157   A forest of television aerials above a block of community flats in Hong Kong: one for every living-room.

158   Home reception is the norm in the West, a pattern reinforced by the advertisers and the electronics industry. But a different pattern is conceivable, with different implications for social life, exemplified by communal viewing in a village in Rajasthan.

THE OBTRUSIVE IMAGE

The 'image explosion' has accompanied the phenomenal growth of the advertising industry – in the press, on radio, on television and in our daily environment in the form of posters and neon signs. While ostensibly geared to sell goods, its cumulative effect is to recommend a life style that uses those goods. We are, moreover, not free to see or not to see these images – they are infiltrated into our consciousness with all the skill that artistry and psychology can command.

159 A race-track at Reims, France, with a parade in progress. The advertisements are placed where they will catch the eye of the television camera as it follows the cars. The viewer may be quite unaware of seeing them, but research suggests that they can exert their influence at less conscious levels.

160 'Power and Goodness': the two heads in the Guinness advertisement are about ten times life size. Hard to ignore, though these Nigerians at a sports rally are doing their best.

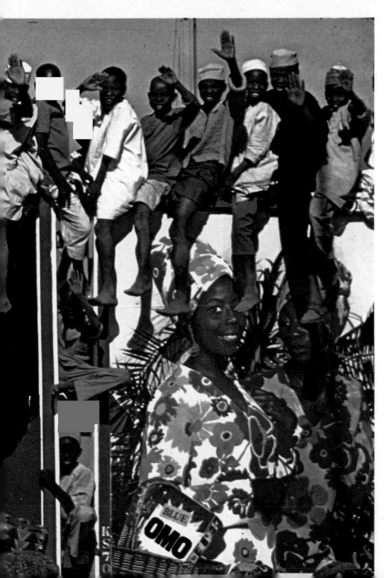

BONNE DOUBLE BIÈRE.

Perdez le ventre.

SIREN VOICES

Many advertisers have learned to work by association rather than by assertion. On this spread all the products have to do with appeals to the senses – beer, cigarettes and scent – but hardly any of them do it directly.

222

161–6 The first French beer advertisement, c. 1840; 'Schätz Jòzsef' – a Hungarian beer, associated with the pleasures of the beer garden; 'Mosselpron', a Russian beer ('pivo'), a poster of the 1920s by Rodchenko; 'Perdez le ventre': the advertiser's weapons turned against him – drink a certain low-calorie beer and lose your paunch; Guinness, an Italian advertisement: a straightforward attempt to associate the product with the peaceful countryside; Long Life Beer: founded on the rock and wreathed in sea-mist, the beer-can outfaces the storm.

167–72 Love Tobacco: an interesting advertisement from just after the American Civil War, suggesting tobacco as a means of reconciling North and South; Marlboro Cigarettes: a German version of a widespread American campaign; Winston Cigarettes: something 'big' to go with a 'big' flavour – the Brooklyn Bridge; 'Satin' and 'Dea': top-hat, evening dress, high life, sophistication, elegance … cigarettes; 'Milde Sorte': amid all the complexities of modern life, tobacco offers a moment of relaxation; Lord Extra: appeals to the outdoor image and to fashion are among the most common.

173–6 Dior: snob value; Parfums Guy Laroche: 'Woman is an island, Fidji is her perfume'; 'Cialengo Balenciaga': fantasy at a more basic level; 'Eminence', a toilet water for men – 'qui frappe fort'.

IX
COMMUNICATIONS TECHNOLOGIES AND SOCIAL INSTITUTIONS

Raymond Williams

177 Telecommunications are producing their own architecture – strange forms that seem to belong to outer space as much as to earth. This huge transmitting aerial is near Mainflingen in West Germany. These worldwide networks make it increasingly difficult for governments to exclude the voices of other nations. New developments in satellite transmission will accentuate this trend, but there is still a vital question of who will be speaking – who can afford to speak – from these 'open skies'.

COMMUNICATIONS TECHNOLOGIES AND SOCIAL INSTITUTIONS

When we think of modern communications we think at once of certain technologies. A whole series of effective inventions seem to have changed, permanently, the ways in which we must think of communication. Yet, at the same time, communication is always a form of social relationship, and communications systems have always to be seen as social institutions. It is then necessary to think, very generally but also very precisely, about the real relations between communications technologies and social institutions.

Consider first one common and influential way of thinking, or appearing to think, about these relations. People say 'television has altered our world', or 'radio altered the world', or, reaching further back, 'printing altered the world'. And we usually, at first, know what these statements mean. Evident and widespread social effects have undoubtedly followed the uses of all these inventions. But then, in expanding the statements in this way, we have already – and sometimes without noticing it – introduced a further category: that of 'uses'. The argument can then go in several directions. It can be said that what has altered our world is not television or radio or printing as such, but the uses made of them, in particular societies. Against this, or partly against it, it is then often said that once the invention has been made it will be used, and that the general effects of its use are at least as important, and may indeed be much more fundamental, than more local and more particular applications.

There are no simple ways out of the argument at this point. One main reason is that the terms in which such initial propositions are made are inadequate. A very complex set of relations and interactions is being reduced to interpretation in two simple terms: 'technical invention' and 'society' ('the world'). Using these simple terms, we can make such opposing statements as that 'technical inventions change society' or that 'society determines the uses of technical inventions'. But then the argument often gets stuck at this stage of apparently opposing assertions, or at the further stage when selections of the historical and empirical evidence are assembled in support of either. For what the terms and their assumptions often prevent us from seeing is that technical inventions are always made *within* societies and that societies are always more than the sum of relations and institutions from which, by a falsely specializing definition, technical inventions have been excluded.

These fairly obvious facts are further obscured by the common tendency to use the terms 'technical invention' and 'technology' as if they were equivalent. This is particularly so in the adjective, when people describe some element of the development of a device – in engineering, for example – as a technological problem or a technological breakthrough. But the distinction between techniques and technologies is crucial, especially in the context of this general inquiry. A technique is a particular skill or application of a skill. A

Printing as access to the power of knowledge, radio and television as poison: two views of communication technology in a 19th-century printer's motif and a contemporary critique of the French state broadcasting corporation.

technical invention is then a development of such a skill or the development or invention of one of its devices. A technology by contrast is, first, the body of knowledge appropriate to the development of such skills and applications and, second, a body of knowledge and conditions for the practical use and application of a range of devices.

These two definitions of technology can be theoretically distinguished, but they are in fact substantially connected. They relate to overlapping stages: the body of knowledge, both theoretical and practical, from which the skills and devices (technical inventions) come, and the body of knowledge and conditions from which they are developed, combined, and prepared for use. What matters, in each stage, is that a technology is always, in a full sense, social. It is necessarily in complex and variable connection with other social relations and institutions, although a particular and isolated technical invention can be seen, and temporarily interpreted, as if it were autonomous. As we move into any general social inquiry, we then find that we have always to relate technical inventions to their technologies, in the full sense, and, further, that we are starting from one kind of social state or institution – a *technology* – and relating it to other kinds of social state and institution rather than to a generalized 'society' so pre-defined as to separate or exclude it.

Two kinds of resource in communication

The general technology of communications is full of fascinating examples of these real relations. Yet, before we can properly understand them, we have to take account of one fundamental distinction in human communications in general. The earliest forms of human communication, like the forms of almost all animal communication, made predominant if never perhaps exclusive use of inherent, evolved and constituted, physical resources. The human body, in its full sense, is the set of resources from which this major kind of communication was developed. This is true of both verbal (oral) and non-verbal (physical expression and gesture) forms. It would be confusing to speak of the systems that were developed from these inherent physical resources as 'technologies', yet we can never afford to overlook the important systems of knowledge, skill and training, applied in the development of these inherent resources – the great systems of rhetoric and of training in acting are the most visible because most specialized forms – alongside the other systems that we can designate as imitation, custom or habit.

This point becomes very important when we come to emphasize the fundamental qualitative change in communications systems which occurred when men began using and adapting – and in the end quite extraordinarily extending – objects and forces outside their own bodies as major means of communication. For, even as we insist on this qualitative change – the beginning of the true *technology* of communications – we have of course to recognize that those earliest forms, dependent primarily on immediate and inherent physical resources, are still today, in many kinds of social relationship – the family, the immediate community, everyday business and travel – either predominant or central. Even in other kinds of social relationship – larger societies and larger economies – they are combined with specific technologies which reinforce them. Meanwhile, of course, other systems, quite differently based, have acquired an increasing importance. These developments and their problems were more generally discussed in the first chapter of this book. But the distinction between systems based on inherent physical resources and systems based on the development and application of objects and forces outside the human body is fundamental to understanding the complex history, including the social history, of communications technologies.

We can now make some preliminary distinctions of the most general types of communications systems, by function. Thus some systems are of an *amplifying* kind – megaphoning or telephoning or broadcasting the still autonomous human voice; transmitting voices, expressions, gestures and actions, as in television. Other systems are of a *storing* kind – recording in more or less permanent form actual human voices, as in sound recording, or expressions, perceptions, gestures and actions, as in much painting and sculpture, or both aural and visual elements in videotape and film. Still other systems are *instrumentally* alternative to the use or representation of inherent physical resources, even when they offer to be equivalent to them, such as the record and transmission of information and ideas in locally autonomous material systems, as in writing, printing and teletext.

These are not simple distinctions between 'ancient' and 'modern' communications. Some uses, however simple, of each of these types occurred very early indeed in human cultural evolution. There were and still are skills of pitching the voice to carry long distances, and methods of choosing prominent places to amplify voices and gestures. There was 'lasting' representation, 'storing' at least in effect, of such human actions as hunting, as in the cave paintings. There were also very early instrumental communications, as in the setting up of stone markers or the making of marks on trees, and again in the adaptation or invention of physical objects to transmit sound, as in shells, drums and horns. All these very early skills and devices presuppose social relations, but it was in the storing and especially the instrumental types that they moved most evidently towards systems. For obvious reasons, it is in the storing and some of the instrumental modes that there has been most survival into later periods, yet it is notorious that many of the surviving marks and representations are very difficult to interpret, largely because their elements of inherent system have been lost. The possibility of interpretation is, indeed, quite precisely related to the extent to which such elements became fully systematic, rather than conventional processes still directly attached to lived and living social relations.

But we can see very early, in some cases, some direct relations between systems and institutions, as distinct from more general relations between skills or devices and the fact of social relationships. Thus we find the mnemonic, indicative or initiation devices of early calendars and genealogies, topographical plans, and above all cult modes and objects, discussed by Professor Goody in relation to tribal and advanced tribal societies. There can be no doubt that these are discretely systematic, in direct relation to social organization. But there is then an intensification of system, and a move towards its generalization, in the development of writing systems in the temple cities and then in the extending trading areas. It is significant that these major advances in what was already becoming a communications technology are predominantly of an instrumental kind, and there are direct relations (as already in tribal societies, in the case of the cults) between the increased complexity and efficiency of the system and its social specialization: 'it was the complexity of the writing that confined its systematic use to a well-trained set of "scribes",' whose position also rested upon the fact that they were largely trained by priests. At the same time the primary uses of the system were directly related to the same form of social organization: 'the records mainly refer to the property and accounts of temples'. The further development of writing systems was directly related to the development of specific kinds of urban economy: 'nor was it simply a consequence but also a condition of that development'. But with the expansion of trading areas, new writing systems, and above all the alphabetic, took the possibilities of instrumental communication beyond local institutional systems, extending at once its range and its content, and indeed making possible the general social dimension rather than the specialized craft of literacy.

Techniques and their realization

Yet there is then an evident asymmetry between the social possibilities of the new instrumental system and the actual institutions which could alone provide access to it. For many centuries, though writing had spread beyond the specialized scribes to a more general educated class, it still spread only to minorities of the actual populations in which, in matters of law, property, history and ideas, it was now a major organizing force. Thus, not for the first or the last time, a communications system and its technology stood in contradictory relations to the institutions which employed and controlled it. In the earliest human communications, use of and access to the various systems, whether amplifying, storing or instrumental, had been relatively generalized, since the relations between the systems and quite general immediate social skills and resources were necessarily close. The increasing complexity of the systems, indeed the movement from techniques to what can properly be called early technologies, made the new relations at best problematic. It was not now by being a person in a place that relative access to the central communications systems of the group was assured. Increasingly, in certain important areas of life, there was a network of institutional arrangements, most evidently in selective educational institutions, which determined the possibility of full communicative resources and access, and this organization of differential access to the most developed communications systems both corresponded to and was itself an integral part of general social organization.

The increased range and the greatly expanded content of written communications only deepened this stratification. For a very long time after writing systems developed, large areas of cultural life were still primarily oral: But, alongside these, the power and continuity of written bodies of law, history, social and religious thought and literature were steadily increasing. By the time of the invention of printing, and its first applications, the asymmetry between the abstract possibilities of the new technologies and their actual, institutionally controlled uses was remarkable. The alphabetic script, the pre-print technologies of reproduction and distribution of writing, and then the printed book itself all contained abstract possibilities (all eventually to be realized in certain societies). At each stage of the development of the actual techniques and technologies these possibilities were not only not fully used but were in many cases deliberately arrested. A simple history of the developing technologies, considered in isolation, might indicate a steady generalization and strengthening of human communication. But technologies, as we saw earlier, can never be considered in isolation. The technique of writing is one thing, but the *technology* of writing involved not only the development of writing instruments and materials, but also the development of a wider body of knowledge, and specifically of the skills of reading, which was in practice inextricable from the most general forms of social organization. Thus it should come as no surprise to find

Professor Martin showing us that 'access to books has contributed to the structuring of a hierarchical social order'. Effective use of the new technology, at the level of reading, required a 'long apprenticeship' which presupposed, for several centuries, a relatively privileged social position: an initial privilege which, as Professor Martin further argues, 'yielded returns which could be reinvested to further advantage'. Thus the relations between a technology and its most general institutions became the ground, first, of specific social differentiations and later, inevitably, of social conflict.

Between the invention of printing, in the 15th century, and our own day, there has been a long and complex series of institutional changes and conflicts in the uses of this powerful and often decisive technology. Frequently these changes and conflicts have represented major issues in the whole development of societies. Thus the long and seemingly endless battle for the freedom to write, print and distribute our own thoughts has been, in one society after another, a key issue in the development both of free intellectual inquiry and of political democracy. Every kind of measure has been adopted against it, from systems of state licensing and the ecclesiastical controls of the *imprimatur* through to general legal provisions in such areas as security, libel and obscenity and organized political censorship. Important gains have been made in some constitutional provisions for the freedom of the press, but in world terms the freedom to print is still extremely uneven and in many societies still does not exist. The tangled and bitter history of the struggle for freedom to print is of course inseparable from the related struggle for the freedom and capacity to read. Yet these relations are not always direct. Some of the most bitter struggles against state licensing and ecclesiastical controls occurred when the majority of people were still unable and unlikely to read. On the other hand, in certain societies, the balance eventually struck between freedom of the press and a minority reading public was deeply disturbed when social and technical changes were beginning to expand the reading public. A good example is the political crisis of English newspapers in the early 19th century. After repeated struggles, most importantly over the right to report the proceedings of Parliament, the relative freedom of some minority newspapers had been established. But in the political crisis from the 1790s a whole new press, written for and often by the new urban working class, grew up alongside newspapers of the older type, and new and severe legislation was enacted against them. As Lord Ellenborough explained for the Government, at the time of the 1819 Stamp Duties Act, 'It was not against the respectable Press that this Bill was directed, but against a pauper press.' This was still at a time when less than half the population

Two views of the struggle for freedom to print. The writer in chains: a satirical cartoon in response to punitive legislation in Britain, 1819.

The pen dipped in blood: a poster for an exhibition of Soviet *samizdat* literature secretly circulated in typescript.

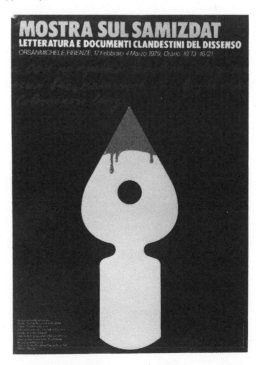

could read. Comparable situations and struggles can be found in, for example, the Germany of Bismarck and early-19th-century Spain.

But of course the distribution of print was not limited by ability to read. In the early 19th century, at once because of reading difficulties and because of the expense of buying books and newspapers, formal and informal group reading – reading aloud – was very common. The interaction between written and oral forms was indeed very complex. The church sermon, often later printed, retained a central importance. Its secular successor, the public lecture, was just entering its major social development, and it is remarkable, for example, how much important 19th-century social thought in England – from Coleridge through Carlyle and Ruskin to Matthew Arnold and William Morris – was first delivered in lectures and only later printed in books. In these varying ways, the real public for what was in effect the combined operation of oral and printed communication was becoming very large. It was a quite different social situation from that of the relative predominance of print in the period 1890–1940.

By the later period, in the most advanced societies, systems of near-universal education in literacy had been established. This relative specialization of education to literacy of course had its own effects. Since the Renaissance, though then for more limited numbers, the defining quality of education had been this mastery of reading print, by comparison for example with the substantial elements of oral training, as in the great systems of rhetoric, in the medieval curriculum. The problem of the relations between this newly central skill and the other relevant skills of adult life became acute as education was extended to whole populations. Some of the consequences of these particular relations are still being critically experienced in the late 20th century. There was of course much resistance to the institution of popular education, on anti-democratic political grounds. But, sometimes confused with this, there were both generous and ungenerous questions about the relations between this central skill of reading and most types of adult work. What eventually carried the day for reading was a combination of three rather different considerations: first, and perhaps especially in the Protestant countries, the desire for moral instruction and moral improvement by the capacity to read the Bible; second, the increasing need, in the new industrial economy, to read printed information and instructions; and, third, the political need for access to facts and arguments in a developing political democracy (a case made from both sides: by the popular forces, that the press was the engine of liberty; by the anti-popular forces, at this late stage, that the new voters must be properly instructed). There were many

social complications. Some of those arguing that the poor must be able to read the Bible, as a means to their moral improvement, overlooked the fact that there is no way of teaching a man to read the Bible which does not also enable him to read the radical press. The consequent disillusion was considerable. Again others argued that the poor should be taught to read, in the interests of moral improvement and working efficiency, but that there was no need at all to teach them to write, beyond the capacity to append a signature, since it was evident that they would have nothing to communicate on their own account. Out of these mixed motives and considerations a system of general literacy eventually emerged. Elementary literacy in England, for example, rose from some 50 per cent in the 1820s to some 90 per cent in the 1890s, and this trend is broadly characteristic of other West European societies in the same period.

Types of popular culture

But there were now quite new problems in the relations between the technology and the institutions. Over a long period, as is clear from Professor Martin's account, elements of an earlier oral culture – 'ballads and "street literature" ' – had been incorporated into print, and new popular print forms, such as almanacs, had been developed. This long period marks the phase of an established popular culture being translated and developed into printed forms. Early popular newspapers bear many of the marks of this inheritance. But the eventual establishment of a widely distributed commercial popular press inaugurated a new phase in the relations between oral and printed cultures. This phase is of course inseparable from general social changes, and in particular the rapid development of predominantly urban and industrial economies. Organized sport (mainly football and horse-racing) and organized commercial entertainment (popular theatres and eventually cinema and television) were not only newly important institutions in urban industrial societies; they became major items of news of all kinds in the new popular press. Their combination with earlier kinds of item – reports of notorious crimes and of scandals – produced a distinctive modern cultural form which still, very obviously, makes some definitions of 'newspaper' ambiguous. The claim of the press to be a 'fourth estate' in political life was sustained by one kind of newspaper, which took its central material from political and economic affairs. By contrast, much of the new 'popular press', though including some of this material, became a specific form which offered to represent, at its chosen level, the general cultural interests of the whole society. These alternative forms of development, important everywhere, are especially evident in the history of the press in the United States, which produced the most influential examples of the latter form. The transition from a 'folk culture', or indeed from a 'popular culture' in the older sense, to a modern type of 'popular culture', now basically derivative from organized central institutions, is a remarkable example of the interaction between a major technology and major social institutions: a history in print which has since been widely repeated in later media.

It is in this perspective that we have to look again at the complex relations between communications technologies and social institutions. For of course this new popular press was made possible only by significant technical developments: steam printing, cheaper production of paper, the telegraph for news-gathering, the railways for rapid distribution. The first two of these were specific to the development of the press, and were, as inventions, specifically sought; in neither area was there mere random technical discovery, which then changed a wider world. On the other hand, their development was closely bound up with the more general changes which were producing the conditions in which the new social and cultural form was necessary: changes which were by no means fully foreseen. Steam printing was an evident application of the more general development of steam engineering for pumping, textile manufacture and locomotion. Improved paper production was a development within the general advance of the chemical industry. Improvements in type-setting and graphic reproduction, on the other hand, were more specific. Improvements in signalling systems had originally been sought mainly for military purposes, but the coincidence of the electric telegraph with the new situation of the newspaper was decisive. The railways, of course, were primarily developed for moving people and goods, but, once built, transformed the social relations of newspaper distribution. The whole interaction is exceptionally complex, with no simple cases of cause and effect, either way.

Yet the general consequences of these interrelated technical and social changes included, in largely unforeseen ways, important changes in the character of the cultural institutions. The amounts of capital required to take full advantage of the new technical and social opportunities led to profound changes in the social character of the press. The English example is extreme but not unrepresentative. In the second half of the 19th century the ownership and control of newspapers moved, in the majority of cases, from small and often local family businesses to a more concentrated corporate stage, in which whole strings of newspapers and magazines were owned and controlled by a few powerful individuals or groups. This contradiction between the democratic potentials of the technology and the specific social and economic conditions which determined its full application and development has been very important indeed, throughout the 20th century.

Communications in the new market

Moreover, within this type of development of the press, there was to be a further development of a major and novel communications system. In many early newspapers, the taking of small commercial notices – what we now call 'classified' advertising – had been a significant factor in revenue and an important element of the newspaper's services. Such advertising was characteristically related to small businesses and to certain novel imported products. The great changes in manufacturing which occurred in the 19th century were very late in being reflected in newspapers. Indeed the new larger-scale advertising looked for every other way to reach its new urban public, from processions and hoardings to fly-bills, since the newspapers, with their quite rigid column layouts, were unwilling to include the 'display' advertising which the new larger manufacturers wanted and which they were already exhibiting elsewhere. But in the last years of the century, with great consequent change in both the layout and the economics of newspapers, display advertising at last penetrated the press. Page layout, type sizes and graphics were all affected, and there was a complex interrelated development of new advertising and journalistic styles (the headline and the slogan; the designed page rather than the assembly of columns; altered relations and proportions between images and print). Increasingly, in the 20th century, income from advertising became a major rather than, as earlier, a minor factor in newspaper economics. Circulation studies and media market research developed in attendant institutions. Advertising agencies changed from booking offices to skilled originators of material and whole campaigns. By the mid-20th century the suitability of a newspaper for effective advertising was to become a major, and in some cases a dominant, criterion for its survival in its original function. Criteria for economically viable circulation changed remarkably. To sell a million copies of a popular newspaper was, by the 1950s in England (where the concentration of 'national' papers was extreme, by international standards), not nearly enough, though to sell less to a public whose buying habits were of more interest to advertisers, as in local newspapers or papers read mainly by higher-income groups, was still quite effective. Thus the specific interrelations of a technology and its social and economic conditions produced results which were in no sense determined by the nature of the technology as such, and which might even, as in this case, in some respects contradict it. The technology which had promised both extension and diversity had, in these circumstances, produced a remarkable and specific kind of extension (what came to be called the 'mass' public) and, by comparison with its own earlier stages, an actually reduced diversity.

Yet while this was the major and indeed dominant line of development, it was always possible to maintain a certain level of oppositional and alternative production. The battle for the big publics had been won by the most advanced print technologies in a context determined by centralized capital, combine ownership and distribution, and a planned interlock with corporate advertising. Yet in the 19th century, as in the 17th century, the culture of the pamphlet and the oppositional newspaper was still intensely active. Indeed at the level of production its technical means were continually improved and made more accessible; it was mainly at the level of distribution that it had been outclassed and in effect marginalized. This situation persisted in the 20th century, but from the 1960s there were important changes. Because of competition from other media, the high point of development of the 'mass newspaper' had been passed, though, within an overall decline of circulation, more intense competition and still further simplification, towards the standard 'tabloid', were evident. In the most centralized print cultures, and especially in Britain, the 'mass' newspaper market began to shrink and there was a flow of new vitality at two different levels: the commercial local press, and new kinds of community and alternative publications. While the centralized press went through fierce and sometimes disabling internal conflicts, significantly centred on the problems of adopting the new, faster, capital- rather than labour-intensive electronic print technology, these other sectors were able to make relatively rapid (in the case of alternative publications, extremely rapid) use of new printing and reproductive techniques.

These are still only marginal changes in the inherited general situation, but they probably indicate the lines of a more general change. They are a useful reminder of the fact that while there can be historical plateaus in which there are settled and apparently permanent relations between a developed technology and certain social conditions and relations of production, there can also be sudden scarps in which a whole set of institutional arrangements, exploiting a technology in determined and established ways, can be seen to be in crisis: a crisis which may at first be seen in isolation, as problems *within* such institutions, but which shows itself eventually as a very complex interaction of innovating

technologies and quite general social and economic factors. In the case of print, such a plateau occurred not only in the history of the newspaper but in the history of the book. From the late 18th century to the mid-20th century, improvements in printing and paper and binding technology made possible a remarkable expansion and also a remarkable cultural diversity in publication and readership. But from the mid-20th century onwards, certain crucial cost factors in the traditional technology began moving the other way, and there were more or less rapid institutional and cultural changes. On the one hand there was a sharp and persistent move towards combine publishing, as distinct from the earlier range of small to medium independent publishers: a move which repeated, structurally, what had happened to newspapers in the second half of the 19th century. At the same time there was the decisive innovation of the paperback book, at first as cheap reprints; later, though still insufficiently, as original titles. At the level of technology alone, the paperback represents a decisive lowering of costs, but of course the technology never does stand alone. The determining factor of distribution, at the level of a new equation between production cost and selling price, led in combine conditions to quite new definitions of the effective size and speed of sale of editions. These definitions, rationalized as the technology but in fact a combination of the technology with determinate economic institutions, brought market considerations to a much earlier stage in the planning and writing of books. At the same time, while institutions of increasing size and cultural predictability came to dominate the general market, there were new opportunities, in the many left-over areas, for new kinds of

Who sells the pasta fasta?

From sandwich man to ad-man: marketing ('mass' marketing) is now enthroned at the heart of our most important communication systems. (Cartoon by R. O. Blechman.)

232

small publishers using new electronic and reproductive technologies. This complex development, in book publishing, is still at this stage occurring within a general expansion, by contrast with the beginnings of a general recession in newspapers.

The interaction of technologies

It is convenient to follow the relations between technologies and institutions in a single medium, as here with print, but of course the real situation has for nearly a century been much more complex and interactive. The crucial modern developments of the technologies of extended sound and extended image, described by Professor Pool and Dr Jowett, have had very deep but also diverse institutional effects. Thus it is interesting, as Professor Pool shows, that by contrast with the centralizing and standardizing institutional effects of the 'popular' press and later broadcasting, the telephone was a technology which not only permitted but encouraged direct person-to-person communications. Much the same can be said of the private photograph, within extended and now often separated families. These are especially interesting cases, in that we can see the problems of cause and effect in an unusually long sequence. Thus both the telephone and the photograph were consciously sought, as inventions, though as usual in such cases the precise forms were not always exactly foreseen. The social and economic conditions which made both technologies desirable were thus already present, as a shaping general context.

In the case of the telephone, the proximate causes are more evident: the general increase of trade, and social specialization into desirable and undesirable residential districts, within the turbulently expanding industrial cities. These were already the effects of other productive technologies and their specific social relations. But then the telephone, designed for this business use, contributed directly to an acceleration of the newly emerging patterns of settlement – as in Professor Pool's example of the business quarter, the skyscraper and (here quite subsidiary to transport technologies) the commuter suburb. Moved beyond its business use, it was then an available technology for personal contact within the new conditions of dispersal of friends and families.

The proximate causes of photography are more predominantly scientific and technical, though the intense interest in reproducible images – and especially in images of persons – is almost certainly itself a response to quite new problems of perception and identification within a society characterized by wholly unprecedented mobility and change. To these basic factors were then added the effects of the vast dispersal of families in the generations of emigration, colonization and urbanization. Within this dispersal, the cheaply reproducible personal image took on a quite new cultural importance, at the same time that more internal cultural effects, in the new social psychology of the image, were also strengthening.

But then the use of the private telephone and the private photograph, within this socially and economically determined area, were the means to new kinds of contact and response, of an assuring and confirming kind. We have only to imagine a modern large-scale metropolitan society without the technologies of the personal telephone and the personal photograph (and the associated personal letter of modern postal systems) to realize that these technologies, produced and developed within a vastly dispersed and (in received terms) dehumanizing social tendency, were seized on as at least to some degree mitigating such conditions; and, more, were the means to wider and more varied personal and social contacts than had been possible within older and more settled communities.

But then, at a quite different level, the predominant general (as distinct from individual) technologies of extended sounds and extended images passed at the same time, though in quite different ways, into new kinds of social and cultural institution. The case of the cinema is especially interesting. For here already, within the new urban and metropolitan conditions, there had been a remarkable expansion, quite pre-dating cinematic technology, of new institutions of everyday entertainment. It was in the 16th century that drama changed, as a social process, from an occasional to a regular provision. The performance of plays at set times of the year, usually as part of a religious festival, came to be replaced by a repertory of productions in new kinds of theatre. In England, for example, the first commercial theatres were built in the last quarter of the 16th century, significantly at the approaches to the City of London, to catch a passing as well as a resident trade. Their physical structure followed precedents in performances in the courtyards of inns. Thus the transition from the occasional drama to regular drama was directly associated with a more mobile, trading society. In different social conditions, in 16th-century Spain, municipal professional theatres were rapidly extended beyond the capital city. The subsequent development of theatres of this modern type was closely associated with the development of modern cities, first metropolitan, then provincial. The major period of general expansion was in the urbanizing and industrializing societies of the 19th century.

Continuity and transformation in city entertainment: the Roxy cinema is a *theatre*, and looks like one, but picture and (with the newly-arrived Vitaphone) sound are reproduced products of centralized institutions (United Artists) with their money-making star system (Gloria Swanson).

The arrival of the motion picture was within this structured phase. At first it occupied the fringes of the show-business world, as had the music-halls and 'out-of-town' theatres of earlier decades. But the power of the motion picture, and especially its capacity to realize effects which had been repeatedly attempted, but with more limited success, in the advanced technology of the stage-theatres, soon brought a decisive central establishment: the 'motion-picture theatre' – 'movie house' or 'cinema'. A crucial technical advantage – rapid multiple distribution of a filmed production – then put it almost at once ahead of the stage-theatres. The same technical factor made possible, and in important ways led to, a novel centralization of production and, in relation to the capital costs of these reproducible productions, conditions of relative monopoly: not only within societies but, because of the factor of rapid reproductive distribution, paranationally, as in the relative monopoly of American production.

Thus the institutions of everyday entertainment, long associated with the city and with the form of the stage-theatre, were at once extended, with a certain continuity – the distribution of films, until a much later stage, with the predominance of television, was through *theatres* – and, in the process, from the factor of centralized production of indefinitely reproducible performances, transformed. Cultural tendencies towards monopoly from a fashionable centre, clearly visible in European and American stage-theatres throughout the 18th and 19th centuries, were heavily reinforced by the new centralizing technology and then by the specific paracultural qualities of the North American cultural process: the simultaneous integration of newly urbanizing and newly immigrant people. The conjunction of these conditions pushed the institutions of cinema in a certain direction (that of relative monopoly) and selected, for dominance, certain modes of artistic use of the technology. At the same time, in relatively subordinated or protected or privileged areas, other artistic uses of the technology became evident, though the problem of the relations of such 'minority' films to the predominant institutions was persistent and often insoluble.

In the same period, though always at a relatively later phase, the technology of sound broadcasting entered its own problematic institutional development. Professor Pool shows (Chapter 7) how closely the development of the actual technology was related to pre-existent official and business uses. And in this case there was no prepared alternative, as in the music-halls and theatres, to take in and adapt to the new technology. Instead, a new set of social conditions both made possible, and in a sense required, new kinds of communicative relations. Theatres and cinemas (like sports

stadiums and commercial and cultural exhibitions) had belonged to the phase of urban and metropolitan accumulation. They depended on bringing together, by prior assembly or by new regular transport systems, significant numbers of people in designated public places. Yet there were now two further factors. Within the cities there were very many people, at many times of the day and night, who were unable, for various reasons – hours of work, family responsibilities in homes, shortage of money – to go, at all regularly, to the places of regular public entertainment. Moreover, outside the cities, and outside the suburbs, there were large numbers of people for whom opportunities of this kind were still, in effect, occasional at best, non-existent at worst, yet who, because of the decisive general development of predominantly urban and industrial cultures, were already or were becoming socially, culturally and politically attuned to the dominant centres. The technology of radio broadcasting, initially developed for quite different purposes, was adapted to these conditions by investment-directed development of the domestic receiver. Soon the whole range of pre-existent communicative relationships – the long-standing and now fully-developed institutions of public assembly, from theatres and concert halls to public meetings and lectures, but also the second-phase institutions of centralized production and rapid physical distribution or reproduction, such as the press and the cinema – was challenged by this new set of relationships: the domestic receiver in direct relation to a centre or centres of regular broadcasting; the inclusion of several hitherto separated functions – news, opinion, music and drama – within a single technology, first in radio and then, even more powerfully and generally, in television.

Types of large-scale communication

It is crucial to distinguish between these two phases of modern communications institutions, which are usually blurred by the overriding and vague concept of 'mass communications'. There are decisive social differences between three types of communicative institution: (i) public assembly; (ii) variable distribution of reproduced central products; (iii) direct distribution of a centralized range of

Radio's ability to provide free listening outside the hours of regular public entertainment is neatly summed up in this Radio Luxembourg advertisement mimicking a cinema programme display: 'Nonstop show, admission free, from 6.00 in the morning to 1 o'clock at night.'

products. It is open to argument whether the metaphor of 'mass' is best applied to one or other of these phases. Its first application was to (i), public assembly, with the 'mass meeting' taking on new social tones in an epoch of democratic mobilization. Its second application was in a context of reproductive centralized ('mass') production – specifically, the automobile assembly line – corresponding to (ii). But this shaded, within particular marketing conditions, into considerations of the size and generality of the public reached, with effects from the centrally-determined character of the product and from the integration of hitherto separated cultural functions – as in (iii). The reduction of all these variable factors, relations and historical phases to the single concept of 'mass communications' obscures these crucial and effective distinctions. It also encourages simple, all-purpose responses to a very complicated set of phenomena. It tries to assimilate a set of very different technologies, with inherently variable functions and potentials, to a generalized 'mass communications technology' which then appears to have determinate rather than, as in fact, specifically determined and both variable and alterable social and institutional effects.

The need to retain the real distinctions, and to resist the reductive generalizing concept, is, as it happens, especially evident in the case of broadcasting. It is well known that even in societies which chose the eventually predominant form of the domestic receiver – as distinct from societies like Nazi Germany which made major use of radio as a form of street address – the nature of broadcasting institutions varied considerably. Variable answers were given to the questions raised by the social character of the new technology: its relations to official communications channels; its problems of funding. The latter question was acute. Earlier types of institution, whether those of public assembly or of the distribution of reproduced products, could operate direct charges for each use. This was impracticable, at that stage, in broadcasting (though it has since become technically practicable in television systems). The solutions adopted did not follow, except at this most general level, from the character of the technology, but from the predominant political and economic institutions of different societies. Thus there could be direct State funding, with corresponding State control of output, as in communist and some other systems; indirect State licensing, controlling both transmission and reception but, within the degree of indirectness, permitting relatively independent but still largely centralized production; or, as in the United States, funding by a complex interaction of the manufacturers of domestic receivers and general advertising interests. Each funding solution had

inevitable effects on productive content, which, as the cultural history of radio shows very clearly, was in only very general ways determined by the technology alone.

What is particularly striking about the history of broadcasting is that, unlike all earlier communications technologies, it was available as a major distributive system before there was any important definition of what was to be distributed. It took many years to move broadcasting from its two earliest practices – *amplifying* sound events which were already occurring, in other institutions and forms; or simply *filling-in*, with improvised material, to maintain the service or retain the audience – into what was eventually specific autonomous production. In news, opinion and drama, especially, radio and television eventually produced work of very high quality – as well as much else, of course. In music, interacting with the new technology of sound recording by disks and eventually cassettes, it radically changed both the distributive relations and eventually some important elements in the production of music. But, by this time, the generality of its systems was such that the technology was, at least potentially, a common carrier.

To understand the opportunities and the problems of this stage we have to look again at some fundamental distinctions between communications systems. From the beginning of writing through to the 19th century there were certain inevitable relations between uses of the technologies and the acquisition (itself socially determined or controlled) of the relevant specific skills. Even with the eventual coming of general literacy, there was a continuing direct relation between a specific training and the uses of print. What then happened, or can appear to have happened, was a radical shift of the relations between systems of social training and access to the products of the new technologies. The most basic social skills, of a kind acquired in quite primary development and relationship, gave access to the motion picture, the radio broadcast, the television programme, at the level of reception, while very easily learned skills gave more general access, including some production, to the photograph and the telephone.

Thus the new technologies were inherently more general, and less apparently subject to systems of training. Much of their popularity undoubtedly derived from these facts. The para-national character of much of the cinema, the developed para-national character of some radio, took people across some cultural frontiers and barriers, but of course still largely in determined conditions. It was not only that the institutions of the new technologies, in the very course of their development, and especially of autonomous production, became, in themselves, training systems. In immediate ways, types of speech, points of view, catch-phrases, jingles, rhythms were in effect taught. Less immediately, some conventions of relationship, of behaviour, of personal and social perspectives, were disseminated by reiterated practice. What had been true of all communications systems was now more generalized by the very fact that the new systems meshed so readily with unspecialized receptive skills. And then the further area of determination, at this stage, was the unprecedented relative monopoly, for audiences of this size, both within and across national societies. Major uses of the new technologies came to depend on unprecedented concentrations of communications capital, and there were then very complex and at times contradictory relations between these new systems and the more normal (State, church, school, family) networks of social and cultural training.

No simple balance can then be struck. In some ways, themselves highly variable according to the character of local institutions, new cultural choices, and effective if still limited

processes of cultural mobility, were undoubtedly achieved. The relatively late case of the portable transistor radio, taking the machine out of the family home again, is striking. In other ways, at the stage of relative monopoly – local, national or international – some, perhaps many, of the new choices and mobilities were much more deeply determined than those who first experienced them realized. Some at least of the new horizons were put there to be found: programmed and indeed marketed.

One crucial response to this complex situation was the development of new or adapted institutions – from censorship, through codes, through advisory committees, to media research and education – which sought to control, monitor, or even, occasionally, understand what was happening. Typically much of their attention went to children, who were only the most evident case of those many who now had alternatives, or apparent alternatives, to the normal systems of social and cultural training. For many of the urgent issues being discovered in media practice were at least

Reading calls for training: radio is easily accessible to all. A German cartoon extolling the advantages of a new station broadcasting to Turkish immigrant workers.

forms of deeper issues of social and cultural change in a much wider dimension. To the extent that this is realized, the usefulness of monitoring and critical responses can be at once affirmed and defined. For they are necessary responses to communications as centralized propaganda or centralized marketing systems, yet until they have engaged with the real processes and the really new technologies of social change and mobility they cannot be much more than marginal.

From the 1960s, and now at what is technically a rapidly increasing pace, certain factors of the technologies have begun to change. The high capital costs of the productive and reproductive technologies, following in part from the centralizing directions in which they had been steered by investment, but following also in some respects from the actual technical stages, are beginning to be succeeded by a period in which (in part from the development of the next stage of the high-capital productive market) *means of production* (as in video) *are themselves being distributed,* or are becoming accessible to more diverse, more autonomous, more voluntary and self-organizing institutions. The problems of this phase are still complex and still emerging. Some of the new 'means of production' are, like most photographic cameras, effectively a stimulus to the use of relatively centralized and profitable processing facilities. Others are a kind of unloading of new domestic machines as marginal consumer products. Neither development, of this kind, implies any significant institutional change.

Yet there could, with enough thought and effort, be quite radical institutional innovations. Many of the details of these are discussed in the next chapter. The epochal change, if it could indeed be achieved, would be a movement beyond the two previous major stages of communications technologies and institutions. The stage of minority instrumental systems (writing and printing) has already been joined and in some sectors succeeded by majority systems (print in generally literate societies, cinema, radio, television) in which the typical relation is one of a few producers to many consumers:

a repetition, in new technical forms, of a major division of labour: the reproduction, in communications, of profound social divisions, and of effective (if relative and changing) social domination and subordination. In this second stage, the limited distribution of specialized products has been overtaken by the wide distribution of generalized products. What may now be possible is a qualitative change to the wide distribution of *processes*: the provision of equitable access to the means and resources of directly-determined communication, serving immediate personal and social needs. The limited mobility of choice between specialized and generalized products could be steadily and in some cases dramatically extended to the full mobility of a range of communications processes which in all their aspects – amplifying and connecting, storing and reminding, alternative and extending – would be the means and resources of a qualitatively different social life.

It will not happen without precise thought and effort, nor without very widespread discussion and quite public decision-making: the inescapable means to its specific end. The institutions of direct democracy and of personal liberty – and of their complex interrelations in self-managing communities and societies – are in communications, as more generally, still largely to be explored. But we are now at one of those historical moments when the relations between communications technologies and social institutions are a matter not only for study and analysis, but for a wide set of practical choices. It is not only (though it will often be presented as) a matter of instituting new technologies. The directions in which investment in research and development should go are now, in this field, fundamental social decisions. The effort to understand and take part in them is more likely to be made, as against the bewildered reception of new products and processes which 'just happen', if enough of us realize the scale of the communicative and thus social transformation which is now becoming, though still in ways to be decided, technically and institutionally possible.

Cartoon by R. O. Blechman

The Electronic
Cornucopia

Man's eyes and ears remain, and must always remain, the central mechanism of all communications systems. The links connecting the transmitter of a message with the receiver grow more complex every day – satellites, micro-miniaturized computers, optical fibres, electronic retrieval networks – but in the end everything has to be translated back into audible sounds and visible shapes and colours. The human mind is indeed more than the sum total of its perceptions, but those perceptions are the raw material from which it creates its version of the world – a reassuring thread to hold as we enter the bewildering labyrinth of modern technology, where the prospects of both extending and manipulating the means by which we exchange information and ideas seem practically infinite.

In this last picture section we confront one of the great problems of our century: knowledge, more than ever before, is power; but whereas in the past the success of attempts to control communication, whether by totalitarian states or by dogmatic religions, has inevitably been partial, in the future there is some danger that it may become total. Computer services, the storage of records, the press, radio and television are now so centralized and so expensive that a strong government could effectively ration some important areas of the information available to its people. Will the shining prospects opened up for us by the technological revolution turn out to be a prison? Or can the new processes be used to uphold and extend the liberties and opportunities of information and communication?

178 The Belgian graphic artist Folon brilliantly captures the sinister ambiguity of our situation – the brain, fed with the products of machines through the senses, becomes a machine product itself.

UN NOUVEAU MOYEN DE COMMUNICATION: L'AUDIO-VISUEL

MIND UNDER SURVEILLANCE

The way in which the media are controlled in different parts of the world will vary according to the prevailing ideologies. In China and Cuba control is exercised in the name of the people. In the West it ranges from the overtly capitalist (commercial television, support of the press by advertisers) to the benevolent paternalism of the BBC at its best. But everywhere the tendency is to create an élite which restricts the freedom of individuals to communicate.

179   A poster displays Chinese leaders holding books, symbols of enlightenment and authority. That authority derives, in theory, from the people, but the workers with bent backs remain workers. Someone else decides who writes the books and whether they are published.

180   Fidel Castro is among those statesmen whose methods of government makes full use of the media. The first objective of many modern revolutionary movements is to seize the radio station.

181   A controller sits in front of his battery of screens and switches which represents a massive investment of capital. What we see at the other end depends on which button he presses.

182–4   Three warning images of power abused: a poster by the Polish artist Marian Nowinski – a book (by Pablo Neruda) nailed shut and the nails bent over; a novel road sign by the Paris student movement, 'Attention. Radio tells lies'; and a television set as gendarme, another comment from the radical left.

242

ATTENTION
la radio ment

MIND AT LIBERTY

To make any independent statement using the modern media demands a certain level of expertise. To address a public meeting was easy; to print a pamphlet needed only modest equipment; to put out a radio or television programme is more complicated but learnable. A recent development in the electronics industry has been to make the necessary 'hardware' available more cheaply than in the past.

185 A West Indian boy helping to make a record in a Caribbean youth club.

186 'Citizen Band' in the USA uses the resources of radio to reinforce community links. Open to all, it can operate to entertain, to call for help, to assist the law or even – for instance in warning fellow motorists about police traps – to defeat it.

187 Children making a video film. Such small-scale enterprises – a novel feature of the media scene – save the media from being completely monolithic.

188 Home video frees the viewer from the broadcast schedules. This machine includes devices for slow-motion and freezing the image.

KEYBOARD CULTURE

The computerized future promised to us by the electronic engineers seems at first inhuman, even mindless, but like all such innovations it is morally neutral. By making a greater range of information available to us very much faster than previously, these machines will doubtless quicken the pace of life; they will also – less directly – be among the factors influencing its quality.

189 Video-conferencing. With television and simultaneous translation, people from all over the world can confer as if they were sitting in the same room.

190 Every kind of information, from recipes to book reviews, from world events to football results, can now be made available on television screens. (It is interesting to see that the advertiser here, Prestel, thinks it desirable to keep the human touch – the coffee cup and the message 'Your lunch is ready'.)

191   Status, a computer developed by the United Kingdom Atomic Energy Authority, closely follows the human method of searching and browsing to unearth wanted facts – but in seconds rather than hours.

192   At the international news agency Reuters, keyboard and television screen enable an editor or staff writer to plug in to a central computerized news file fed by reports from outside.

193   A similar device in use in the London Stock Exchange. Using a micro-miniature digital computer, it provides a continuously updated account of 750 leading share prices.

194   An Olivetti advertisement: a jumble of keyboard symbols catches the eye of the layman.

X
THE FUTURE
OF THE MEDIA

Ederyn Williams

195   Each apparent miracle succeeds the last with bewildering rapidity. The newest revolution is to replace metal wires carrying electrical impulses by glass fibres carrying light **impulses. Now a hundred thousand messages can be transmitted simultaneously. This greatly magnified detail shows the 'nerve-ends' of a number of fibres, which would be bound together and insulated to form a cable. Optical fibre transmission is only the latest of a series of techniques all of which increase the capacity of communications channels. It is possible that in the near future the placing and movement of some kinds of worker will become of secondary importance – an office switchboard could be in a different city; professional colleagues could work as easily 1000 miles apart as next door; and every kind of detailed information will be instantly available everywhere in the world.**

THE FUTURE
OF THE MEDIA

As we enter the 1980s, we seem to be on the threshold of a period of quite unprecedented change, during which new communications media will appear with bewildering frequency. Many of our basic preconceptions about the nature of human communication and about the role of the existing media are likely to be overturned. There will be many surprises, though for someone who understands the fundamentals of human communication, outlined in Chapters 2 to 4, they may not be quite so surprising.

The new media are the product of a convergence between systems of transmitting information – telecommunications – and systems of storing and processing information – computers. Technical and technological breakthroughs within these two domains, ranging from miniaturized electronic circuits to satellites launched by rockets, are continually reducing costs and adding to what the systems can do – often in ways that are not immediately obvious to us. For example, the telephone seems, to a user, much like it was in 1876 when Bell invented it. Yet behind the scenes there have been enormous strides. Already, one channel on a satellite or a wave-guide link can carry 100,000 telephone calls simultaneously, and still newer systems, based on glass fibres, may soon greatly exceed even that performance.

We have all noticed the rapid fall in the price of calculators: a programmable calculator can now be bought for less than the price of a week's groceries, yet it has the power of some of the early computers that filled a whole room and cost more than a helicopter. It is rapidly becoming true that the cost of the plastic case, the buttons and the batteries is greater than the cost of the electronic circuitry. Mini- and microcomputers in the home and on office desks are now a reality, and many other devices benefit from the same developments. These advances are the product of the micro-miniaturization of electronic components. It is now possible to pack thousands of transistors and resistors into a few square centimetres, to give a smaller, cheaper and more reliable product than the old valve technology could possibly achieve.

Progress has been just as stunning in information storage. Even now, you could carry around the complete works of Shakespeare in your pocket (using slips of miniaturized film called microfiche) and you could store all the information from the biggest library in a small room. Newer technology, using lasers, promises even more densely packed information, and it seems that it will not be long before we can get the whole of *Encyclopaedia Britannica* into a matchbox.

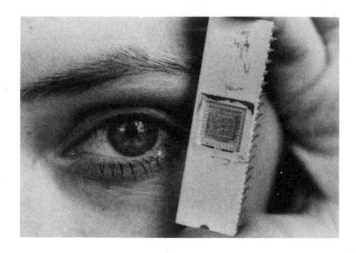

The miracle of micro-miniaturization: a silicon chip containing many thousands of electronic switches or 'gates', mounted with its connections and terminals, is held up for comparison in size with the human eye.

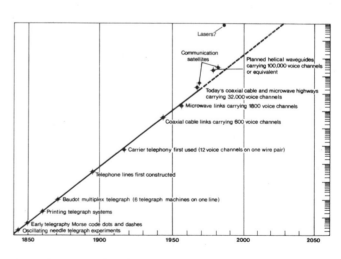

The explosive growth in the carrying capacity of telecommunications links in a century. A unit of 1 telephone call is represented on the scale at the point marked 'Telephone lines first constructed'. Already now one channel on a communications satellite can carry 100,000 telephone calls simultaneously.

It seems that there are no technical limits to the electronic cornucopia which will engulf us before the year 2000.

In order to organize the myriad of possible new communications devices, I shall group them into four classes: entertainment systems (present examples are television and radio); information and calculation services (encyclopaedia, calculator); message-sending systems (post, telegram); and person-to-person communication devices (telephone).

Entertainment systems

Most people in the developed world have now made the transition to colour television. Several further advances are now on the market to tempt us.

Projection television, with a picture expanded to 3 ft × 3 ft (1 m. × 1 m.), or even 15 ft × 15 ft (5 m. × 5 m.), is becoming quite common in bars in the USA, and attracts customers who would otherwise stay at home to watch the big sporting events. In the home, the cost (£1000 or $2000), and the fact that the television lines become visible when a large screen is viewed close up, will probably prevent widespread adoption of this innovation.

Video-cassette recorders can be used either for repeated playing of films in an educational or training context, or in the home, to record programmes for future use. Growth has been slowed by the incompatibility of the recorders developed by different companies, but video cassettes are already replacing home movies. However, the tapes will always be relatively expensive (£10 or $20). Video disks have two great advantages over tapes: they can be stamped out in less than

a second, while tapes have to be played through to be reproduced, and they allow random access, that is you can rapidly find a place anywhere on the disk. Recently announced video-LP machines use laser technology, and the disks (which are made of plastic, and thus cheap) will store up to an hour of film or several thousand pages of text.

A little further into the future, we can expect three-dimensional television which, being based on laser photography, will not require special spectacles as did the unsuccessful 3-D cinema films.

More television channels will also become available to us. In the USA, Canada and Belgium many people are now connected to special cable networks that provide them with fifteen to twenty channels. These additional channels are mostly used for imported television: in Belgium they watch Dutch, German, French and British channels as well as their own. The increased number of channels may not add greatly to the diversity of the types of programme available: one American viewer is said to have remarked sourly that he now had the choice of watching Perry Mason at 190 pounds, 210 pounds or 235 pounds. Nevertheless, in some cases quite new services are being offered. Recent films, for which a payment is required, effectively supply cinema in the home: this seems to attract many customers. With the advent of portable videotape recorders and cameras, it is now easy for anyone to become an amateur television programme maker. Local television stations in places such as New York and Genoa encourage people to make their own programmes for transmission by cable to the local area. Finally, in some localities cable television is used to provide information services: for instance, Reuter's Wall Street Prices are available on Manhattan Cable.

Striking advances are less likely for sound-only entertainment systems. Radio seems to have captured the niche of entertainment for the mobile: car drivers and people doing housework have their visual channel busy, but can still listen. Apart from an increase in the numbers of local radio stations, however, radio seems likely not to change very much. The evolution of the record player and tape recorder seems almost to have stopped: quadraphonics (four-track music) was a dismal failure, and the quality of reproduction is now so high that further improvements would be virtually undetectable by the human ear. Apart from the integration of these systems into music centres, no radical change seems likely.

Videogames like TV tennis are popular now and seem likely to become more so as more powerful computing facilities become available in the home. Perhaps it is fortunate that the initial intense appeal of games soon wears off and we can escape from them back to more natural social activities.

More television channels may not necessarily mean a greater variety of programmes.

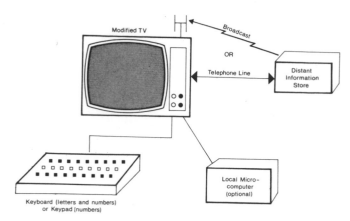

A schematic diagram of a home communications console and its links to outside information stores.

Information and calculation services

A number of novel television-linked information services use elements of the system shown in the diagram above.

The teletext services, which started in Britain in 1974 and in France and Germany soon after, use a broadcast signal over the air. Anyone with the right kind of special television can receive several hundred pages of writing and simple diagrams, telling him about the weather, the latest news, stock exchange prices or special events. He can get these at any time by the press of a button, so he does not need to fit his information needs to the broadcasting schedules. The pages are broadcast every twenty or thirty seconds, being continually updated from the central studio. As the page is broadcast the specially adapted set freezes it and displays it to the user. On-demand information at the touch of a button, previously only available to prosperous businesses using expensive computer systems, can now reach every home.

International interest in teletext systems has been considerable. Apart from Ceefax and Oracle in the UK, there are now Videotext and Bildschirmzeitung in West Germany, Antiope in France and Telset in Finland. Similar systems are also being run in the USA over cable television (the example of Reuter's Wall Street Prices has already been referred to). Japanese activity has been hindered by the complexity of their script (each letter is generated by its own micro-electronic circuit), but they are now making progress with their Captains system.

A further development on teletext is the viewdata (or videotex) system. This uses telephone lines, rather than the airwaves, to carry the information pages, which has one great advantage and one disadvantage. The advantage is that the user can instruct by button presses a computer which stores the information data bank. The store can contain several million pages of information, but computer control allows him to find quickly the one he wants. These much larger data banks can store local as well as national news, and detailed company accounts as well as just share prices. Even an encyclopaedia, consisting of 10,000 pages, has been put on the British version of viewdata, called Prestel. Again, international interest is considerable, with the Germans, French, Dutch and many other nations experimenting with viewdata systems. Prospects look promising, but we must not forget the major disadvantage: the user will have to pay extra not only for a modified television (expensive now but perhaps only £25 or $50 in five years' time), but also for the telephone call, and possibly for the information pages as well. With teletext, on the other hand, there is no means for the customer to pay for the information he gets, and lack of revenue-earning capacity is a factor inhibiting its growth.

Once someone is on-line to a computer, new horizons open up to him. He can have the computer do complex calculations, or even relatively simple calculations which are not beyond the power of a pocket calculator, but for which the user needs extra guidance. If the television has a credit card reader, or there is some similar security system, he can check his bank balance, transfer money or pay bills. He can play games against the computer (e.g. chess), or against an opponent with the computer maintaining the rules or introducing random factors.

In some cases, it would be more cost-effective for the user to have his own microcomputer rather than be on-line to a distant computer. Microcomputers for a few pounds, controlling their own data store on an audio-cassette recorder, are not far off. However, most people could not be expected to programme their own microcomputer: they

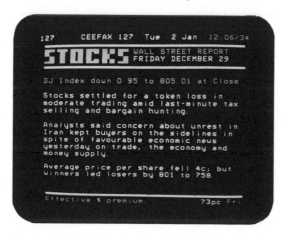

Financial news by teletext.

would either buy cassette tapes of programmes, or the microcomputer would be programmed at a distance from a teletext or viewdata information store (by what is called 'telesoftware').

At present, teletext and viewdata services have fairly crude graphics and a limited number of colours. Future developments will include improvement to both of these, though the price of this is that a more detailed picture takes longer to build up on the television screen. If there was a very broad channel into the home, such as optical fibres, then this would not be important, but it certainly is a limitation while most of us have only the ordinary telephone lines.

To many people, typed input and text output may seem an awkward means of communication. However, to develop machines that can understand human speech is quite difficult, and to produce comprehensible computer-synthesized speech is not much easier (see p. 256). We will have to be satisfied with typing for some time yet.

Message-sending systems

At present, most of us depend on the mail, plus the occasional telegram, for messages. Some businesses, however, now have telex and facsimile machines.

Telex machines are like communicating typewriters. A message typed in at one machine is sent via a special network to one or more other machines, which receive the message without a human operator. Messages can be prepared on punched tape to reduce the time that the line is open. Only the symbols on the keyboard can be sent, not pictures or diagrams.

Facsimile machines are like communicating duplicating machines. A page, with typing, writing or diagrams, is fed into one machine and is then transmitted over a telephone line to a similar machine at a distant location. The main disadvantage is that it takes between 1 and 6 minutes to send a single page, which makes on-peak long-distance use very expensive.

Facsimile machines will probably continue in use in various specialist businesses – for example, to send newspaper pictures or engineering drawings. Telex is likely to be gradually replaced by communicating word processors.

The word processor is a relatively recent concept, and depends again on advances in electronics. In essence, it is an advanced typewriter, designed to make the process of producing a typewritten document less time-consuming. It has been found that typical typists, although their typing speed may be rated at 50 to 60 words per minute, in practice only produce 10 or 15 words of final copy per minute. The rest of their time is spent in correcting errors (dismally slow with most existing methods) and retyping documents where drafting changes have been made. A word processor makes these activities much easier and quicker – and therefore more efficient, since it allows the typist to correct an error merely by overtyping the correct letters; to insert or delete a word or phrase, and shuffle all the rest of the text round so that the insertion or deletion can no longer be detected; to move whole blocks of text from one place to another, again with automatic shuffling so that no spaces are left; and to change the format of the text, e.g. the length of line or the spacing.

The more advanced word processors are computer-controlled, and the draft versions appear on a television-type screen. They are thus very like the home communications console shown in the drawing opposite.

Word processors are already having a considerable impact in the printing world, as well as in offices. Newspapers could make considerable savings if journalists input their stories directly on to word processors: the stories could then be reformatted and edited while in computer store, and the computer could control the printing process. It is this 'new technology' that has caused industrial disputes such as the one that lay behind the suspension of publication of the London *Times* in 1978 and 1979.

In offices, word processors are usually used to compose a document that is then printed out and sent through the mail. However, use of the mail is not essential: the message in computer store might be sent via a telephone line to the point of delivery, where it would be printed out or displayed on another television screen. Already delivery by telephone is cheaper, as well as faster, than delivery by mail within a local call area (this is true within London and New York). For many decades the cost trends have been against the mail and for telecommunications. The following table shows the relative movement of prices since 1948:

	1948	1958	1968	1978
Telephone call (3 minutes long distance)	100	59	38	28
Letter	100	77	96	129

This trend seems likely to continue, and the impact on the viability of the mail service as a whole may be marked. In Australia, for instance, about 37 per cent of mail is from one business to another, compared with 15 per cent from one home to another. Business mail is also cheapest to service, with bulk postings and bulk delivery to central locations. If this more profitable part of the mail usage switches to telecommunications, the unsubsidized survival of the rest would be in serious doubt.

Person-to-person communication media

At present, most of us are used to only two methods of talking to other people: by telephone and face-to-face. Multi-person telephone conversations have been available since the 1930s, though most people are unaware of this facility, and various further developments have been demonstrated.

The video-telephone (or videophone) was first used in 1927 between Washington and New York. The Bell System tried to introduce it more widely in 1971, but – despite its seeming inevitability judged by all the science fiction we read or see – it was a commercial failure. In part this was owing to cost, which was particularly high because the videophone signal takes up the equivalent of 250 telephone channels. However, there are also real doubts, based on psychological evidence, as to whether people want the videophone at any price. It is fairly certain that most of us will not be using videophones by the year 2000.

Audio conferencing, on the other hand, is becoming more and more popular. There are now various devices for holding discussions between two or more groups at different locations. Some are relatively small and can sit on a desk. Others are more elaborate, giving better quality sound and extra facilities but inevitably at greater expense and with less mobility. All have the great advantage that they can use one or two telephone lines, so the cost of the call itself is not much different from the cost of a telephone call.

Video conferencing or conference television has also been tried in several parts of the world. Various configurations of seats, microphones, cameras and television monitors have been tried, and in a few cases projection television has been used. The cost of transmitting the video picture is high, since it can take up the equivalent of 1000 telephone channels. Nonetheless, video conferences can sometimes be as effective as, but cheaper than, face-to-face meetings, and the costs of telecommunications can be expected to fall relative to the cost of travel in the future, provided previous trends continue. The changes since 1948 in the price of two sample indications of travel costs relative to the cost of the telephone call referred to in the previous table are shown below (the falling behind in real terms of petrol prices by 1978 has now been made good):

	1948	1958	1968	1978
Telephone call (3 minutes long distance)	100	59	38	28
Gallon of petrol	100	137	148	116
Typical tube (subway) fare	100	101	149	279

Computer-mediated conferencing, where a conference is composed of a series of messages put into a central computer store by individuals at dispersed terminals, has been used extensively in the USA and Canada. In some ways it is rather like a message service and it includes the facility of sending private one-to-one messages, but it seems more like a conference in practice. One advantage is that participants can put in contributions or read the proceedings any time that they wish (very convenient when different time zones are involved); also there is a permanent record of the conference, which can be searched, with the aid of the computer, for all entries by a particular contributor, on a particular topic or on a particular date. Finally, computer conferencing systems can be used for joint authorship and other collaborative efforts between people who cannot normally meet face-to-face. One disadvantage is that contributions have to be typed in; and discussion is sometimes rather disorganized as people enter and leave the conference and topics are raised and dropped haphazardly.

Teleconferencing, and a related development, remote polling, have been seen by some as offering opportunities for greater public participation in decision making. In remote polling, people in their homes, after being posed a question on radio or television, can respond by pressing buttons to give their opinion. The choices are transmitted back, through telephone or cable television links, to a computer which accumulates the votes and almost instantaneously displays the result.

Citizen Band (CB) radio illustrates another dimension of development. Now prevalent in the USA, Citizen Band radios are devices like walkie-talkie radios that can be bought by anyone. A small number of channels is available, and these can be used by anyone, so that a disorganized, but sometimes fruitful, multi-way conversation can develop. With the wavebands now used transmissions normally carry only a few miles, but CB radio has nonetheless come to be very popular, especially amongst people on the move. In cars and trucks, people were previously isolated unless they could afford an expensive mobile telephone. Now that they can obtain a cheap CB radio (only about £100 or $200), usage has rocketed. A CB language with special call codes has developed – 10/4 means 'I have got your message' and 'Smokies' are the police – and claims are made that hundreds of lives are saved each year as people in distress call fellow CB users.

Outside the USA, the growth of CB radio has been prevented by many Governments' denying suitable wavebands. Although some of the technical reasons for this denial are valid, the social benefits of CB may outweigh them.

Social limits to the 'electronic encounter with the world'

The reaction of people to the prospect of the electronic cornucopia varies. Some relish the possibilities, like American sociologist Suzanne Keller: 'We are moving ... toward the electronic encounter with the world. This should permit us to experience the world in a far less fragmented manner than heretofore and may restore to us a wholeness and richness which the first industrial revolution destroyed.'

Others, like Ogden Nash, are distinctly less enthusiastic:

> Someone invented the telephone
> And interrupted a nation's slumbers
> Ringing wrong, but similar numbers.

It has been argued that new communications media affect our lives very little. The medium, it is said, is merely a communication channel, to be used for good or evil, democracy or tyranny, pleasure or pain according to the wishes of the users.

Marshall McLuhan attacked this viewpoint: '... a few years ago, General David Sarnoff made this statement: "We are too prone to make technological instruments the scapegoats for the sins of those who wield them. The products of modern science are not in themselves good or bad; it is the way they are used that determines their value." Suppose we were to say, "the smallpox virus is in itself neither good nor bad: it is the way it is used that determines its value." ' Certainly, examples of effects that are specific to the nature of the medium can be found: some are described in Chapters 7 and 8. The same is likely to be true for the newer media, and we can be fairly certain that our lives will be affected by their introduction, whether as individuals or as members of a family, a work organization, or even society in general.

Psychological problems in the new media

Face-to-face is the medium which most of us learn to use from childhood. Most, but not all, people also learn to communicate by letter and telephone, but it is clear that this is not always an easy process. The need to learn how to exploit fully the newer media is demonstrated by the 'television charm schools' which exist to teach people how to present themselves adequately on television. The knack of projecting oneself on television, film, radio or even the telephone has become a highly prized and highly paid skill; people who cannot achieve this skill are becoming as handicapped as illiterates. With more and more media

bursting upon the scene, the pressure to learn how to manipulate them will become intense, and human adaptability may be stretched to the limit. This is one example of Alvin Toffler's 'Future Shock' which he describes as 'a time phenomenon, a product of the greatly accelerated rate of change in society. It arises from the superimposition of a new culture on an old one.... This is the prospect that man now faces. Change is avalanching upon our heads and most people are grotesquely unprepared to cope with it.' It seems likely in fact that the limiting factor determining the rate of adoption of innovations will be the rate at which ordinary people can adapt their habits and behaviour. If the medium requires the user to be active (as opposed to the passive soaking up of television or radio), then it will only secure rapid adoption if it is very easy to use. This fact is often ignored by system designers, who think that if a communication system is more potent (that is, if it can be used to do previously impossible things), is feasible and is of reasonable cost, then people will 'automatically' adopt the innovation. They ignore human reactions at their peril, and we can already see a history of failed media, such as the videophone.

The ability to change communicative habits is very limited because these habits are so deep rooted. As we saw in Chapter 3, much of human non-verbal communication can be observed in babies and apes. These behaviour patterns are virtually immutable and function at a subconscious level. If new media interrupt these processes it is hardly surprising that users respond unfavourably. For example, eye contact (eye-to-eye gaze between two people) is an important part of face-to-face communication. Yet it is impossible in a videophone call, as may be seen in the drawing below. Because the camera is above the screen, when one looks directly at the eyes of the other person (i.e. at the centre of the screen) one appears to him to be looking downward. The only way to give the other person the impression that one is looking directly at him is to look away from his face towards the television camera.

The differences between face-to-face communication and a variety of technologically-mediated types of communication have been studied in a series of psychological

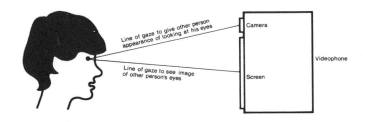

One reason why the videophone did not catch on: it is impossible to look the person at the other end in the eye.

experiments. The systems studied were video link, telephone and communicating typewriters. It turns out that there are marked differences between all these media, especially when social relationships are important to the communication. Getting to know someone, forming impressions of the other person, negotiation and persuasion are all radically changed. These effects seem to be due to the disruption of the normal channels of non-verbal communication, and to a psychological remoteness that occurs in telecommunication. There is some scope for minimizing both of these problems, by giving voices a more life-like quality and producing visual images life-size and in full colour, but the difference between, for instance, the best teleconference system and face-to-face communication is still marked. An anecdote from a user of conference television makes the point clearly: 'Over the TV, we felt the four of us were against him. For example, we had arranged for coffee or tea to be served at our end . . . and he didn't have any. We sat there drinking our coffee and passing the biscuits round, and he looked increasingly gloomy.'

The media that require person-to-computer communication also cause psychological problems, associated with their restriction to typed input and output. Most people would prefer to speak and listen to computers, but to date only limited progress has been made with computer synthesis of speech. A computer can be given a bank of syllables or words, and programmes specifying ways of combining these, so that fairly comprehensible speech can be produced (though computers are not yet at the stage where their speech would be mistaken for human). On the input side, however, progress is much slower. In English, as in virtually every other language, there are numerous homonyms, where one sound has several meanings (e.g. 'to', 'too' and 'two'). In addition, the same word can be pronounced very differently by different speakers (for example, the word 'hurt' can be pronounced as 'hurt', 'urt', 'hoit', 'herd' and in several other ways). Speech cannot be understood by breaking it down into minute parts and dealing with the parts one at a time, which is the way computers normally carry out tasks. Instead, global understanding is required, and so far it has been impossible for computers to achieve this to any satisfactory degree. It seems, then, that even the best-designed computer system will for some time be communicating in a way that people find fairly cumbersome and unnatural.

There are, however, some psychological advantages in the new media. For instance, the telephone has been found to be more effective than face-to-face communication in changing another person's opinion. There is anecdotal evidence that many people find it easier to be rude or negative or to give bad news if they are not face-to-face. It is also easier to omit social niceties, so mediated communication can be quicker and more efficient. The anonymity of communication with computers has been found to be of advantage in medical history taking, since people find it easier to reveal personal or embarrassing details to an impartial machine. Computers can also be made infinitely polite and patient – very useful characteristics in many quasi-social situations.

Social life and the 'telecommunity'

The effects of telecommunications on social life seem mainly to be a matter of changing the balance between the two types of social relationship known to sociologists as community and society, *Gemeinschaft* and *Gesellschaft*. According to this distinction, community relationships (which include family relationships) are characterized by emotional cohesion, depth, continuity and fullness and tend to be enjoyable in their own right, while social relationships tend to be impersonal, temporary, functional and of value only as a means to an end.

Many people's immediate response to telecommunication is to say that it is impersonal, mechanistic, inhuman and a destroyer of human relationships. This judgement has been applied at various times to telephone, television and radio, and it is so consistent that it deserves careful consideration. Certainly more traditional societies without modern machines do seem to have a stronger community life; and the people with greatest access to modern telecommunications are the fast-moving city businessmen of today, whose shallow social life has often been noted.

Has television killed the art of conversation, and is the telephone destroying our chance of obtaining fulfilling social relationships? Are we heading for a future so impersonal that we will be able to distinguish the people from the machines only by their physical appearance?

In Ray Bradbury's *Fahrenheit 451* the fireman, Montag, has to burn books so that people will not be distracted from the multi-screen life-size televisions in their parlours. Real and video people are barely distinguishable:

the wife . . . sat in the middle of the parlour talking to an announcer, who in turn was talking to her. 'Mrs Montag', he was saying, 'This, that and the other' . . . The converter attachment, which had cost them one hundred dollars, automatically supplied her name whenever the announcer addressed his anonymous audience, leaving a blank where the proper syllables could be filled in. A special spot-wavex-scrambler also caused his televised image, in the area immediately about his lips, to mouth the vowels and consonants beautifully. He was a friend, no doubt of it, a good friend. 'Mrs Montag – now look right here.'

New communications technology: bane or benefit? The Japanese cartoonist U. G. Sato presents a frightening vision of the dehumanizing possibilities of telecommunication, but it could also offer many new networks of human contacts and relationships.

This vision may be too pessimistic. New telecommunications could be very valuable in strengthening the community. The essential difference from traditional society is that this community may not be based in a locality. There may have been a tendency to confuse neighbourhood and community, perhaps thanks to the ambiguous way in which town planners use the terms. A person may know none of his neighbours, and be involved in no local groups or societies, but still be strongly involved in the life of a community: for his community may spread over a whole city or country, based upon common interests in scuba diving or left-wing politics or jazz, rather than upon a common geographical location.

The dispersed community, which has been called an 'invisible college' in the academic field, is critically dependent on new telecommunications. Future advances will strengthen such communities and, if this happens at the expense of communities based on local districts, it may merely be because most people prefer to have friends with similar interests, rather than rely on the people who just happen to live nearby. In Reading, Pennsylvania, for example, there has been an experiment in which old people, as groups or individuals, are brought together by two-way video transmitted over cable television circuits.

Even at the family level, it is possible to argue that telecommunications will strengthen family relationships. Two centuries ago, when a member of a family left for another part of the country or, even worse, emigrated, communication was so difficult that he might as well have died. Today, limited geographical moves do not necessarily break up family relationships, and one can foresee that in the future it may not matter much if mother is in Australia, daughter in Great Britain and grand-daughter in the USA.

Of course, the fact that contacts can be maintained by telecommunications does not mean that the quality of contact is unchanged, and we have already mentioned the loss of quality revealed in psychological studies. But, as was argued in the last chapter, whether in general new technologies enrich or impoverish social and communal relationships depends on the socially-determined uses that are made of them as much as on their inherent characteristics.

City and country

Some have seen an even more positive benefit for family and local community life. At present, almost every worker has to go to work, yet for more and more people work involves no contact with physical materials, but rather consists of communication. Why not bring the information to the worker, rather than vice versa? Some people, like freelance journalists and authors, do already work at home and enjoy the benefits: no time wasted in commuting, more contact with family and neighbours, and greater control over their own work habits. With cheaper and more capable telecommunications systems, more of us will be able to work at home, and a new form of 'cottage industry' will be born.

Peter Goldmark, inventor of the long playing record, sees telecommunications as allowing the reinvigoration of rural life: 'It is our belief that all necessary inventions have already been made, and broadband communications systems now can be imaginatively applied to the needs of business, government, education, health care and cultural pursuits to stimulate the development of the new rural society.... . We would like to give all Americans an opportunity to work and live in small but attractive communities. The persons who choose to settle in these communities will become the new rural society.'

The terms 'community communications centre' and 'neighbourhood work centre' envisage a facility of the future where a small building at the end of the street would contain a concentration of advanced communication devices. Video, audio, data and facsimile links to other centres and to the metropolis would allow people to carry on office-type work for organizations whose headquarters were far distant, and would also allow high-quality health care, education and even entertainment to be brought to the neighbourhood. Several demonstration projects have already indicated the efficacy of tele-medicine, and tele-education is used regularly in the Universities of Wisconsin, Quebec and Illinois. These are interactive forms of communication using long-distance telephone links, in which the doctor or teacher communicates directly with patient or students. The problems seem to be financial; at present video-telecommunications are rather too expensive to justify bringing work, social services and education to the people, rather than vice versa. However, there do seem to be unexploited possibilities in audio-only communications, which are much cheaper than video, and often just as effective. As the figures quoted above show, moving information may soon become much cheaper than moving people. The New Rural Society may soon be a goal within reach, to the benefit of city and country – and the people in both.

Life in the office of the future

A more extreme step would be for everyone with a non-manual job to work at home. In the UK there is already a computer software company whose employees nearly all work at home; some of the employees are physically handicapped and would find it difficult to manage any other kind of job. The nature of the work makes this an especially appropriate case, but typing, much clerical work and some information jobs (such as answering telephone inquiries) could equally well be done at home. Extra expense in telecommunications could be minor compared to the savings in office rent, heating, lighting and commuting expenses.

One implication of a massive shift to home working could be the strengthening of home life and the local community – contrary to the tendency mentioned above for 'telecommunities' to replace communities based on place. The workers of the community would no longer disappear to the central city, leaving a desolate dormitory area where the housebound (whether tied by children, age or handicap) wither away. Of course in some cases, if husband and wife were together all day, every day, there might be extra tension; but there might also be more equality of roles, in which paid employment and housework were more evenly shared.

A shift towards work at home could have a disastrous effect on the central city. Both office buildings and public transport systems could quite quickly become surplus to requirements. There are already signs that New York office development may have been over-expanded, as fear of crime and high local taxes drive out those firms who can carry on their business by telecommunications. Rapid transit systems are still being built to carry a concentrated stream of commuters from the suburbs to the central city, but many of these seem barely viable financially. If expanding use of telecommunications causes this concentrated traffic to fall off by 20 per cent or more, the commuter lines could become totally uneconomic.

Telecommunications may affect not merely the location of offices, but the whole structure of the work organization. The jobs of many workers will change; the most noticeable example we can already see is the effects of the new technology on journalism and printing. Multinational companies are usually very heavy users of telecommunications, and it is reasonable to argue that they could not exist without them. Certainly telecommunications have made it easier to centralize control – 'running the company from Detroit' – and to leave very little freedom of action or power to branch managers. In previous centuries, communication was so poor that power had to be decentralized: the Viceroy of India was effectively as powerful as a king, because virtually all his decisions were made at his discretion, with no real possibility of referring back to Britain for instructions from a higher authority. Telecommunications have changed all that, and have made it possible for one man, at the centre of a communications network, to have day-to-day control of a worldwide organization.

It does not necessarily follow that we shall all eventually become part of an enormous multinational conglomerate company, controlled by a small clique with access to the most advanced telecommunications. Improved communications can also encourage the small, professional, extremely specialized organization. Recently, I have come across a company whose sole work is finding names for new products, and another company that specializes in reducing telephone bills. Such companies are totally dependent on maintaining a wide range of contacts, and each advance in telecommunications makes their job easier. In a more familiar way, small firms of shipping agents, solicitors, consultants, publicity agents and brokers are usually the first to adopt new communications services, as they know that their livelihood depends on it. With more powerful communication systems, many people with such specialized skills who now rely upon a large company to bring them work can strike out on their own. More and more of us may be able to become our own bosses, running our own small businesses from our multi-purpose home communications consoles.

Telecommunications and democracy

It is not inevitable that improved communications should lead to increased power at the centre, though this is the main way that they have been exploited to date. In other circumstances, it may help the man at the centre to be more responsive to outside influences. The early Presidents of the United States were essentially unknown to most of their countrymen, who had little opportunity to exchange opinions with them. Today, they can see their President every day on television and, although he may often be mouthing platitudes, sometimes he will be explaining his values, opinions and plans to the people. They in turn may influence him by letters and telegrams or through opinion polls. Occasionally, they may be able to engage him in direct conversation during phone-in broadcasts. Although this may favour Presidents with charismatic visual presence, it should lead to better agreement between Government and people, providing two-way communication is allowed to develop freely. The live broadcasting of Parliamentary or Congressional proceedings may have an even greater impact, as the public is enabled to follow actual decision-making processes. Immediate public opinion feedback via a simple button-press device, as described above, is feasible now. Some would say this could encourage demagogy, but it is so clearly in the tradition of direct democracy that it will surely have great attractions for most Western voters.

An even more radical idea for direct democracy by telecommunication has been suggested by the sociologist Amitai Etzioni. Telephone conferencing could be used as a means of bringing together small groups of, say, six to thirty people to discuss topical issues. They could all participate from home and could elect representatives, who could in turn meet by telephone conferencing. A network of *ad hoc* representative groups could be built up which might achieve policy solutions corresponding closely to the considered popular view. Everyone would be involved, everyone would contribute to policy-making and no one would be discouraged by the physical constraints that are often the cause of what looks like political apathy.

Telecommunications and environmental resources

Opponents of new technology in general concentrate on two main arguments. The first – that technology is mechanical and dehumanizing – does seem to have some validity in the sphere of the new telecommunications media, as we have seen. However, the second – that technology is polluting and destructive of non-renewable resources – is very far from true in this area. Indeed, it is reasonable to argue that greater use of advanced telecommunications may become essential if our society is not to break down under the impact of the resource and pollution constraints which we will inevitably face in the next century.

Compared with transport or heavy manufacturing industry, telecommunications use very little energy. A television uses about as much energy as a light bulb, and those who spend an evening watching television are far, far kinder to the environment than those who go for a drive. The average telephone exchange, serving thousands of people, uses about the same amount of energy as one car, serving one or two people. At Cornell University, it has been calculated that the energy used in a return flight from New York to Los Angeles could provide 63 hours of videophone conversation, or several thousand hours of ordinary telephone conversation. Low energy usage also means low pollution (including noise pollution), and telecommunications do, of course, cause few accidental deaths.

All these considerations suggest that, as travel becomes more expensive and energy resources scarcer, and greater precautions against pollution and accidents are required, telecommunications will increasingly become a substitute. Even where social and psychological factors suggest that telecommunications are an inferior alternative, cost and convenience will force the decision in their favour. Live theatre was largely replaced by the cinema, which in turn has been largely replaced by television, yet no one would claim that television gives a more accurate representation of the original performance: its picture quality compared with that of the cinema is abysmal. But while live theatre costs over £2.50 ($5) per audience person per hour, cinema costs only about 50p ($1) and television (including the costs of the home apparatus) no more than about 5p (10 cents). Television has the additional advantage of being available in the home. It is thus hardly surprising that it has very rapidly replaced the other media. Similarly we may expect several existing transport and communications media (such as the mail, cars and air transport), as they become more expensive because of energy, resource and manpower limitations, to be replaced by the electronic media, where technological advance is the only major constraint.

Will the electronic media themselves suffer from limits to growth? We have already mentioned their energy usage, which is uniformly low. Manpower requirements are also relatively modest, since a high level of automation is involved. Material requirements seem fairly insignificant. Some rare elements are used (germanium for transistors, gold or platinum for contacts) but, with the strong tendency towards miniaturization, demands are not likely to increase greatly. The biggest need is for copper. Within the apparatus, it is used for windings and connections, but the use for transmission, as in telephone wires, is even greater. Cable television and submarine cable systems also contain many tons of copper. Nonetheless, it appears that even this constraint will be removed by technological progress. Satellites are taking more and more of the load of long-distance transmission, and microwave beams are being used instead of cable. The most significant development of all is optical fibre transmission. A single glass fibre of great purity can now carry the equivalent

Aerial No. 1 at the British Post Office's Goonhilly earth station in Cornwall, part of the global network of satellite communication stations of the international commercial communications organization, Intelsat.

of thousands of telephone conversations for several kilometres without amplification. Glass, of course, is made out of one of the commonest materials in the world, sand (silicon dioxide). Optical fibres are not merely a replacement for copper cables, but are vastly superior in information-carrying capacity. It thus seems probable that in the 21st century the streets of London and New York will become the most prolific copper mines in the world, as copper cabling is torn out to be replaced by optical fibres.

One final resource, which is renewable but in practice is sharply limited in supply, is paper. At present many of us feel we are being buried in a mountain of paper: the average per annum consumption is about 45 kilos per head in the UK and it is even higher in the USA. The impact of this ever-growing demand on the world's forests cannot be borne much longer, and the fact that the 'paperless office' will soon be possible is thus vitally important. Files, messages and notes can all be held in computer store and accessed via a visual display unit. The history of computing shows the way: at first, users put in punched cards and got out mountains of print-out – an enormous consumption of paper. Gradually, on-line work was introduced, though the remote terminals produced hard copy so that quantities of paper were still produced, 90 per cent of it containing aborted runs and fit only for the waste paper basket. However, now that visual display units have been introduced, neither data input nor inaccurate output consumes paper; at most the final clean results are printed out. Just as the telephone replaced the telegraph with a consequent saving of paper, so all the other bits of office paper will tend to be replaced by data files held on computer, viewed electronically, and only printed out when absolutely necessary. Even when printed out, output will often be to microfiche with 64 pages on a single photograph rather than to paper. In the home, consumption of newsprint is likely to decline, partly because of the increasing relative cost of newsprint, but also because of teletext and viewdata.

In summary, it appears that progress in telecommunications is unlikely to be constrained by resource or environmental problems: on the contrary, electronics are likely to become a potent force in overcoming these problems.

Old media never die, they only fade away

If all the newer media described above come into widespread use, what will happen to the existing media – books, newspapers, mail, telephone, radio, cinema, tape and disk, television? The sociologist Richard Maisel, in an article entitled 'Decline of the Mass Media', suggested that several of our familiar forms – national newspapers, network television and the general-interest magazine – will tend to die away in favour of more specialized media that take full advantage of technological opportunities. Thus a publication or a television programme with an audience of millions would become a thing of the past; as choice increased, audiences would become more fragmented, and only the media that could provide specialist information for specialist interests would survive.

It would be over-pessimistic to expect any of the media to die completely. The telephone has not yet wholly replaced telegrams, nor is live theatre dead. Instead, the old media tend to shift away from providing a general service towards finding a particular niche. Cinema, under the impact of television, has ceased to provide a full range of programmes, but tends to concentrate on disaster or science-fiction spectaculars that translate poorly to the small screen, or on sex or violence that would not pass the stricter television censorship. Similarly, radio has not been destroyed by television but has become more local and specialized.

A similar process is likely to take place with the media that are now in the ascendancy. National newspapers, as already mentioned, are likely to fare poorly under the impact of increasing newsprint costs and of teletext and viewdata systems; the high wages and restrictive practices in some parts of the newspaper industry will accelerate the decline. Local papers may thrive, however, together with various specialist weeklies (from *Motorcycle Weekly* to *Gay News*). Television on a national scale seems bound to suffer from a declining audience share as more channels open up, and other uses of the television (games, teletext, videodisk) spread. However, if the major networks use their initiative, they may be able to attract a considerable audience for programmes such as national news or live sporting events. The mail will undoubtedly undergo a decline in traffic: this trend is already apparent in many countries. As electronic mail grows, the cost of postage will rise and speed and frequency of delivery of conventional mail will suffer. It may even be necessary to abolish all home deliveries, with mail being collected from the nearest post office: yet the mail will not die, since it will be competitive for a long time in the delivery of periodicals, parcels and bulky letters.

Only the telephone and books seem quite safe into the 21st century. The videophone seems on present evidence to be no competitor for the telephone; even if there was little cost differential, which seems unlikely in the next two decades, many people would still prefer the telephone. Instead development will be towards more capable telephones: capable of allowing multi-person calls, short code dialling, automatic call-back, mobile operation and other useful additions to the basic service. Books and magazines may suffer a little under the impact of microfilm and viewdata alternatives, but since their subject matter is generally less ephemeral than that of newspapers, their present form is likely to remain attractive, especially as they retain the potential for portability and high-quality illustration.

The communications-rich society

What will be the wider effects of these communications developments on society and the world? There are three particular trends that contemporary commentators have discerned.

The first is towards what Marshall McLuhan called the 'global village'. The Vietnam war highlighted the trend towards an integrated world; for the first time the bloody details of the reality of war could be seen on television. The public revulsion against the war was strengthened by its visibility. With the exception of a few closed countries, the internal politics of every nation are open to the view of the world. Under UN auspices, Norwegian troops are in the Lebanon, and Ghanaians are in Cyprus. At a less serious level, events from the Eurovision Song Contest to the Olympic Games bring the world into everyone's home. Just as hotels in the Holiday Inns chain are the same from Newark to Nairobi, in time we may find that Bangkok seems as familiar as Birmingham, and telecommunication will take much of the credit (or blame, depending on your point of view).

Then there is the tendency for new communications systems to reinforce existing social inequalities, at least for a time. The sociologist Natan Katzman has argued that 'with the adoption of a new communication technology, people already having high levels of information and ability will gain more than people with lower initial levels.' As each new medium is introduced, some people get it first, and these people tend to be richer, better educated, better informed and more communications-oriented. If the medium gives further education, information and communication opportunities, the net effect is a widening of the gap between the advantaged and disadvantaged groups in society. Eventually the disadvantaged will catch up, as they have done with literacy and television ownership in most Western countries,

and as they are in the process of doing with the telephone, but the advantaged will have in the mean time opened up a gap in newer media such as viewdata, videodisks or home computing. It has been claimed that, by the 1990s, anyone who cannot programme a computer will be as disadvantaged as if he was unable to spell or do simple arithmetic today. Katzman quotes the case of the American educational children's programme *Sesame Street*, which was intended to help disadvantaged children to learn to acquire basic skills. In fact, the more advantaged children seemed to gain more from it, in part because they were more likely to watch. This tendency is not in itself an argument against new communications media: eventually the gap closes as all social groups achieve access to the medium, and everyone is better off. However, the short-term implications do need careful consideration.

Finally, there is the move towards the information society. Daniel Bell has described the Post-Industrial Society, where labour is no longer concentrated in agriculture or manufacture, but in the service industries. Machines do all the physical, material-oriented work; people become more and more concentrated in intellectual, communication-oriented work. Marc Porat at the US Office of Telecommunications has calculated that in the USA over 50 per cent of jobs now largely or wholly involve communication. This trend, which has been caused by developments in automation and communication, seems likely to continue and even to accelerate with the impact of the technologies we have discussed. Problems are certain to arise, if only because some people may be quite unsuited to communications jobs, as a result of never having learnt the necessary communication skills. Will we be able to find them a place in the communicating society, or will they become unemployable discards?

Let us hope we can control technological progress in communications, the potential benefits of which seem enormous. Greater awareness of the possibilities should help us to avoid some of the more serious psychological and social risks that have been described. With luck and forethought, the communicating society will be a happy experience for everyone.

GLOSSARY

affective mental processes are concerned with 'emotions'; **cognitive** mental processes are concerned with 'knowledge'.

arbitrary signs are defined as having no inherent connection with the thing or quality they refer to; in another definition these are described as **conventional**, indicating that their meanings are attached to them by deliberate or, more commonly, practical agreement (*cf.* pictorial).

cognitive: *see* affective.

conventional: *see* arbitrary.

grapheme: a basic unit of a writing system – word sign, syllabic sign or letter.

linear: made up of arrangements of lines and not of two-dimensional shapes.

metonymic: referring to something by one of its associations or attributes.

morpheme: a basic unit of a language; words can be broken down into morphemes such as root, inflection, prefix, etc.

morphological: to do with the consideration of the forms of a language or system of writing in relation to the way they function within it.

natural index: *see* pictorial.

pictorial (or *iconic*) signs contain some inherent indication of an object or quality; a **natural index** is likewise a sign with an inherent connection with its referent (*q.v.*) (*cf.* arbitrary).

polysemous: having more than one meaning.

referent: thing or quality referred to.

semantic: relating to meaning.

semiotic: having the property of a sign; by extension, as *semiotics*, the study of signs in language and more generally.

stimulus diffusion: the spread of linguistic elements or elements of writing systems as a result of borrowing by geographically adjacent, but not necessarily genetically related, cultures.

transformation: re-composition of material from one form into another.

BIBLIOGRAPHY

1 General Bibliography

Barry, Gerald, et al. (eds) Communication and Language London 1966

Barthes, Roland Image, Music, Text London 1977

Benjamin, W. Illuminations New York and London 1970

Dance, Frank (ed.) Human Communication Theory New York 1967

Gramsci, A. Prison Notebooks London 1970

Hogben, Lancelot T. The Signs of Civilisation London 1959

Innis, H. A. The Bias of Communication Toronto 1964

Miller, Jonathan McLuhan London 1971

Schiller, H. I. Communication and Cultural Domination New York 1976

Smith, Alfred G. (ed.) Communication and Culture New York 1966

Sorokin, P. A. Social and Cultural Dynamics New York 1937

Tunstall, J. (ed.) Media Sociology: a reader London 1970

Williams, Raymond The Long Revolution London 1961

2 Language

Bakhtin, Mikhail (Voloshinov, Valentin N. ?) Marxism and the Philosophy of Language, trs. L. Matejka and I. R. Titunik, New York and London 1973 (Russian original 1929)

Brown, Jason W. Mind, Brain and Consciousness New York 1977

Chomsky, Noam A. Reflections on Language New York 1975; London 1976

Davis, Philip W. Modern Theories of Language Englewood Cliffs, N.J. 1973

Eco, Umberto A Theory of Semiotics Bloomington, Ind. and London 1976

Hewes, Gordon W. Language Origins: a bibliography The Hague 1975

Jerison, Harry Evolution of the Brain and Intelligence New York 1973

Lenneberg, Eric H. Biological Foundations of Language New York 1967

Leroi-Gourhan, André Le geste et la parole, I Technique et langage; II La mémoire et les rythmes Paris 1964–5

Liebermann, Philip On the Origins of Language: an introduction to the evolution of human speech London and New York 1975

Luria, Aleksandr Romanovich Cognitive Development: its cultural and social foundations, trs. Martin Lopez-Morillas and Lynn Solotaroff, Cambridge, Mass. and London 1976

Lyons, John Introduction to Theoretical Linguistics Cambridge 1968

McCormack, W. C. and S. A. Wurm (eds) Language and Thought: anthropological issues The Hague 1978

Moore, Timothy E. (ed.) Cognitive Development and the Acquisition of Language London and New York 1973

Morris, Charles W. Signs, Language and Behavior New York 1946

Rossi-Landi, Ferruccio Il linguaggio come lavoro e come mercato Milan 1968; English ed. forthcoming

Sapir, Edward Selected Writings of Edward Sapir in Language, Culture and Personality, ed. D. G. Mandelbaum, Berkeley, Cal. 1949

Saussure, Ferdinand de Course in General Linguistics, trs. W. Basin, New York, Toronto and London 1966 (French original 1915)

Schaff, Adam Introduction to Semantics, trs. O. Wojtasiewicz, Oxford 1960 (Polish original 1962)

Thao, Trân duc Recherches sur l'origine du langage et de la conscience Paris 1973

Vygotsky, Lev Semenovich Thought and Language, trs. Eugenia Hanfmann and Gertrude Vakar, Cambridge, Mass. 1962 (Russian original 1934)

Whorf, Benjamin Lee Language, Thought and Reality, selected writings, ed. John Carroll, New York and London 1956

Yakobson, Roman Selected Writings (7 vols) The Hague 1962

3 Non-verbal Communication

Argyle, Michael Bodily Communication London 1975

—— The Psychology of Interpersonal Behaviour Harmondsworth 1978 (3rd ed.)

Argyle, Michael and M. Cook Gaze and Mutual Gaze Cambridge 1976

Birdwhistell, R. L. Kinesics and Context Philadelphia, Penn. 1970; Harmondsworth 1973

Eibl-Eibesfeldt, I. Love and Hate London 1971

Ekman, Paul Darwin and Facial Expression: a century of research in review London 1973

Ekman, Paul and W. V. Friesan Unmasking the Face: a guide to recognising emotions from facial clues London 1975

Hall, E. T. The Hidden Dimension London 1969

Harper, R. G., A. N. Wiens and J. D. Matarazzo Nonverbal Communication: the state of the art New York and Chichester 1978

Hinde, R. A. Non-verbal Communication Cambridge 1972

Kendon, A., R. M. Harris and M. R. Key Organisation of Behaviour in Face-to-Face Interaction The Hague 1975

Laing, R. D. Interpersonal Perception London 1966

—— Self and Others Harmondsworth 1971

Mehrabian, Albert Nonverbal Communication Chicago and New York 1972

—— Public Places and Private Spaces New York 1976

Morris, Desmond Manwatching London 1977

—— The Naked Ape London 1967

Morris, Desmond, P. Collett, P. Marsh and M. O'Shaughnessy Gestures London 1979

4 Signs and Symbols

Arnheim, Rudolf Art and Visual Perception Berkeley, Cal. 1954

Berenson, Bernard Seeing and Knowing Greenwich, Conn. 1969

Collingwood, R. G. The Principles of Art London and New York 1958

Diethelm, Walter Signet, Signal, Symbol: handbook of international signs Zurich 1970

Dondis, Donis A. A Primer for Visual Literacy Cambridge, Mass. 1973

Dreyfuss, H. and H. Buckminster Fuller (eds) Symbol Sourcebook New York 1972

Eco, Umberto Il segno Milan 1973

Ehrenzweig, Anton The Hidden Order of Art Berkeley, Cal. 1967

Firth, Raymond Symbols, Public and Private London 1973; New York 1975

Freud, Sigmund The Interpretation of Dreams, trs. A. A. Brill, London 1913

Goldsmith, Elisabeth Ancient Pagan Symbols New York 1929

Gombrich, Ernst Art and Illusion London 1968

Hammond, Natalie Hays Anthology of Pattern New York 1949

Hangen, Eva C. Symbols: our universal language Wichita, Kan. 1962

Hogben, Lancelot From Cave Painting to Comic Strip New York 1949

Hogg, James (ed.) Psychology and the Visual Arts Harmondsworth 1970

Jung, Carl G. et al. Man and His Symbols New York 1968

Kamekura, Yusaku Trademarks and Symbols of the World New York 1965

Langer, Susan K. Introduction to Symbolic Logic London 1937

—— Philosophy in a New Key Cambridge, Mass. 1948

Leach, Edmund Culture and Communication: the logic by which symbols are constructed Cambridge 1976

Mumford, Lewis Art and Technics London 1952

Read, Herbert The Meaning of Art Harmondsworth 1961

Ross, Ralph Symbols and Civilization New York 1963

Whitehead, Alfred N. Symbolism. Its meaning and effect Cambridge 1928

Whittick, A. Symbols, Signs and Their Meaning London 1971

Wildbur, Peter Trademarks: a handbook of international designs London 1966

5 Alphabets and Writing

Boas, F. Primitive Art Oslo 1927

Brice, W. C. 'The writing system of the Proto–Elamite Account Tablets of Susa' Bulletin of the John Rylands Library 45.15, 1962

Chadwick, J. 'Introduction to the problems of "Minoan Linear A" ' Journal of the Royal Asiatic Society 143.147, 1975

Clark, J. C. G. World Prehistory Cambridge 1977 (3rd ed.)

Cross, Frank M. 'The origin and early evolution of the alphabet' Eretz Israel 8:8–24, 1967

—— 'Leaves from an epigraphist's notebook' The Catholic Biblical Quarterly 36:490–93, 1974

Dewdney, S. Scrolls of the Southern Ojibway

Toronto 1975

Diringer, D. *The Alphabet, a Key to the History of Mankind* London 1968 (3rd ed.)

—— *Writing* London 1962

Driver, G. R. *Semitic Writing* London 1948

Gelb, I. J. *A Study of Writing* London and Chicago 1952

—— 'Thoughts about Ebla; a preliminary evaluation' *Syro-mesopotamian Studies* 1:1, 1977

—— 'Writing, forms of' *Encyclopaedia Britannica* (vol. 19) 1974 (15th ed.)

Goody, Jack *The Domestication of the Savage Mind* Cambridge 1977

Goody, Jack and I. P. Watt 'The consequences of literacy' *Comparative Studies in History and Society* 5:304–45, 1963. Reprinted in *Literacy in Traditional Societies*, ed. Jack Goody, Cambridge 1968

Gray, J. *The Canaanites* London 1964

Gurney, O. R. *The Hittites* London 1952

Havelock E. A. *Prologue to Greek Literacy* Cincinnati 1973

Hinz, W. 'Problems of Linear Elamite' *Journal of the Royal Asiatic Society* 106–15, 1975

Kinnier Wilson, J. V. *Indo-Sumerian: a new approach to the problems of the Indus script* Oxford 1974

Leach, Edmund *Culture and Communication: the logic by which symbols are constructed* Cambridge 1976

Leroi-Gourhan, André *Le geste et la parole*, I *Technique et langage*; II *La mémoire et les rythmes* Paris 1964–5

Macqueen, J. G. *The Hittites and their Contemporaries in Asia Minor* London 1975

Mallery, G. 'Pictographs of the North American Indians – a preliminary paper' *Fourth Annual Report of the Bureau of Ethnology to the Secretary of the Smithsonian Institution 1882–83* Washington 1886

—— 'Picture-writing of the American Indians' *Tenth Annual Report of the Bureau of Ethnology to the Secretary of the Smithsonian Institution, 1886–89* Washington 1893. Reprinted by Dover Publications, New York 1972 (2 vols)

Mulder, J. W. F. and S. G. J. Hervey *Theory of the Linguistic Sign* The Hague 1973

Naveh, J. 'Some Semitic epigraphical considerations on the antiquity of the Greek alphabet' *American Journal of Archaeology* 77:1–8, 1973

Oates, J. 'The emergence of urban civilization in the Near East' *Cambridge Encyclopaedia of Archaeology* Cambridge *forthcoming*

Parpola, A. 'Tasks, methods and results in the study of the Indus script' *Journal of the Royal Asiatic Society* 178–209, 1975

—— 'An ostracon of the period of the Judges from 'Izbet Sartah' *Tel Aviv* 4:1–13, 1977

Roch, E. 'Human categorization' *Advances in Cross-cultural Psychology*, ed. N. Warren, (vol. 1) London 1976

Schmandt-Besserat, D. 'The earliest precursor of writing' *Scientific American* 238:38–47, 1978

Ucko, P. J. and A. Rosenfeld *Palaeolithic Cave Art* London 1967

Author's Acknowledgment
In a field as extensive, as changing, and as linguistically demanding as the early history of the written word, one's debts to one's friends and acquaintances are necessarily great. I am pleased to acknowledge my debt to John Alexander, Martin Bernal, Aaron Demsky, Gilbert Lewis, Shlomo Morag, Joan Oates, James Kinnier Wilson, and anyone else (and their name is legion) who wittingly or unwittingly has saved me from wallowing too deeply in the Slough of Ignorance.

6 Printing

D'Ainvelle, V. *La Presse en France* Grenoble 1965

Aldis, G. *The Printed Book* Cambridge 1941 (2nd ed., revised and brought up to date)

Altick, Richard D. *The English Common Reader. A social history of the mass reading public 1800–1900* Chicago 1957; Chicago and London 1963 (reduced reprint of 1957 ed.). In an appendix there is a table of printings and editions of books, magazines and newspapers which is of great interest.

Arendt, Hannah *The Crisis in Culture, Between Past and Future* London 1961

Ayerst, D. *The Guardian: biography of a newspaper* London and Ithaca, N.Y. 1971

Bergonzi, Bernard *The Situation of the Novel* Harmondsworth 1972

Bland, D. *The Illustration of Books* London 1951

Briggs, Asa *Essays in the History of Publishing* London 1974

Burch, R. M. *Colour Printing and Colour Printers* London 1910

Butler, P. *The Origin of Printing in Europe* Chicago 1940

Clair, C. *A Chronology of Printing* London 1969

—— *A History of Printing in Britain* London 1965

Coleman, D. C. *The British Paper Industry, 1495–1860* London 1958

Cook, E. T. *Delane of The Times* London 1915

Curran, James, George Boyce and Pauline Wingate (eds) *Newspaper History: studies in the evolution of the British press* London 1978

Febvre, L. and H.-J. Martin *The Coming of the Book* London 1976

Frank, Joseph *The Beginnings of the English Newspaper 1620–1660* London and Cambridge, Mass. 1961

Gedin, Per *Literature in the Marketplace* London 1977

Goldschmidt, E. P. *The Printed Books of the Renaissance* Cambridge 1950

Graza, Sebastian de *Of Time, Work and Leisure* New York 1962

Hobson, H. et al. *The Pearl of Days: an intimate memoir of The Sunday Times* London 1972

Johnson, A. F. *Type Designs, Their History and Development* London 1934

Knightley, Philip *The First Casualty – the War Correspondent as Hero, Propagandist and Myth Maker from Crimea to Vietnam* London and New York 1975

Kobre, S. *The Development of American Journalism* Dubuque, Iowa 1972

Leavis, Q. D. *Fiction and the Reading Public* London 1932; reissued 1965

Madison, Charles A. *Book Publishing in America* New York 1966

Moran, James *The Composition of Reading Matter* London 1965

—— *Printing in the Twentieth Century* London 1974

—— *Printing Presses* London 1973

Morison, S. *The English Newspaper, 1622–1932* Cambridge and New York 1932

Mumby, F. A. and Ian Norrie *Publishing and Bookselling* London 1974 (5th ed.)

Seymour-Ure, Colin *The Political Impact of Mass Media* London and Beverly Hills, Cal. 1974

Singer, C., E. J. Holmyard, A. R. Hall and T. L. Williams *A History of Technology* Oxford –1978 (7 vols)

Smith, A. C. H. *Paper Voices: the popular press and social change, 1935–1965* Totowa, N.J. 1975

Smith, Anthony *The Newspaper: an international history* London 1979

Steinberg, S. H. *Five Hundred Years of Printing* Harmondsworth 1974

The Times *History of The Times* London 1935–52 (5 vols)

Watts, Ian *The Rise of the Novel* Harmondsworth 1972

Weill, G. 'Le journal, origine, évolution de la presse périodique' *L'évolution de l'humanité* vol. 95, Paris 1934

Wickwar, W. *The Struggle for Freedom of the Press, 1819–1832* London 1928

Wolfe, Tom *The New Journalism* New York 1972

7 Extended Speech and Sounds

Baker, W. J. *The History of the Marconi Company* London 1979

Barnouw, Erik *A Tower in Babel* New York 1966 (3 vols)

Briggs, Asa *The History of Broadcasting in the UK* London 1961 (4 vols)

Bureau of Applied Social Research *The People Look at Radio* Chapel Hill, N.C. 1946

—— *Radio Listening in America* New York 1948

Cantril, H. L. *Invasion from Mars* Princeton, N.J. 1940

Cantril, H. L. and G. W. Allport *The Psychology of Radio* New York 1941

Cantril, H. L. and J. B. Whitton *Propaganda by Short Wave* Princeton, N.J. 1942

Durham, F. G. *Radio and Television in the Soviet Union* Cambridge, Mass. 1965

Emery, W. B. *National and International Systems of Broadcasting: their history, operation and control* East Lansing, Mich. 1969

George, A. *Propaganda Analysis* Evanston, Ill. 1959

Hale, Julian *Radio Power: propaganda and international broadcasting* London 1975

Katz, E. and G. Wedell *Broadcasting in the Third World* Cambridge, Mass. 1977; London 1978

Klapper, J. T. *The Effects of Mass Communication* Glencoe, Ill. 1960

Kris, E. and H. Speier *German Radio Propaganda* London 1944

Lackman, R. *Remember Radio* New York 1970

Lazarsfeld, Paul F. *Radio and the Printed Page* New York 1940

Lazarsfeld, Paul F. and Frank Stanton *Radio Research 1942–1943* New York 1944

—— *Communications Research 1948–1949* New York 1949

Lerner, D. *The Passing of Traditional Society* Glencoe, Ill. 1957

Liu, A. P. L. *Communications and National Integration in Communist China* Berkeley, Cal. 1971

Merton, R. K. *Mass Persuasion: the social psychology of a war bond drive* New York 1947

NHK *The History of Broadcasting in Japan* Tokyo 1967

Paulu, B. *Radio and Television Broadcasting on the European Continent* Minneapolis, Kan. 1967

Settel, I. *A Pictorial History of Radio* New York 1976

White, L. *The American Radio* Chicago 1947

Wood, R. E. *Shortwave Voices of the World* Park Ridge, N.J. 1969

8 Extended Images

Aldgate, Anthony *Cinema and History* London 1979

Arts Enquiry Report *The Factual Film* London 1947

Bachlin, Peter *Histoire économique du cinéma* Paris 1947

Bakewell, J. and N. Garnham *The New Priesthood: British television today* London 1970

Barnouw, Erik *The Sponsor* London and New York 1978

Bawden, Liz-Anne (ed.) *Oxford Companion to Film* London and New York 1976

Brownlow, Kevin *The Parade's Gone By* New York and London 1968

Ceram, C. W. *The Archaeology of the Cinema* New York and London 1965

Cooke, Alistair (ed.) *Garbo and the Night Watchmen*, a selection made in 1937 from the writings of British and American film critics, London 1971

Educational and Cultural Films Commission *The Film in National Life* London 1932

Elliot, Eric *Anatomy of Motion Picture Art* Territet, Switzerland 1930

Feininger, Andreas *Roots of Art* London 1975

Fielding, Raymond (ed.) *A Technological History of Motion Pictures and Television* Berkeley, Cal. 1967

Fletcher, Winston *The Ad Makers* London 1973

Gabriel, J. *Thinking about Television* London 1973

Garnham, N. *Structures of Television* London 1973

Gernsheim, Helmut and Alison *The History of Photography* London 1978

Harris, Ralph and Arthur Seldon *Advertising in Action* London 1962

Ivins, William *Prints and Visual Communication* Cambridge, Mass. and London 1953

Jarvie, Ian *Towards a Sociology of the Cinema* London 1970

Jowett, Garth *Film: the democratic art* Boston, Mass. 1976

Kleppner, O. and I. Settel *Exploring Advertising* Englewood Cliffs, N.J. 1969

Kracauer, Siegfried *From Caligari to Hitler* Princeton, N.J. 1966

Lindgren, Ernest *A Picture History of the Cinema* London 1960

—— *The Art of the Film* London 1970 (2nd ed.)

Lindsay, Vachel *The Art of the Moving Picture* New York 1922

Low, Rachael and Arnold R. Manvell *A History of the British Film, 1896–1906* (vol. 1), *1906–14* (vol. 2) and *1914–18* (vol. 3) London 1948–50

McConnell, Frank *Storytelling and Mythmaking: images from film and literature* London and New York 1979

Mayer, J. P. *Sociology of the Film* London 1946

Mees, C. E. K. *From Dry Plates to Ektachrome Film* (Eastman Kodak Company) New York 1961

Packard, V. *The Hidden Persuaders* London and New York 1957; Harmondsworth 1960

Pollack, Peter *The Picture History of Photography* London 1977

Quigley, Martin (jnr) *Magic Shadows: the story of the origin of motion pictures* Washington, D.C. 1948

Rhode, Eric *A History of the Cinema from its Origins to 1970* New York 1976

Robinson, D. *The History of World Cinema* New York 1973

Rotha, Paul *Celluloid: the film to-day* London 1931

—— *The Film Till Now* London 1930; 1967 (4th ed., enlarged and revised)

—— (ed.) *Television in the Making* London and New York 1956

Schuneman, R. Smith *Photographic Communication* London 1972

Scott, J. F. *Film, the Medium and the Maker* 1975

Singer, C., E. J. Holmyard, A. R. Hall and T. L. Williams *A History of Technology* Oxford –1978 (7 vols)

Stauffacher, Frank (ed.) *Art in the Cinema* San Francisco, Cal. 1947

Thorp, Margaret Farrand *America at the Movies* London 1946

Tudor, A. *Image and Influence* London 1974

—— *Theories of Film* London 1975

Vedrès, Nicole *Images du cinéma français* Paris 1945

Williams, Raymond 'The Magic System' *New Left Review* July 1960

—— *Television: technology and cultural form* London 1974

Wollen, Peter *Signs and Meaning in the Cinema* London 1969

Wollenberg, H. H. *Fifty Years of German Film*, trs. Ernst Sigler, London 1948

Wright, Basil *The Long View* London 1974

—— *The Use of Film* London 1948

9 Communications Technologies and Social Institutions

Cherry, Edward C. *On Human Communication* Cambridge, Mass. and London 1966

Gouldner, A. *The Dialectic of Ideology and Technology* London and New York 1976

Lerner, D., F. Frey and W. Schramm (eds) *Handbook of Communications* Chicago 1973

McLuhan, Marshall *The Gutenberg Galaxy* London and Toronto 1962

Singer, C., E. J. Holmyard, A. R. Hall and T. L. Williams *A History of Technology* Oxford –1978 (7 vols)

Williams, Raymond *Television: technology and cultural form* London 1974

10 The Future of the Media

Australian Telecommunications Commission *Telecom 2000* Melbourne 1976

Braun, E. and S. MacDonald *Revolution in Miniature: the history and impact of semiconductor electronics* Cambridge 1978

Dickson, E. M. and R. Bowers *The Video Telephone: a new era of telecommunications services* Ithaca, N.Y. 1973

Elton, M. J. C., W. A. Lucas and D. W. Conrath *Evaluating New Telecommunications Services* New York and London 1978

Evans, Christopher R. *The Mighty Micro: the impact of the computer revolution* London 1979

Gillespie, G. *Public Access Cable Television in the United States and Canada* New York and London 1975

Giraud, A., J. L. Missika and D. Wolton *Les réseaux pensants: télécommunications et société* Paris 1978

Johansen, R., J. Vallee and K. Spangler *Electronic Meetings: technical alternatives and social choices* Reading, Mass. and London 1979

Katzman, N. 'The Impact of Communication Technology: promises and prospects' *Journal of Communications* 24, 1974

McHale, J. *The Changing Information Environment* London 1976

Maddox, B. *Beyond Babel: new directions in communications* London 1972

Martin, James *Future Developments in Telecommunications* Englewood Cliffs, N.J. and London 1971 (2nd ed.)

—— *The Wired Society: a challenge for tomorrow* Englewood Cliffs, N.J. and London 1978

Meier, R. L. *A Communications Theory of Urban Growth* Cambridge, Mass. 1962

Nilles, J. M., F. R. Carlson, P. Gray and G. J. Hanneman *The Telecommunications-Transportation Tradeoff: options for tomorrow* New York and London 1976

Nora, S. and A. Minc *L'informatisation de la société* Paris 1978

Pool, I. de Sola *Talking Back: citizen feedback and cable technology* Cambridge, Mass. and London 1977

—— *The Social Impact of the Telephone* Cambridge, Mass. and London 1977

Research Institute of Telecommunications and Economics *The Coming Society and the Role of Telecommunications* 1975

Short, J., E. Williams and B. Christie *The Social Psychology of Telecommunications* London and Chichester 1976

Smith, R. L. *The Wired Nation: cable TV, the electronic communications highway* New York 1972

Toffler, A. *Future Shock* London 1970

Warner, M. and M. Stone *The Data Bank Society* London 1970

Winsbury, R. *The Electronic Bookstall* London 1979

ILLUSTRATION ACKNOWLEDGMENTS

Text illustrations are referred to by page numbers; other references are to illustration numbers in the picture sections.

Museums and Libraries

Amsterdam, Rijksmuseum p. 146
Athens, National Archaeological Museum p. 59(a), p. 115(a)
Barcelona, Archivo de la Corona de Aragón 30
Berlin, Islamisches Museum 53
—— Museum für Indische Kunst 100
—— Preussische Staatsbibliothek 104
—— Rundfunkmuseum p. 14, p. 239
—— Staatliche Museen p. 108(a), p. 112, p. 113(a), p. 122, p. 130
Bern, Burgerbibliothek p. 129
Bonn, Rheinisches Landesmuseum 18
Boston, Museum of Fine Arts p. 124(a)
Brussels, Bibliothèque Royale 106
Calgary, Glenbow-Alberta Institute p. 107
Cambridge, Museum of Archaeology and Ethnology 95
Châteauroux, Museum p. 25
Coblenz, Bundesarchiv 132
Delos, Archaeological Museum p. 120(c)
Dijon, Musée des Beaux Arts 108
Istanbul, Archaeological Museum p. 120(a)
London, The British Museum 33, 49, 50, 52, 69, 70, 111, 113, 134; p.23, p. 80, p. 110(b), p. 113(b), p. 114(a), p. 119, p. 123(b), p. 140(a–c), 141(a–b), p. 142, p. 184, p. 186, p. 187(b)
—— The British Library 78, 115–16, 119, 132, 161–63, 167; p. 23, p. 62, p. 109(b), p. 124(b), p. 132(a–b), 134(a–b), p. 135(a–b), p. 139(a–b), p. 144, p. 145, p. 147, p. 148, p. 175(a), p. 181
—— The Museum of London 63
—— National Gallery 13, 99
—— National Portrait Gallery 149
—— Science Museum
—— St. Bride's Printing Library p. 143(a–c)
—— Tate Gallery 37
—— Victoria and Albert Museum 46, 109, 136, 145–7, 170; p. 77(b)
Mainz, Gutenberg Museum p. 131
Munich, Bayerische Staatsbibliothek 96
Münster, Westphälisches Landesmuseum 32, 55
New York, Brooklyn Museum 112

—— Metropolitan Museum of Art 151
—— Public Library p. 145(b), p. 191(a), p. 187(b)
Oxford, Bodleian Library 54, 56, 110
Paris, Bibliothèque Nationale 58; p. 106, p. 109(a), p. 128, p. 136(a–b), p. 137
—— Louvre p. 77(a), p. 78, p. 110(a)
—— Musée de L'Homme 41
—— Musée des Arts Décoratifs p. 145(a)
—— Musée des Arts et Traditions Populaires 107
—— Musée Guimet 71
—— Petit Palais 31
Perigeux, Museum p. 25
Pittsburgh, Carnegie Institute p. 115(b)
Prague, National Museum 47
Princeton N.J., University Library 102, 103
Rome, Museo delle Terme p. 78
Rhodes, Archaeological Museum p. 59(b)
Santander, Museum p. 25
Siena, Cathedral Treasury 39
St. Gallen, Stiftsbibliothek p. 125(b)
St. Germain-en-Laye, Musée des Antiquités Nationales, p. 106
Taipei, National Palace Museum p. 116(a–b)
Treviso, Museo Civico, Salce Collection 135
Utah, Museum of Natural History p. 28
Valetta, Malta, National Museum, p. 120(b)
Vienna, Kunsthistorisches Museum 1, 76

Special photography for Thames & Hudson by J. R. Freeman & Co. and Ray Gardner

Photographers

Berenice Abbott/Side Gallery, Newcastle-upon-Tyne 68
Aerofilms 138
Alinari/Mansell Collection, London 81, 97; p. 125(a)
Archives Photographiques p. 74
Associated Press 88; p. 58
Krystina Baker/Night Gallery: Photographic Training Centre, London 26–29

Bruno Barbey/John Hillelson Agency 160
Roloff Beny, Rome 40, 144, 152
Ian Berry/John Hillelson Agency 14
Paul Brierly, Harlow 195
G. Bruckner, London 66; p. 72, p. 73
Bulloz, Paris 31
David Burnett/Colorific 44
Camera Press 157, 191
H. Cartier-Bresson/John Hillelson Agency 15, 17, 142, 181; p. 9
Harold Chapman, Gignac, France 36
Bob Chase/Inter-Action, London 185, 187
Gerry Cranham, London 10–12
Financial Times, London 117
Werner Forman Archive, London 45, 77, 91–94; p. 17
Jean Gabus, Neuchâtel 2–9; p. 26–27
Giraudon, Paris 84
Ray Green, Liverpool 48
Ernst Haas, New York 86, 129
Richard Harrington/Camera Press 180
David Harris, Jerusalem 51
Paul Harrison/Camera Press 38
John Hillelson Agency 90
Hirmer Fotoarchive, Munich 98; p. 184
V. Hinz/Stern 137
Takeji Iwamiya, Osaka 20–25
Mas, Barcelona 30, 34, 59; p. 30(a)
Fred Mayer/John Hillelson Agency 159
J. Mazenod p. 114(b)
T. McGrath/*Observer* p. 250
R. & S. Michaud/John Hillelson Agency 65
B. Mitchell, Oswestry p. 30(b)
Ikko Narahara, Japan 128
National Film Archives 145, 146, 147; p. 194(a–c)
OBS/Camera Press p. 11
A. O'Kamura/Life & Time Life Inc. 19
Doros Partassides/Cyprus Broadcasting Corporation 35
Josephine Powell, Rome 60–62, 125; p. 31, p. 72, p. 120(a), p. 123(c)
Radio Times Hulton Picture Library 153, 154; p. 175–78, p. 191, p. 197
Paul Raffaele/Camera Press 101
Mario Ruspoli, Paris 64
Scala, Florence 39
Roger Schall, Paris 42
Roger–Viollet, Paris 131
Emil Schultess p. 17
Score, Paris 118
B. Silverstein/Camera Press p. 126
H. Silvester/Camera Press 87

Sven Simon/Camera Press 179
Ragbuhor Singh/John Hillelson Agency 158
Karel van Straaten, DSM Holland 67
Homer Sykes/Camera Press 89
United Press International 133
H. Vassal/Gamma/John Hillelson Agency 16

By courtesy of the following individuals and firms:

Otl Aicher p. 85
AT & T Archives, New York 123–4; p. 175(b)
R. O. Blechman/Metromedia Radio p. 238
R. O. Blechman/CBS p. 232
British Rail p. 81(b–c–d)
Christie's, London 79
Cinema Vision, London p. 12
Dalgety Ltd., p. 70
Esso Petroleum Co. Ltd. p. 75
Ferranti Ltd. 192
I. M. Folon 127, 178
General Post Office 130, 190; p. 252, p. 260
Hughes Aircraft Company, California 155–6
JVC UK Ltd. 188
Kodak Archives 141; p. 190
S. Lissitzky Collection, Novosibirsk 43
Bryan McAlister/*Guardian* p. 251
Nasa, Washington DC 57; p. 68
Marian Nowinski, Poland 182
Collection D. Mookerjee p. 124(b)
Olivetti (UK) 194
Oswin/Bandespostamt, Berlin p. 14, p. 237
Purnell & Sons Ltd. 120–21
Radio Luxembourg p. 235
Reuters 189
M. Roche/Editions Seuil p. 38
U.G. Sato p. 257
R. Savignac 114
Dr. M. Sijelmassi 72
Sotheby's, London 143, p. 65
Ivan Steiger/Börsenblatt p. 150
Saul Steinberg/*New Yorker* p. 32–4
Welsh Arts Council p. 81(a)

INDEX